KAISER WILHELM II, 1859–1941

A Concise Life

Kaiser Wilhelm II (1859–1941) is one of the most fascinating figures in European history, ruling Imperial Germany from his accession in 1888 to his enforced abdication in 1918 at the end of the First World War. In one slim volume, John Röhl offers readers a concise and accessible survey of his monumental three-volume biography of the Kaiser and his reign. The book sheds new light on Wilhelm's troubled youth, his involvement in social and political scandals, and his growing thirst for glory, which, combined with his overwhelming nationalism and passion for the navy provided the impetus for a breathtaking long-term goal: the transformation of the German Reich into one of the foremost powers in the world. The volume examines the crucial role played by Wilhelm as Germany's Supreme War Lord in the policies that led to war in 1914. It concludes by describing the rabid anti-Semitism he developed in exile and his efforts to persuade Hitler to restore him to the throne.

JOHN C. G. RÖHL is Emeritus Professor of History at the University of Sussex.

Wilhelm Imperator Rex: the Kaiser at the height of his personal power.

KAISER WILHELM II,
1859–1941

A Concise Life

JOHN C. G. RÖHL

TRANSLATED BY SHEILA DE BELLAIGUE

 CAMBRIDGE
UNIVERSITY PRESS

CAMBRIDGE
UNIVERSITY PRESS

University Printing House, Cambridge CB2 8BS, United Kingdom

Cambridge University Press is part of the University of Cambridge.

It furthers the University's mission by disseminating knowledge in the pursuit of
education, learning and research at the highest international levels of excellence.

www.cambridge.org
Information on this title: www.cambridge.org/9781107420779

© John C. G. Röhl 2014

First published 2014
4th printing 2015

Printed in the United Kingdom by TJ International Ltd, Padstow, Cornwall

A catalogue record for this publication is available from the British Library

Library of Congress Cataloguing in Publication data
Röhl, John C. G.
Kaiser Wilhelm II, 1859–1941 : a concise life / John C. G. Rohl ; translated by
Sheila de Bellaigue.
pages cm
ISBN 978-1-107-07225-1 (Hardback) – ISBN 978-1-107-42077-9 (pbk.)
1. William II, German Emperor, 1859–1941.   2. Germany–Kings and rulers–Biography.
3. Germany–History–William II, 1888–1918.   I. De Bellaigue,
Sheila, 1945– translator.   II. Title.
DD229.R6412413 2014
943.08′4092–dc23
[B]
2014010879

ISBN 978-1-107-07225-1 Hardback
ISBN 978-1-107-42077-9 Paperback

To the memory of my sisters, Angela and Nora

Contents

Figures

Acknowledgements

Figures 1, 5, 6 and 7 (Hessische Hausstiftung, Archiv und Bibliothek Schloss Fasanerie)

Figures 2, 3, 9, 10, 13 and 18 (The Royal Archives, © Her Majesty Queen Elizabeth II)

Figures 4, 17 and 20 (Ullstein Bilderdienst, Berlin)

Figure 8 (Bildarchiv Preussischer Kulturbesitz, Berlin)

Figure 11 (© Das Bundesarchiv)

Figures 12 and 28 (Author's private collection)

Figure 14 (Radio Times Hulton / Getty images)

Figures 15 Eulenburg, Philipp zu, *Mit dem Kaiser als Staatsmann und Freund auf Nordlandsreisen*, Carl Reissner Verlag, Dresden

Figure 16 (Landesmedienzentrum Hamburg)

Figures 19 and 33 (J. A. de Jonge, Wilhelm II, Amsterdam 1986)

Figure 21 (*Illustrated London News* / Mary Evans)

Figure 22 (Maurice Baumont, L'Affaire Eulenburg, Geneva 1973)

Figure 23 (IWM London)

Figure 24 (Adolf von Achenbach, Unser Kaiser: Fünfundzwanzig Jahre der Regierung Kaiser Wilhelms II., Stuttgart 1913)

Figures 25 and 29 (Viktoria Luise, Duchess of Brunswick-Lüneburg, *Bilder der Kaiserzeit*, Göttingen 1970)

Figures 26 and 27 (Süddeutsche Zeitung Photo)

Figure 30 (Brigitte von Klitzing)

Figure 31 (Nederlands Filmmuseum)

Figure 32 (Hulton Archive / Stringer / Getty images)

Preface to the English edition

This brief life of Kaiser Wilhelm II, Queen Victoria's eldest grandson, who led the powerful German Reich into the abyss of war in 1914, is based on some fifty years of original archival research, the results of which I have published, first in German and then in English, in three large volumes totalling some 4,000 pages.[1] The present book summarises the salient points of the much more detailed biography in miniaturised form and, while providing an interpretation of the last German emperor's personality and policy in its own right, can also be used as a vade mecum to the more substantial work by anyone wanting further information. The notes provide a guide to the relevant pages in the three-volume biography.

Inevitably, given the Kaiser's central role in the decision-making of his powerful empire, the book is also intended as a contribution to the current very lively centennial debate on the origins and nature of the First World War. When this slender book was published in Germany in 2013, historical scholarship had long since reached something of a consensus on the trajectory underlying German history from unification under Otto von Bismarck in 1871 to utter destruction under Adolf Hitler in 1945. In this generally accepted interpretation, the dynamic energy generated by the united Prusso-German empire at the heart of Europe was by the end of the nineteenth century perceived by its neighbours as an existential challenge to the European system of states, to which first France and Russia and then Great Britain responded by drawing closer together, eventually to form the Triple Entente – a development regarded in Germany in turn as 'encirclement' and increasingly as an unacceptable constraint on her rightful future development. To have managed this burgeoning 'German problem' would have required exceptional wisdom, restraint and tact on all sides, and particularly in Berlin – qualities that were spectacularly absent under the erratic personal military monarchy of Kaiser Wilhelm II. The root cause of the First World War (and, by extension, of the Second World War too) was thus seen to lie, by German historians as well as by British and American scholars, in this fundamental conflict between Germany's elemental drive for supremacy and the determination of Britain along with her continental partners to uphold the existing balance of power in Europe. The decision – which was to have such catastrophic consequences for everyone, and not least for Germany herself – of Kaiser Wilhelm II and his military and civilian advisers to use the growing antagonism between the moribund multinational Habsburg monarchy and her small irredentist South Slav neighbour Serbia in July 1914 as a pretext for a carefully prepared strike against first France and then Russia had all been meticulously documented, and an international consensus along these lines had been reached.[2]

In the past commemorative year this paradigm has been challenged, by a number of influential accounts of the origins of the First World War that tell a somewhat different narrative, preferring a horizontal (pan-European) rather than a vertical (Germanocentric) perspective in order to highlight the warlike tendencies present in all European societies by 1914, so focusing far less on the intentions of the rulers in Berlin.[3] It is as if, after fifty years of preoccupation with Germany's (and to a lesser extent Austria-Hungary's) responsibility for the catastrophe, these historians are returning to the interpretation favoured in the 1920s and 1930s: that in the summer of 1914 the nations of Europe had unintentionally 'slithered over the brink into the boiling cauldron of war', as David Lloyd George famously put it in his memoirs.[4]

These two versions of how and why the terrible European civil war of 1914–1918 occurred are not entirely mutually exclusive, for, of course, the policies of Germany's leaders cannot be understood in isolation – their mentalities and policies were very much a response to what was going on, and perceived to be going on, around them – and in this sense the new emphasis on Europe as a whole is invaluable. But, even so, there remains an irreducible conflict between the two paradigms. The view that in July 1914 the great powers all stumbled unwittingly into war like sleepwalkers, none of them more culpable for the disaster that ensued than the other, is in the end irreconcilable with the view that the Kaiser and his paladins conspired with their allies in Vienna deliberately to begin a war in what were deemed to be advantageous circumstances, with the aim of breaking out of the intolerable constraints of the so-called 'concert of Europe' in order to establish supremacy on the Continent before it was too late. In this latter interpretation, France, Russia, Great Britain and, of course, Serbia were fighting the war not for some wanton, incomprehensible reason but to safeguard their very existence – and paying an unimaginable price in the process, as they were to do again in the 1940s. It is my contention that the 'slithering' into the First World War thesis can be sustained only by the deliberate omission or marginalisation of much well-known, cast-iron evidence to the contrary, striking examples of which I cite in this life of the Kaiser.

Kaiser Wilhelm II, imperious, impulsive, imbued with antiquated notions of the divine right of kings and of Prussia/Germany's God-given trajectory to greatness, while at the same time insecure and hypersensitive to perceived slights to his imperial dignity or his dynastic mission, was arguably the very last person who should have been entrusted with the immense powers of the Hohenzollern military monarchy at such a critical juncture in Germany's and Europe's history. Nevertheless, he stood at the apex of the Kaiserreich's policy-making pyramid for thirty years, from his accession at the premature death from cancer of his father in June 1888 to his ignominious flight into exile in the Netherlands in November 1918. All the generals and admirals, chancellors, ministers and ambassadors who served under him were appointed by him and dependent on his 'All-Highest favour' while in office. Wilhelm followed events at home and abroad with a nervous intensity that on occasions bordered on insanity, issuing orders and covering diplomatic dispatches with often furious diatribes, which have survived in their thousands in the archives. His own words and deeds mark him out as in many respects a forerunner of Hitler, not least in his vitriolic anti-Semitism in exile. And it was of course he, Prussia's Supreme War Lord, who, having on several occasions beforehand urged the Austrians to attack Serbia, gave the fateful order on the night of 3–4 July 1914 that led to disaster.

This slender volume brings together some of the most striking evidence on Wilhelm's traumatic birth and upbringing, his accumulation of personal power after the dismissal of Prince von Bismarck in 1890 and his dangerous susceptibility to sycophantic flattery and backstairs intrigue, which left him and his court so vulnerable to scandal. Above all, the book traces the Kaiser's breathtaking ambition to lead his country to what he himself termed 'Napoleonic supremacy' – by peaceful means if possible, by war if necessary – that lay at the heart of the great European crisis of the first half of the twentieth century. Looking back at his own reign at the end of his life, the Kaiser in exile greeted Hitler's conquest of Norway, Denmark, the Netherlands, Belgium and France in 1940 as the fulfilment of his own supremacist ambitions. In jubilation, he exclaimed in English to an American friend: 'The brilliant leading generals in this war came from *my* school, they fought under my command in the [First] World War as lieutenants, captains and young majors. Educated by Schlieffen they put the plans he had worked out under me into practice along the same lines as we did in 1914.'[5] His words speak for themselves.

JOHN RÖHL

SUSSEX, 27 JANUARY 2014

Preface to the German edition

Until not so very long ago Wilhelm II was dismissed as a *Schatten-kaiser*, a shadowy figure without power and of little historical significance. The man who, as German emperor, King of Prussia and Supreme War Lord, ruled for thirty years (from 1888 to 1918) over the mighty Prusso-German Reich, at the heart of Europe, was largely ignored by German historians. None of them paid serious attention to this grandiloquent, sabre-rattling monarch with the provocative moustache in his shimmering eagle-helmeted uniform, who sacked Prince Bismarck, the founder of the German Reich, in 1890, built up a gigantic battlefleet against Britain, and in 1914 led his flourishing empire into the First World War. One does not need to be a Sherlock Holmes to get to the bottom of this startling omission: as treacherous as the silence pervading *The Hound of the Baskervilles*, the taboo imposed on all mention of Wilhelm II during the Weimar Republic and the Nazi era was part of the campaign in German historiography to reject the 'war guilt lie' of Versailles. In the last three decades, however, our understanding of Kaiser Wilhelm II's place in German history has gained infinitely more depth. His flawed personality, his angry view of the world, his autocratic methods as ruler and his ambitious naval and world power policies now stand at the heart of a lively debate over continuity and disruption in the history of the first German nation state from 1871 to 1945. Biographies saturated with new archival evidence have appeared, together with volumes of documents running to a thousand pages, scholarly editions of his speeches, monographs on his relationship with the armed forces and with religion, art, science, film and the world of industry and technology, and psychological and socio-anthropological examinations of his circle of friends or the scandal-ridden Hohenzollern court; all these subjects have been put under the microscope. True, there is still work to do – very little attention has been paid to the evidence on Wilhelm in the Russian and French archives, for instance – and no general consensus has yet been reached: Wilhelm II continues to divide opinion. But anyone who honestly searches for the truth, rather than hankering after an idealised golden age, will find the scope for interpretation severely reduced by the proven facts. This volume attempts to summarise what we now know about the last German emperor and king of Prussia. The picture that emerges from all this research has grown several shades darker.

Acknowledgements

Since this is an essayistic distillation of a lifetime's work on the Kaiser and Wilhelmine Germany, my debt of gratitude to all those friends, colleagues, archivists and critics who have helped to shape my views over the decades is far too great to be itemised here without defeating the book's chief purpose, which is concision. To all of them, and my family, I have expressed my appreciation in earlier volumes. For this slim book in particular I wish to thank the usual experts: my Lektor at the C. H. Beck Verlag, Dr Stefan von der Lahr, who, after guiding all three volumes of the major biography through to publication in Germany, suggested I write a very much briefer survey of Wilhelm II's life for the general reader; Sheila de Bellaigue, who, not content with having translated all of the second and most of the third volume of that massive biography into her elegant English, agreed to translate this short overview as well; and Douglas Matthews, master indexer of the monumental third volume, *Into the Abyss of War and Exile*, who has again worked his magic on this book to guide the reader through the maze of names, places and events. As ever, my thanks are also due to Isabel Hull, Ragnhild Fiebig-von Hase, Annika Mombauer and Hartmut Pogge von Strandmann for their unrivalled knowledge of the sources and their unstinting willingness to share their insights with me over very many years. Finally, I thank all the good people at Cambridge University Press, my English publishers now since 1982, including my copy-editor, Mike Richardson, for his forbearance in accommodating my whims, and my production editors, Caroline Mowatt and Amanda George, not least for tracking down the resplendent portrait of the young Kaiser by Ferdinand Keller that adorns the cover.

Overview: Wilhelm the Last, a German trauma

Kaiser Wilhelm II was born on 27 January 1859 in Berlin and died on 4 June 1941, at the age of eighty-two, in exile in the Netherlands. Chronologically, therefore, his life coincided almost exactly with the rise and fall of the first German nation state, which Bismarck founded through the wars of 1864, 1866 and 1870–1 and which came to a dire end with the catastrophe of the Second World War. Wilhelm II was anything but a silent spectator of the momentous events of his lifetime. From his accession in the so-called Year of the Three Kaisers in 1888 until his abdication and flight to the Netherlands on 9 November 1918 he ruled the German Reich and its hegemonial constituent state, the powerful military monarchy of Prussia, not only as its figurehead but in a very direct and personal manner. Indeed, given his parvenu insecurity, aggressively inverted into a superiority complex with an unbounded craving for acceptance, Wilhelm has seemed to some as a 'representative individual', a personification of the newly united German Reich.

However that may be, Wilhelm was not a dictator. He was always obliged to come to an accommodation with the incumbent Reich Chancellor and minister-president of Prussia, the Prussian Ministers of State, the Reich secretaries, the Reichstag and the Prussian parliament, as well as the allied governments of the other German kingdoms, grand duchies, duchies and free cities in the federation. Increasingly, too, public opinion, as expressed through political parties, churches, trade unions, special interest groups, pamphlets, press criticism and popular demonstrations, acted as something of a brake on his personal influence. But at the centre of power, and above all in the conduct of personnel, military, foreign and armaments policy, Kaiser Wilhelm's was very much the determining voice until the decision to go to war in 1914 – a decision in which he took a leading part. It is true that during the First World War his role was quickly overshadowed by that of the generals, but even then he retained the last word on all matters of importance.

The young Wilhelm II inherited the basis of his power from his grandfather and father when he acceded to the throne on 15 June 1888, not long after his twenty-ninth birthday, for Bismarck had succeeded in preserving the 'personal monarchy' of the Hohenzollerns, as he boasted, from the 'constitutional thumbscrews' that had condemned the crowned heads of the monarchies of northern, western and southern Europe to being mere 'signature machines' under parliamentary control. Wilhelm went much further, however. Not only did he 'drop the pilot' – Bismarck – in 1890 so that he could take the wheel himself, but in the course of the 1890s he steadily built up his personal power to the most astonishing extent, secretly advised by his fawning favourite, Philipp Count zu Eulenburg-Hertefeld. At the same time, despite his wide-ranging interests and his undoubted gifts, this highly emotional and restless monarch quite simply lacked the sense of proportion, the judgment and the shrewdness to provide reliable leadership for what was rapidly becoming the most dynamic and powerful empire in Europe. His antiquated insistence on his divine right, his ostentatiously autocratic rule, his sabre-rattling militarism, his startling narcissism and the obsequious servility to which it gave rise at court (and even among the most senior public servants) all created the impression of a throwback to the eighteenth century, and were widely felt to be an affront to his own people. The scandals and crises that many had predicted at the very outset of his reign did not take long to materialise. Equally doomed to failure were Wilhelm's sly attempts to use his blood relationship with the British royal family on the one hand and the Russian imperial family on the other in order to disguise his hegemonial ambitions in Europe. Via the Kruger telegram of 1896, the seizure of territory in north-eastern China in 1897, the battlefleet building programme initiated in 1898, the Russo-Japanese war of 1904–5, the first Moroccan crisis in 1905–6, the Bosnian annexation crisis of 1908–9, the Agadir crisis in 1911 and the two Balkan wars in 1912–13, the twisting road led finally into the abyss of the First World War.

With his ignominious flight into exile in the Netherlands in November 1918, Kaiser Wilhelm lost every shred of influence over the formulation of German policy. He fought successfully against being handed over to be tried as a war criminal at a tribunal of the victorious powers, which would have condemned him, if not to the death penalty, then at least to banishment on Devil's Island or the Falklands or the Dutch East Indies. In the twenty-three years of his exile the embittered ex-Kaiser developed a paranoid racial delusion and an anti-Semitism so intense that it ranks with the savagery of the National Socialists' hate campaign against the Jews. He would have joined Hitler with all flags flying, had the Führer only been prepared to put him back on the throne. Thus the chapter on the Kaiser's powerless years in exile also provides a lesson on continuity in German history in the first half of the twentieth century. But let us begin at the beginning, with the fateful birth of the future sovereign on 27 January 1859.

PART I

1859–1888: The Tormented Prussian Prince

CHAPTER I

The 'soul murder' of an heir to the throne

The marriage of Wilhelm's parents in London in 1858 was intended to herald a close relationship between Great Britain, with its vast overseas empire, and the rising (and also largely Protestant) kingdom of Prussia on the Continent. The seventeen-year-old Princess Victoria, known in her family as Vicky, was the oldest child of Queen Victoria and Prince Albert of Saxe-Coburg-Gotha, the Prince Consort; her bridegroom was Prince Friedrich Wilhelm ('Fritz'), the only son of the sixty-year-old Wilhelm, Prince of Prussia, who had recently become Regent for his mentally ill and childless brother, King Friedrich Wilhelm IV. With the birth of a son, on 27 January 1859, the future of the Hohenzollern dynasty and the peace of Europe seemed to be secured for decades ahead. Significantly, the newborn Prussian prince was also given the names of his English grandparents: Friedrich Wilhelm Viktor Albert.[1]

The birth took place on the top floor of the Kronprinzenpalais on Unter den Linden in Berlin. The circumstances surrounding the delivery of the child, for a long time shrouded in speculation, are now clearly established on the basis of documents in the royal family archives. The labour pains began in the afternoon of 26 January. Early that evening the father, who never left his wife's side during her confinement, sent a letter by the ordinary post (!) to alert the leading Berlin gynaecologist Professor Dr Eduard Arnold Martin. At that point no one yet realised that the child was in the breech position – bottom first, with the arms stretched upwards over the head. When this complication, life-threatening for both mother and child, was recognised the following morning, the Crown Prince sent a messenger to fetch Professor Martin – who had not yet received his letter. The gynaecologist thus found himself confronted with a grave emergency when he hurried up the palace stairs into the delivery room. On his instructions the suffering mother was given a large dose of chloroform by the Scottish doctor Sir James Clark, whom Queen Victoria had sent to Berlin. As he deemed the contractions to be insufficiently effective, Martin gave orders for ergot (in fact an abortion-inducing substance) to be administered, and then tried to extract the child, who was in danger of asphyxia as the umbilical cord, supplying oxygen, was being crushed by the head in the birth canal. During his attempt to pull down the baby's left arm, which was stretched up above his head, and to rotate the body 'by means of the same [arm]', as Martin wrote in his report, the nerve complex in the neck was torn. Thus the future king of the military Prussian monarchy and the man destined to rule as emperor over the mighty German Reich came into the world not only 'suffering to a high degree from foetal asphyxia' but also with what is technically referred to as a brachial plexus injury or Erb–Duchenne palsy.[2]

Over the next weeks and months it became clear that the little prince had been seriously injured during his birth. A distinct crease developed between the left upper arm and the shoulder area. While the arm was pulled tightly to the shoulder, the arm itself hung limply down with the elbow joint, stiff and inflexible. Compared with his right arm, his left arm was cold and shorter, the difference becoming ever more visible as time went by. His left hand also remained smaller than the right, with unusually pointed fingers that curled inwards in a claw-like fashion. The cause of this worrying malformation remained a mystery at first. It was assumed to be due to a contusion of the muscles that would heal with time, and washing in cold water, rubbing with spirits and passive movements of the crippled arm were recommended. The royal physician also gave orders for the infant's right arm to be tied to his body so as to encourage him to use the left arm – proof enough of how little was then known to medical science about the nervous system. Only gradually did the doctors become convinced that the paralysis had been caused not by muscle injury but by damage to the brain or the nerves, and was therefore incurable.

On the basis of the mistaken diagnosis, treatments that now seem grotesque were tried out. When the infant was six months old Professor Bernhard von Langenbeck of the Charité hospital in Berlin

1 Wilhelm on his tenth birthday; a glove is used to make the left arm appear longer and the left hand larger; the Crown Prince ordered the plate of this photograph to be destroyed, but one print has survived.

prescribed 'animal baths'. Twice a week Wilhelm's left arm was inserted into the body of a 'freshly slaughtered hare' for half an hour, in the hope that the wild animal's warmth and vigour would be transferred to the arm.[3] At this point one already wonders what psychological effects this cruel and gory procedure, which was kept up for several years, might have had on the future German Kaiser. It certainly brought no physical benefit. As his paralysed arm made it difficult for him to balance, Wilhelm's attempts to walk were painful, especially since his right arm was still regularly tied to his body. He reacted with frustration and rage. Soon after Wilhelm's first birthday, in addition to the 'animal baths' Langenbeck prescribed malt baths and electromagnetic therapy. His arm was electromagnetised for the first time on 11 April 1860, but it remained cold and numb and dark red in colour. Later electrotherapy was carried out on the neck using constant galvanic current, as Wilhelm could not tolerate the alternating magnetic current on this sensitive spot. For his arm both types of current continued to be used daily 'for a great length of time' and 'with considerable intensity', as Queen Victoria's doctors noted in 1865.[4]

When Wilhelm was four years old he developed yet another clinical condition: torticollis. The unharmed neck muscles on the right side were pulling his head downwards to the right, twisting his chin towards the paralysed left side. In April 1863, as his father recorded, a specially constructed 'machine for Wilhelm's neck' was tried out.[5] This 'head-stretching machine', which the prince had to wear for an hour a day, as his horrified mother wrote to the queen, consisted of

a belt around the waist to the back of which an iron bar is fixed. This bar leads up the back to something which looks exactly like a horse's bridle. The head is then fixed in this and positioned as desired by means of a screw which adjusts the iron bar.

The Crown Princess added a drawing of the instrument; it was dreadful, she lamented, 'to see ones [sic] child treated like one deformed'.[6] This treatment, the psychological effects of which one can again well imagine, also proved useless, and an operation became necessary. On 23 March 1865, when Wilhelm was just six years old, Langenbeck cut through the tendon between the neck muscle and the collarbone on the right side. A few days later a second muscle was severed, because it was pulling his chin to the side and distorting his

2 The 'head-stretching machine'.

face: his right eye and right cheek had grown disproportionately large, his mouth was crooked and his left eye was half closed.[7]

As Wilhelm could not move his left forearm at all – it remained locked stiffly at the elbow – in 1868 it seemed that another operation might be necessary, this time to cut through the biceps tendon. In the end, however, it was decided not to do this, since the stiffness was judged to be due to a deformity in the bone of the elbow joint. Instead of an operation, the 'arm-stretching machine' that the prince had been forced to endure since his infancy was applied even more frequently; twice a day, and also during his lessons. It was only for fear that it might induce epileptic attacks that he was not obliged to wear it at night too. With the aid of the arm-stretching machine and a 'fixing frame', from 1866 onwards Wilhelm was able to do remedial gymnastics three times a day under the supervision of Captain Gustav von Dresky, the effects of which proved beneficial for the development of his crippled arm.[8]

As if this (naturally, well-meant) torture were not enough for the delicate prince, further physical defects appeared over the years, which the doctors likewise attributed to his difficult birth or to the treatment of his birth injuries. The defective sense of balance that had been noticeable in his infancy led to dislocations of the knee on several occasions in his youth, and sometimes kept Wilhelm in bed for weeks. From the autumn of 1878 onwards he suffered for years from a recurring, life-threatening infection of the right inner ear, with polypoid growths and foul-smelling pus. When an alarmingly severe attack of the ear infection occurred in 1886, accompanied by dizziness and buzzing in the ears, the doctors prescribed a ten-week cure at Bad Reichenhall in southern Bavaria. In October of that year the previously healthy left ear also became inflamed, and the eardrum had to be perforated. Rumours that the growths were cancerous proved unfounded, but in later years fears continued to be expressed to the effect that this otological malady might be the underlying cause of the Kaiser's peculiar behaviour. In August 1896 a radical operation to remove the eardrum in the right ear proved essential because of the danger that meningitis might develop. Even after the operation the Kaiser suffered all his life from chronic middle ear catarrh, which he removed vigorously every morning with a cotton swab on a wooden splint fashioned by himself, followed by a small strip of gauze inserted into the ear canal with a pair of tweezers.[9]

All these ailments, and the way in which they were handled, are meticulously documented in the sources; the facts are clear. But other explanations for Wilhelm II's peculiarities put forward by his contemporaries or by biographers remain speculative. Whether he suffered a (minimal) degree of brain damage during his birth, which might account for his distorted face, must remain an open question.[10] His sexual orientation, and the possibility that he had suppressed homosexual tendencies (which has also sometimes been suggested), will be examined later in connection with his marriage and friendships. There are indications, not conclusively proved as yet but strong enough to be taken into consideration, of a hereditary illness that afflicted the royal families of Hanover and Great Britain from the Stuarts onward, namely porphyria. Wilhelm's great-great-grandfather, King George III, is thought to have suffered from porphyria, which led to that monarch's occasional bouts of rage and periods of dementia. The fact that the dominant gene causing this transmissible 'royal malady' crossed from the British royal family into the house of Hohenzollern through the marriage of Wilhelm's parents has recently been proved beyond doubt through DNA analyses, which confirmed the presence of the mutation in his eldest sister, Charlotte, and her daughter, Feo.[11] Whether Wilhelm himself was affected remains open to question. What can be said for certain is that leading doctors and statesmen in London became convinced quite early on that 'the taint of George III is in his blood' and that he would always be subject to sudden bouts of rage, which would become more frequent and violent with age.[12] Much more obvious than such suppositions, however, are the consequences that Wilhelm's birth injuries and the various measures taken to treat them, which over-shadowed his entire childhood, had on the development of his character.

CHAPTER 2

Ambivalent motherhood

These consequences cannot be fully understood without taking into account the consternation felt by Wilhelm's young mother at the birth of a son who was, in her eyes, 'deformed' or 'crippled'. Vicky, known in Prussia as 'the Englishwoman', was barely eighteen years old. Proud of her status as Queen Victoria's daughter, intelligent, well read, liberal and astonishingly progressive in her ideas and a passionate anglophile, she made no secret of her feelings of superiority at the antiquated, reactionary Prussian court, and was correspondingly unpopular and isolated there. Defiantly, she counted on the accession of her beloved soldier husband Fritz to the throne in the near future, followed by the introduction of a more modern – parliamentary – constitution and an alliance between Prussia and her powerful mother country. With the expected birth of her son it seemed certain that these bright hopes would bear fruit well into the twentieth century. But the little prince had come into the world 'crippled', and the Crown Princess felt a constant, almost intolerable sense of shame that he was imperfect. 'I feel so sore on the subject that when other people make remarks about it I wish myself under the ground or in my shoes or any where [sic],' she lamented.[1] The flaw had to be removed – and, if the measures prescribed by the doctors failed, the physical handicap would have to be corrected through the child's upbringing. With the inevitability of a Greek tragedy, these unrealisable hopes led to a vicious circle of reciprocal disappointment, which was to degenerate, on Wilhelm's side, into hatred and rejection of his mother's liberal ideals. Many years later, after the catastrophe of the First World War, Sigmund Freud was to pinpoint Vicky's inability to bond with her handicapped son as the root cause of their fateful estrangement. 'It is usual,' he observed in 1932, 'for mothers whom Fate has presented

10

with a child who is sickly or otherwise at a disadvantage to try to compensate him for his unfair handicap by a superabundance of love. In the instance before us, the proud mother behaved otherwise; she withdrew her love from the child on account of his infirmity.'[2]

From the outset Vicky took little pleasure in her firstborn child. It is pitiful to see how her distress at his shortcomings spoiled her happiness as a young mother. Years later she still remembered vividly how upset she had been at his christening because he had to be 'half covered up to hide his arm wh. [sic] dangled without use or power by his side'.[3] It was particularly painful for her to watch Wilhelm playing with healthy boys. 'When I see other children clapping their hands and then I see his poor little arm hanging listlessly by his side without any use in it, it distresses me so much.'[4] 'The idea of his remaining a cripple haunts me,' she wrote to her father on Wilhelm's first birthday.[5]

The frustration engendered in little Wilhelm by his disability and the agonising therapies he had to endure soon expressed itself in 'violent passions', which did little to endear him to his mother.[6] 'Poor Willie is so tormented with all these machines and things, that it makes him cross and difficult to manage, poor child really he is sadly tried,' she reported in 1863.[7] No less disturbing in her eyes was her son's increasing arrogance – doubtless another compensatory reaction – which she tried in vain to 'correct'.[8]

The boy is so impertinent & obstinate that at times I really do not know what to do with him – & I find it so difficult to control myself when he aggravates me this way. [. . .] I am constantly threatening him with the cane, and I will in fact use it (that is, if I do not lose heart at the last minute, which is most likely).[9]

Mentally, too, the little prince lagged far behind his mother's expectations. 'He has a marvellous memory, but in other respects I don't find his mind particularly developed. [. . .] He talks for the sake of hearing his own voice, without making any effort whatsoever to think or to express a particular thought,' she complained when Wilhelm was five years old.[10]

His mother's disappointment could not be concealed from the prince. More lasting than the threat of the cane were the verbal blows that the Crown Princess dealt him. As she herself admitted later,

3 Wilhelm with Queen Victoria on the Isle of Wight in August 1864.

'[W]hen Wilhelm was still a child & often spoke & acted & bragged in such a complacent manner, I would always say to him in order to tease him *no* lady will ever have *you* with your black finger etc... – to which he usually responded with scorn.'[11] It was a barb that wounded him deeply, as Wilhelm showed in 1880 when he became engaged and told his tutor, Dr Georg Ernst Hinzpeter, that he had never thought it possible that 'a lady could ever take any real interest in him' on account of 'his unfortunate arm!'.[12]

The Crown Princess's grief over her eldest son's handicap and his development was increased immeasurably by two further strokes of fate: the deaths of her beloved sons Sigismund in 1866 and Waldemar in 1879. From then onwards her family, like that of her widowed mother in England, was haunted by a sorrow that cast its shadow over everything else. Her surviving elder children, Wilhelm, Heinrich and Charlotte, could never live up to the idealised memory of the two dead princes, Sigi and Waldi. As a result, the Crown Princess was to lavish all the more affection on her three younger daughters: Victoria ('Moretta'), Sophie and Margarethe ('Mossy').

CHAPTER 3

A daring educational experiment

What the doctors could not achieve with their 'animal baths' and head- and arm-stretching machines therefore had to be accomplished by a purposeful upbringing. Precisely because of her firstborn son's infirmities, it remained the Crown Princess's goal to mould him into an exemplary liberal, reforming monarch. In 1864 she wrote to Queen Victoria saying that it was her dearest wish that Wilhelm should grow up to be 'like dear Papa and become a great man, a second Frederick the Great – but one of *another* kind'.[1] In the autumn of 1866, on the recommendation of the liberal diplomat Sir Robert Morier, at that time British minister in Darmstadt, this task was entrusted to the former tutor of Count Emil Görtz in the small Hessian town of Schlitz, Dr Hinzpeter – an eccentric choice in more ways than one. The conditions that Hinzpeter laid down – his pupil had to be entirely 'in my power', and he was not prepared to play the part of a 'play-fellow for a little boy' – showed how rigorously he intended to proceed.[2] His Spartan educational principles, combined with the Crown Princess's high expectations, brought young Wilhelm even more suffering and a joyless childhood. Nevertheless, one should not exaggerate the severity of Hinzpeter's regime in these early years. Thus it is a propaganda myth, concocted by Wilhelm II in the childhood recollections he dictated during his years in exile, that Hinzpeter used appallingly painful methods to teach his pupil to ride, allowing him to fall repeatedly from the saddle for days and weeks on end until he had found his balance.[3] For one thing, it is quite unthinkable that his parents and the doctors would have permitted the disabled heir presumptive to risk serious injury in this way. For another, Sergeant Robert Lucke had already taught him to ride, under the supervision of his military governor, Captain Gustav

4 The 'Doctor': Georg Ernst Hinzpeter, Wilhelm's civil governor.

von Schrötter, well before Hinzpeter took up his post as civil tutor in October 1866. After all, riding lessons for a Prussian prince were a matter for the military, not for a pusillanimous middle-aged schoolteacher.[4]

For ten years, at first at home and then from 1874 to 1876 at the gymnasium (public grammar school) at Kassel, Hinzpeter exercised an uninterrupted influence over the development of the future monarch. In their endeavour to bring up the heir to the throne in accordance with liberal, middle-class, 'English-Coburgian' thinking, the Crown Prince and Crown Princess gave the pietistic 'Doctor' a monopoly over the education of their son and resisted, successfully at first, the interference of the reigning Kaiser and the court generals, who wanted to turn the prince into a traditional Prussian soldier king. Only a few months after Hinzpeter's appointment the military governor, von Schrötter, resigned, offended at the diminution of his role. He was replaced not by a self-confident soldier such as Count Alfred von Waldersee, Helmuth von Moltke's successor as chief of the General Staff with the burning ambition to replace Bismarck, or General Georg Leo von Caprivi, Bismarck's actual successor as Reich Chancellor in 1890, both of whom were under consideration by the court, but by an insignificant, impoverished and (as it later transpired) homosexual lieutenant of Irish extraction called August O'Danne, who did not question Hinzpeter's authority in any way.[5]

At first all went well. The 'Doctor' frequently took his pupils Wilhelm and his brother Heinrich out on excursions and sightseeing visits. The two princes spent the entire winter of 1869–70 in Cannes in the care of Hinzpeter, O'Danne, Dresky and their personal physician Dr Max Schrader; in 1872 they spent the summer at Wyk auf Föhr in the North Frisian Islands; on another occasion they were on the Belgian coast, again without their parents. Hinzpeter became increasingly dissatisfied with the success of his efforts, but the sharpest criticism meted out to the future heir to the throne came from his own mother. She continued to find him wanting in comparison with her ideal, her adored late father Prince Albert. She returned Wilhelm's letters to him with corrections, complaining constantly that

the hand and the spelling are both bad – there was hardly a word without a mistake or a letter left out. [. . .] I think you should take a *little more pains* – or you will get into such a slovenly untidy way of writing, only ask the Doctor whether I am not right. [. . .] Then you begin 'liebe Mama' – which I think is very cool – dont [sic] you think you could find a little word wh.

sounds more affectionate? – Then I think all children should sign them-selves with *respect* to their Parents, you say 'Dein Dich *liebender* Sohn' – this would do to a sister or brother or cousin – but to a Parent you should say 'Dein treuer' or 'dankbarer' or 'gehorsamer' or 'ergebener'. – Perhaps you have forgotten that.[6]

From that point on, Wilhelm's letters began with the address 'My very dear Mama' and ended with the desired closing formula, 'Your obedient son Wilhelm'. But, no matter how much he tried, his mother was still unsatisfied with his spelling. As late as April 1870, when Wilhelm was eleven, she wrote, 'In your letter received the day before yesterday both the handwriting and spelling were so much neglected and the style so incoherent that it was difficult to make anything of it – and I thought to myself – Master Willie finds it very hot and has a lazy fit upon him, was I right?'[7] Gradually Hinzpeter began to wonder whether he was not asking far too much of his pupil. Yet, instead of taking heed of the warning signs, the Crown Princess tightened the educational screw still further.

In a memorandum of October 1870 the tutor put a radical new plan to Wilhelm's parents – a plan that would not only mean a three-year separation from their son, but would almost certainly invite conflict with Wilhelm I and his military entourage. He proposed that, from his fifteenth year until he came of age, young Wilhelm should continue his education in a gymnasium – a public grammar school – far from Berlin, in open competition with pupils from middle-class families. To prepare for this ambitious educational experiment a new curriculum would be introduced. As well as Latin and mathematics Wilhelm was to learn Greek, and external teachers were to be engaged to instruct him in chemistry and biology and to give him lessons in English, French, German literature and art history. From now on other boys took part in some of the lessons and accompanied the two Hohenzollern princes on visits to museums on Sundays. At the request of his parents Wilhelm was also given drawing lessons at the Decorative Arts Museum in Berlin. On 2 April 1873 he passed the examination for the Obertertia – the equivalent of the lower fifth in an English grammar school – but, behind the scenes, anxiety was expressed not only about his fitness to attend the gymnasium but about his character in general.

In late 1870, while proposing this ambitious curriculum, Hinzpeter had already confronted the Crown Prince and Princess with the crucial question of whether their son might not perhaps 'become a happier and more useful man if such high expectations are not placed upon him'.[8] In April 1873 the 'Doctor' again sounded the alarm on his adolescent pupil's development in words that speak volumes. With 'frightening clarity', he declared that he was staring the difficulties that stood in the way of achieving the original aim in the face. He drew attention to the 'very severe sacrifices' that both parents and tutor, but above all his royal pupil, would have to make if he were to continue on the 'high road'. Until he finished his schooling at the gymnasium in Kassel with the Abitur, Wilhelm would have to live apart from his parents and 'seek happiness almost solely in his studies'. If, on the other hand, an easier path were chosen, the prince's life, in close contact with his family, would be much more cheerful and the end result would probably prove more harmonious.[9] After an 'unpleasant' altercation with Hinzpeter, the parents – that is to say, the Crown Princess – opted nonetheless for the 'high road' at the gymnasium, which inevitably entailed the 'Spartan' discipline about which the Kaiser was to complain so bitterly in later years.

By the time of his confirmation, in the summer of 1874, Wilhelm was showing disturbing character traits that could no longer be overlooked. As a defence against the medical torment he had had to suffer, the unfulfillable expectations laid upon him by Hinzpeter and constant put-downs from his parents and especially his mother, he developed a superiority complex – a brittle, narcissistic amour propre combined with an icy coldness and an aggressive contempt for those he considered weaker than himself. The Crown Princess and Hinzpeter blamed each other for the failure of their ambitious experiment. Vicky complained that her son was '*very* arrogant, extremely smug & quite taken with himself, is offended at the slightest comment, plays the injured party, & more than occasionally gives an impudent answer; furthermore, he is unbelievably lazy & slovenly'.[10] 'More than ever, I now notice Wilhelm's rough and arrogant manner,' she wrote to her husband in 1873. 'He copies the somewhat dry & off-handed manner of the Doctor.' He was 'rather gruff, reproachful & dogmatic when speaking to me!'.[11] For his part, Hinzpeter lamented:

No one, but truly no one, has the idea that this boy has a soul like other children, that it requires nurturing, purification, sanctification; it is only I who am pursued by this thought as if it were a nightmare. [. . .] I am sorry for the poor boy. [. . .] Where is *this* person to find love and faith, which he will need more than anyone else?'[12]

Shortly before he and his pupils moved to Kassel the 'Doctor' doubted that it would ever be possible to overcome Wilhelm's 'almost crystal-hard egoism', which formed 'the innermost core of his being'.[13] Many years later, when he had reached the pinnacle of his personal power, the Kaiser confessed to his intimate friend Count Philipp zu Eulenburg: 'Something is missing in me that others have. All poetic feeling in me is dead – has been killed.' 'Experiences and experiments in his youth' had 'artificially dammed the balancing qualities in his nature', Eulenburg observed.[14] All in all, it must be said that the ambitious educational scheme adopted by Victoria and Hinzpeter, with a view to overriding his physical disability on the one hand and preparing him for his challenging future 'profession' on the other, not only robbed young Wilhelm of his right to childhood but, for a sensitive child who had to endure orthopaedic torment hour after hour and day after day, was as inappropriate as it could possibly have been.

Very much against the will of the reigning Kaiser, Wilhelm I, in September 1874 Prince Wilhelm, together with his brother Heinrich, their military governor Major General Walter von Gottberg and Hinzpeter, moved into wretchedly meagre accommodation at the Fürstenhof in Kassel. Wilhelm was to start school in the Obersekunda – the upper fifth form – of the nearby Lyceum Fridericianum. From the outset Hinzpeter's 'experiment without precedent' still aimed, against the odds, at bringing about a fundamental change in his pupil's character. Through privation, iron discipline and pitiless competition he was to be trained in the ways of diligence and dutifulness, while the 'fundamental flaws' stemming from his princely rank and 'the split nature of the Prince's development' were to be overcome.[15] The prince crammed from six in the morning until ten at night, including Saturdays: nineteen hours a week of Greek and Latin, six hours of mathematics, three hours of history and geography, three hours of German and two of English; in addition, from 1875 there were two hours of French and, later, two hours of physics as well, and on top of this, of course, the obligatory religious instruction. The emphasis lay clearly on classical languages, by contrast with the subjects that would arguably have been more appropriate to a modern monarch. No wonder that Wilhelm complained all his life about 'this fossilised and most deadly of all systems'.[16]

The other teachers at the Kassel gymnasium were as disappointed as Hinzpeter with the prince's performance. Wilhelm's German compositions from the lower sixth form, only recently rediscovered, teem with mistakes and not infrequently failed to reach the pass mark; and yet German was his favourite subject.[17] The character change Hinzpeter had hoped for did not materlialise at all. In Kassel the 'Doctor' was as horrified as before by his pupil's 'triviality' and 'immaturity', his 'deplorable self-satisfaction', his 'saucy and conceited nature' and his narcissistic readiness to take offence.[18] When Hinzpeter retired to Bielefeld in 1876 and looked back on his ten years as tutor to the boy who would succeed to 'the mightiest throne on earth' (Philipp Eulenburg) at the age of twenty-nine, he exclaimed to Sir Robert Morier in despair: 'I ought to have known better and to have retired quietly under one of my favourite apple or plum trees to hang myself instead of beginning a hopeless struggle with such perversity of nature and notions.'[19] According to Prince Alexander of Hohenlohe-Schillingsfürst, the 'Doctor' also confided to Morier: 'You have no idea *what an abyss* I have gazed into.'[20]

If one takes stock of Prince Wilhelm's childhood and youth, one cannot fail to see a fundamental conflict. On the one hand, his early years were overshadowed by the painful attempts by the doctors to remedy the injuries he suffered at birth, treatments that will almost certainly have affected the development of his young brain. His proud mother's inability to love her firstborn child because of his physical imperfections; her efforts to make up for his disabilities by pushing him to succeed intellectually, with the aid of a stern tutor; the deliberate adoption of an excessively demanding educational programme aimed at blocking his attempts to assert himself, which were seen as rebelliousness – all these engendered in Wilhelm, as the anxious comments of his parents and Hinzpeter so strikingly testify, a narcissistic but fragile self-love and a brash, guffawing, icy heartlessness. Very soon the direction in which his personality was evolving made itself felt politically, with his glorification of the military feats of the autocratic Hohenzollern dynasty and his corresponding rejection of the peace-loving, cosmopolitan ideals of his English mother. On the other hand, however, as Hinzpeter clearly recognised, Wilhelm developed an insatiable craving for love, praise and flattery, for childish games, stupid pranks and obscene jokes, primarily in male company. His nature was one of extremes, unstable and highly emotional; he lacked the medium tones, the ability to see things in proportion. He could not tolerate opposition; whenever his high expectations were disappointed he felt injured, and reacted with aggressive outbursts of boyish rage or with depressed helplessness. Here we can already see the psychological breeding ground, notwithstanding some strikingly progressive elements instilled in him by Hinzpeter with the encouragement of the Crown Princess, for his vision of the rule of a quasi-absolute military monarch, enthroned by divine right, surrounded by anglophobe admirals and (like his forebear, the 'Sergeant King') by six-foot-tall generals, but at the same time alarmingly open to the backstairs blandishments of his fawning favourites. His unusual education, with its eccentric mix of royal privilege at court and rigorous bourgeois competitiveness at Kassel, would have done little to steady his self-identity. Already in his childhood the course was set for conflict with his liberal parents, with the all-powerful Bismarcks, father and son, with the inexorably rising democratic forces in Germany – and in the end also with the oceanic superpower Great Britain, as guarantor of the prevailing European states system hemming in his burgeoning empire.

CHAPTER 4

The conflict between the Prince of Prussia and his parents

While still at the gymnasium in Kassel the pubescent prince reached out one last time to his mother before breaking with her in haughty disdain and mutual recrimination. In the winter of 1874–5 Wilhelm began a series of letters to his mother – in English, naturally – recounting a recurring 'dream' he was having; letters that are remarkable not only for their evidently incestuous character but also for their fetishistic emphasis on her gloved left hand – a poignant cry for unconditional acceptance and love if ever there was one. 'I have got a little *secret* which is for you alone viz. a peculiar dream,' he wrote to Vicky in March 1875, shortly after her visit to Kassel for his sixteenth birthday.

I dreamt last night that I was walking with you & another lady; in walking you were discussing who had the finest hands, whereupon the lady produced a most ungraceful hand, declaring that it was the prettiest, and turned us her back. I in my rage broke her parasole [sic]; but you put your dear arm round my waist, led me aside, pulled your glove off your dear left hand – which I so often kissed at Cassel – & showed me your dear beautiful hand which I instantly covered with kisses.

Wilhelm hoped that his 'dream' would soon become reality. 'I wish you would do the same when I am at Berlin, alone with you in the evening.' And he continued, craving reassurance: 'Pray write to me what you think about the dream; it is quite *true* as I have written it. You see I always think of you, my dear Mama, I sometimes dream of you; I am so glad that soon we shall sit together in you[r] dear library and cose [sic] together. But this dream is *alone* for *you* to know,' he insisted.[1] Several days later the 'dream' recurred.

5 Wilhelm and his mother in 1876.

I am very glad that you liked my little secret about your dear hands. Since then I have again dreamt about you, this time I was alone with you in your library, when you stretched forth your arms & pulled me down to your chair so that my head rested on your left arm. Then you took off your gloves [. . .] & laid your hands gently on my lips, for me to kiss it [sic] asking me at the same time if I remembered dreaming about you. I instantly seized your hand & kissed; then you gave me a warm embrace & putting your right arm round my ~~shoulder~~ [sic] neck got up & walked about the rooms with me.

He could hardly wait for his dream to be fulfilled: 'In 8 days,' he wrote,

we will go to Berlin & then what I dreamt about we will do in reality when we are alone in your rooms without any witnesses. This is the second *secret* for you, pray write to me what you think about it, & promise to do so really as you did in my dream to me, for I do so love you.[2]

The correspondence continued in this vein for several months. In May 1875 he urged his mother again to 'keep your promise you gave me at Berlin [. . .] *always to give me alone the soft inside* of your hand to kiss; but of course you keep this as a secret for yourself.'[3] With less than four weeks to go before the summer holidays he wrote thanking her for her most recent letter: 'How glad I was to see the promise written down that I could kiss your hands as much as I liked; be shure [sic] of it I shall do it.'[4] Shortly before their reunion Wilhelm could hardly contain his excitement, calculating that it was now only '7 days or 84 hours or in 5040 minutes or in 302400 seconds' before he would be able to embrace his mother again in Potsdam and kiss her 'sweet beautiful hands'.[5] Understandably, the Crown Princess did not quite know how to respond to this effusion. Initially she returned her son's letters to him like an embarrassed schoolmistress, with the spelling corrected;[6] then she indulged him, both on her visit to Kassel and back home in Berlin, by allowing him to kiss her hands. On one occasion she even signed her letter with her child-hood nickname, 'Pussy'.[7] But, of course, the whole project was doomed from the beginning, and soon Prince Wilhelm turned his back on his mother and all she stood for, and infuriated her with his ice-cold indifference and a demonstrative ultra-Prussianism.

After the doctors' tortures and the impossible demands of Hinzpeter's regime at Kassel, the carefree existence of a student at the University of Bonn (1877–9), and even more so the life of an officer in the elite Guards regiments at Potsdam, seemed to the prince like paradise. He had survived, he had triumphed over adversity, he was free! Sought out by his aristocratic fellow students in the Corps Borussia fraternity (though he himself was banned from duelling) and flattered by his military comrades and superiors, the young heir to the throne threw himself heart and soul into the Prussian-nationalistic and militaristic atmosphere of this new world. As a Hohenzollern prince he was promoted as befitted his status: captain in 1880, battalion commander in the elite First Regiment of Guards in 1883, colonel and commander of the Hussar Guards Regiment in 1885. Potsdam was his 'El Dorado', he later recalled; among his regimental comrades he had found a family, friends, interests – everything that he had lacked beforehand. The 'awful years in which nobody understood my individuality' were over.[8] The Crown Princess was horrified by the 'zeal' with which her son dedicated himself to his military service. 'Willy is chauvinistic and ultra-Prussian to a degree and with a violence which is often very painful to me,' she wrote to Queen Victoria in 1880.[9] The liberal Austro-Hungarian Crown Prince Rudolf noted with astonished distaste in 1883 that 'Prince Wilhelm, for all his youth, has become a dyed-in-the-wool Junker and reactionary'.[10] His views were already the polar opposite of what his parents had wanted to achieve through the enlightened upbringing they had tried to give him.

The Crown Princess played one last card in the hope of keeping her influence over her son: the choice of his bride. She persuaded him to give up his wish to marry his cousin Elisabeth (Ella) of Hesse-Darmstadt, almost certainly because the family of her sister, Alice, was affected by the hereditary and lethal blood disease haemophilia. Instead, she suggested one of the two elder daughters of Duke Friedrich of Schleswig-Holstein-Sonderburg-Augustenburg, who had been deposed by the Prussian and Austrian armies in the war of 1864. The family had links to the British royal family through marriage and friendship, but was considered of inferior birth in Berlin court circles, so that this choice inevitably met with fierce resistance, above all from Kaiser Wilhelm I. Prince Wilhelm's marriage to Princess Auguste Viktoria ('Dona') of Schleswig-Holstein, celebrated on 27 February 1881 in the chapel of the Berlin Schloss, in fact brought about neither the change in the prince's political views nor much domestic happiness for Wilhelm himself. Instead of acting as a liberal, anglophile counterweight to the Berlin court clique, as Vicky and Fritz had hoped, Dona turned out to be a stiff,

6 Wilhelm and his bride, Princess Auguste Viktoria of Schleswig-Holstein, known as Dona.

narrow-minded, rigorously orthodox, arch-conservative wife, pathologically hypersensitive about her new royal (and soon to be imperial) status. In later years Wilhelm bewailed his fate to his friend Max Egon Fürst zu Fürstenberg, crying: 'She is a good woman, but terrible. [. . .] She is always afraid of losing face and is always so stiff with everyone. [. . .] You can't imagine what I have to put up with.'[11]

As a dashing colonel of Hussars, however, Prince Wilhelm did not allow himself to be constrained by the conventions of a bourgeois

Christian marriage. From the early 1880s he had a liaison with Emilie Klopp, professionally known as Miss Love, a woman from Alsace whom he later installed in Potsdam for a time as his mistress. Using letters in her possession and claiming that she had had a daughter by Wilhelm, Miss Love was able to extort considerable sums of money by blackmail; the Bismarcks bought up Wilhelm's love letters and poured scorn on the curious intimacies (some involving bondage of the hands) described therein.[12] When he came to write his celebrated memoirs, the bitter old man found it impossible to resist the temptation to mock the Kaiser's exceptionally strong sexual urges.[13] In the two or three years before his accession in 1888, Wilhelm's extramarital adventures became quite notorious in political and military circles. Together with Crown Prince Rudolf he visited the procuress Frau Wolf's brothel in Vienna, where he met two women, Ella Sommssics and Anna Homolatsch, spending several rumbustious nights with both of them together in the Austrian capital and in the Alpine resorts of Mürzsteg and Eisenerz. According to Rudolf, in the winter of 1886–7 the heir to the Prusso-German throne installed Ella Sommssics as his mistress in the Linkstrasse in Berlin. In the summer of 1887, in response to a request from Wilhelm for her to return to Berlin and bring a companion along with her, Ella wrote to him from Vienna (her letter has survived) assuring him that this other woman was indeed 'truly beautiful and also has very beautiful hands, quite in keeping with Your Highness's taste'.[14] Both Ella Sommssics and Anna Homolatsch had to be paid off on Wilhelm's accession to the throne, especially as the latter had borne him a daughter.[15] A fourth woman with whom he had a lasting affair in the mid-1880s, Elisabeth Bérard, the divorced Countess Wedel, was unlucky enough, while attached to the Persian legation in Berlin, to mislay some of the love letters that she had received from Wilhelm, as a result of which she was pursued by court agents for the rest of her life. Suffering severely from paranoia and convinced that she was the rightful German empress, she was eventually admitted to a lunatic asylum in Basel and then bundled over the border at Lörrach into the hands of the German authorities. Wilhelm's missing letters eventually came to light in Teheran after the Second World War. They were printed in facsimile in the German popular press and were without any doubt authentic.[16] There may have been other liaisons in this period the details of which have not come down to us.[17] Certainly, we shall need to bear this evidently rather needy extramarital activity in mind when we come to discuss the persistent rumours, underlined by the embarrassing scandals at his court two decades later, of the Kaiser's homosexuality.[18]

In spite of the birth of six sons and a daughter, Wilhelm's marriage was not a fulfilling one. Dona complained of his frequent long absences and had fits of jealousy when he spent too much time with Eulenburg and his cronies. Her letters show her attempting to coax him back into the family fold with promises of sexual favours of the sort he craved. She wrote to him in 1892:

I shall let you have all your little pleasures. I always have gloves on at night now to take care of my hands! [. . .] You naughty little husband for thinking that I might perhaps not give my little husband such a nice welcome as he imagines. You know how awfully much I love you, and if I am well, *how* willing I am to do everything. Come back as soon as you can my own darling and you will not be disappointed.[19]

Clearly, the Crown Princess's hope that Wilhelm's marriage to Dona would improve his relations with his parents and convert him to their political standpoint proved to be wholly misplaced. Long before his father became terminally ill with cancer, terrible disputes broke out between him and his father and mother, which took on more and more of the threatening character of usurpation. Vicky lamented tearfully that she had spent '*so* much care & love & affection & time' on her 'naughty' son, who now boasted of being 'his grandfather's & Pce B[ismarck]'s favourite' and behaved as if he were the head of the Junkers and of the reactionary *Kreuzzeitung* party. Wilhelm was 'stuck up, vain, proud, narrow minded, insolent & oh – *so* ignorant!', she cried.[20] His father was no less outraged at Wilhelm for being 'absolutely bursting with egoism'; his 'incalculable lack of tact' was 'quite horrifying'; he had absolutely 'no tact & no princely savoire [sic] faire'.[21] On occasions ashen with rage, the Crown Prince even criticised Wilhelm in public, giving vent to his fear that his son and his coterie might be tempted to challenge for the succession to the throne.

The young Prince of Prussia, spurred on by the arch-reactionary, war-obsessed and anti-Semitic Count Alfred von Waldersee, the elder Moltke's deputy as chief of the General Staff, was indeed scheming to

7 Wilhelm's father, Crown Prince Friedrich Wilhelm, in January 1883.

have the succession leapfrog over his parents, or at least to engineer a separation between his father and mother, so leaving the Crown Prince without 'the Englishwoman' at his side. As Waldersee noted as early as in the spring of 1884, it had become clear to Wilhelm, to his horror,

> that his mother never became a Prussian princess, but has remained an Englishwoman, not only with respect to lifestyle & outlook, but also at heart and above all politically. He knows that his mother is deliberately working against German & Prussian interests for the sake of English ones! Given his thoroughly Prussian sentiment, this offends him deeply, and it is often difficult for him to keep his fiery temperament under control.[22]

The way Wilhelm sometimes expressed himself 'sounded as if the thought of imprisonment [of his mother] lurked in the background', remarked Friedrich von Holstein, the secretive but always well-informed Geheimrat (Privy Councillor) at the Auswärtiges Amt, the German Foreign Office in Berlin's Wilhelmstrasse.[23]

Step by step Prince Wilhelm, with the support of the grandfather he idolised, took over the role that the Crown Prince, who was increasingly sidelined, regarded as rightly his. Now fifty-five years old, Friedrich Wilhelm felt humiliated above all by the two visits the young Wilhelm paid to Tsar Alexander III in St Petersburg and Moscow in 1884 and 1886 respectively, during which the young Prince of Prussia spoke out in the most insulting fashion against his parents, Queen Victoria and his uncle the Prince of Wales, the future King Edward VII.[24] On his return to Germany Wilhelm carried on his hate campaign against his parents, the British royal family and British policy in secret letters to the tsar, thus foreshadowing, already under the all-powerful Bismarck, the fatal 'Willy–Nicky' correspondence with Nicholas II through which he was to frustrate the foreign policy of Bismarck's successors as Reich Chancellor.[25] Queen Victoria for her part vented her anger by informing Wilhelm and his brother Heinrich through the Prince of Wales that they would not be welcome in England; for a time it even looked as if she might not invite her eldest grandson to London for her Golden Jubilee in June 1887.[26] To his parents' indignation, at the end of 1886 Prince Wilhelm succeeded in obtaining permission to work in the Auswärtiges Amt, of which Bismarck's son Count Herbert was

8 General Count Alfred von Waldersee.

9 Prince Wilhelm of Prussia in London for his grandmother's Golden Jubilee
in June 1887.

now the head.[27] Under the Bismarcks' influence, one of Wilhelm II's first actions on acceding to the throne would be to banish his uncle, the Prince of Wales, from Vienna for the duration of his own inaugural visit.[28]

It is tempting to detect in this bitter and barely credible conflict within the Anglo-German royal family that drifting apart of Bismarck's Prusso-German Reich from the countries of northern, western and southern Europe, in which parliamentary government prevailed or was taking hold, that many historians have seen as the key to understanding the looming catastrophe of the first half of the twentieth century. Prince Wilhelm's mindset, on the threshold of succeeding to the throne, was characterised by bellicose ambition and contempt for parliaments and political parties – indeed, for civilians in general. 'Britain must be destroyed' was his watchword; and he was already developing a passion for the idea of a strong German navy. But Paris too had to be 'destroyed', he railed.[29] Wilhelm was, 'naturally, very much in favour of war and hopes that it will break out soon', General Waldersee noted with glee on 25 January 1887.[30] Under the latter's influence, the prince also advocated war with Russia. 'That young man wants war with Russia, and would like to draw his sword straight away if he could,' Chancellor Bismarck recorded with dismay in 1888.[31] As if that were not enough, Wilhelm was loud in his criticism of the Jews, the Catholic Centre Party, the cosmopolitan left liberals and the internationalist Social Democrats in the Reichstag, and wrote: 'May the day soon come when the Grenadier Guards cleanse the place with bayonets and drums!'[32]

CHAPTER 5

1888: the Year of the Three Kaisers

On 22 March 1887 Kaiser Wilhelm I celebrated his ninetieth birthday. Seven days earlier Professor Karl Gerhardt had for the first time cauterised a small tumour on the Crown Prince's left vocal cord; it was eventually to become clear that Friedrich Wilhelm was suffering from cancer of the larynx. Suddenly the prospect loomed of two changes of sovereign in rapid succession, or even of the crown passing directly from Wilhelm I to Wilhelm II. Everything needed to be reconsidered. Not only for Bismarck and Waldersee, but even for loyal supporters of the Crown Prince and Princess such as their candidate for the Chancellorship, the liberal Badenese statesman Franz Freiherr von Roggenbach, the accession of a Kaiser Friedrich who was not only ill with cancer but, as a result, unable to speak and thoroughly demoralised could be contemplated only if his 'English' wife could somehow or other be removed from his side, even if it meant conjuring up a major sexual scandal.[1] Their son, Prince Wilhelm of Prussia, whose belligerent and reactionary tendencies the military and conservative forces at court had nurtured with a view to creating a bulwark against what might have been decades of rule by his liberal anglophile parents, now became the focus of everyone's calculations.

With the support of his grandfather, the court, Waldersee and Bismarck, and driven by the conviction that he had to save the divine monarchical principle in its Prussian, militaristic form from imminent takeover by his English–Coburgian mother with her 'sentimental humanitarianism' and her 'unGerman' constitutional principles, Wilhelm stepped up his machinations against his parents. After a dolorous odyssey via Bad Ems, the Isle of Wight, the Scottish Highlands, the Tyrolese Alps and Baveno, the Crown Prince and

Princess had since early November 1887 been staying in San Remo on the Italian Riviera, where by putting on a show of optimism they tried to fend off demands for Friedrich Wilhelm to renounce the throne in favour of his son. As the ninety-year-old Kaiser might die at any moment and the Crown Prince was marooned in Italy 'with his throat cut open', on 17 November 1887 Prince Wilhelm of Prussia was appointed by All-Highest Cabinet Order to act as the Kaiser's representative.[2] Only a few weeks later he was promoted to general – once again in contradiction of the express orders of his despairing father – and posted from Potsdam to Berlin, where he was given a makeshift introduction to the internal administration of Prussia and the Reich.[3]

Meanwhile, there was scarcely any room for doubt that the Crown Prince had cancer. On 11 November 1887, under the influence of his wife, Friedrich Wilhelm had rejected the operation to remove his larynx that the doctors recommended, and that might at least have saved his life, albeit in agonising circumstances; but his condition deteriorated visibly, and on 9 February 1888 Gustav Bramann had to perform a tracheotomy. The hatred for his mother and the English doctors that these tragic events inspired in Prince Wilhelm is palpable from his letter to his friend Philipp Eulenburg:

My poor father, so often deceived, surrounded by lies, deceit, intrigue and scheming, underwent the operation at the last minute, when it was nearly *too late*. He is bearing the dreadful disease like a hero, which, due to the incompetence and malice of the Englishmen, nearly cost him his life. [. . .] Racial hatred, anti-Germanism to the very edge of the grave! [. . .] Satan's bones![4]

When Wilhelm arrived in San Remo on 2 March 1888 to take charge of his father's treatment, however, the latter wrote to him forbidding him to interfere in any way at all.[5]

By now it had become inevitable that the doomed Crown Prince would have to return to Germany, and the decision had already been taken when, on 9 March 1888, a telegram arrived in San Remo from Wilhelm announcing the death of the old Kaiser. Friedrich Wilhelm set off for Berlin as Kaiser and King Friedrich III. At first he took up residence at Schloss Charlottenburg. But the new monarch was to be granted only ninety-nine agonising days on the throne before the crown again passed from father to son. Almost all those who saw the weak, speechless Kaiser came to the conclusion that he ought to abdicate; only Kaiserin Victoria's antipathy towards her son, it was rumoured, could explain why the conduct of affairs had not long since been transferred to their son Wilhelm, who was now of course Crown Prince. Terrible conflicts arose between him and the empress, Victoria. On 12 April 1888, in another bitter letter to Eulenburg, Wilhelm wrote:

What I have endured here in the last 8 days simply defies description and even mocks the imagination! The sense of deep shame for the sunken prestige of my once so high and inviolable House – that is the strongest feeling! [. . .] But that our family shield should be besmirched and the Reich brought to the brink of ruin by an English princess who is my mother – that is the most terrible thing of all![6]

Wilhelm's fear that the 'English' Kaiserin at the side of the dying Kaiser Friedrich III could, with the help of her liberal and Jewish supporters, undermine the Prusso-German Reich as 'the bastion of monarchy' and bring in parliamentarianism in the western European mould was, in fact, completely unfounded. The forces opposed to Victoria, whether around the Bismarcks in the Wilhelmstrasse, at court, in the Prussian officer corps, in the administration or even in her own entourage, were far too strong.[7] All were focused on the 'rising sun' of the twenty-nine-year-old heir to the throne, and were counting the days until his accession. Kaiser Friedrich was no more than a skeleton; he lay in bed with a high fever, expectorated large amounts of pus and had an agonising cough. On 1 June 1888 he was moved by water from Charlottenburg to the Neues Palais in Potsdam. Soon afterwards the cancer perforated his oesophagus. Friedrich III died at 11.30 a.m. on 15 June 1888; at that moment Wilhelm II became German Kaiser, King of Prussia, Summus Episcopus (Supreme Bishop) of the Lutheran–Calvinist Evangelical Church, Supreme War Lord of the most powerful army in the world and commander-in-chief of the nascent German navy. As his first act he had a cordon thrown round the palace by his Hussars, to prevent his mother from smuggling her papers out (although they were in fact in Windsor Castle, where they had been sent via the British embassy some time ago). This act had symbolic significance: far from introducing a form of government appropriate to the modern, pluralistic, industrial society that the united Germany was rapidly becoming, the new Kaiser set about implementing his conception of a monarchical-militaristic autocracy by divine right, for all the world as if he were Frederick the Great.

PART II

1888–1909: The Anachronistic Autocrat

CHAPTER 6

Divine right without end

For contemporaries, the transition from the ninety-year-old Kaiser Wilhelm I to his twenty-nine-year-old grandson Wilhelm II seemed like jumping a generation. Ideologically, however, the Year of the Three Kaisers was more a matter of leaping a chasm of centuries. It is true that the Empress Frederick, as Victoria now asked to be known, with her almost republican convictions, was in many respects far in advance of her time; she could never have gained acceptance for her ideas in the system of 'personal monarchy', which, thanks to Bismarck, was once again firmly entrenched in Germany (and Prussia in particular). Yet the conception of the divine monarchical principle that the young Wilhelm had absorbed, not least as a counterweight to his parents' liberal ideals, belonged to the eighteenth century, to the era before the Enlightenment, the French Revolution and Napoleon. Although Bismarck had prided himself on preserving the Hohenzollern monarchy from the clutches of parliamentarianism and preventing it from degenerating – as in Britain, Italy, Scandinavia, the Netherlands and Belgium – into an 'automatic signing machine',[1] he was compelled to realise, soon after the double change of sovereign in 1888, that by keeping alive the 'monarchical principle' he had put an axe to the roots not only of his own position of power but also of the entire Reich structure he had built up. By ignoring the constitutional aspirations and the centuries-old experience of Europe, he had opened the door to arbitrary rule, sycophantic favouritism and strutting militarism at the court of the Hohenzollerns. If 'personal monarchy' was no more than a legal fiction in Bismarck's eyes, Wilhelm II took it literally and regarded the monarchical principle of divine right as legitimising his autocracy.

10 Oil portrait by Rudolf Wimmer of Kaiser Wilhelm II in the uniform of a British admiral of the fleet on the terrace of Osborne House in 1889.

According to his view of his role as Kaiser and king, he was the intermediary between God and his people: he received his instructions from God and was duty bound, under his 'obligation to God',[2] to carry out the divine will against all criticism. In all seriousness he claimed that crowned heads such as himself were born with the gift of second sight, which all ordinary, mortal statesmen lacked. A monarch who allowed himself to be restricted by the constitution or by parliament deserved only contempt. 'I am accustomed to being obeyed,' he declared in 1890, shortly before Bismarck's dismissal. 'The word of a Kaiser is not to be trifled with.'[3] His quasi-absolutist pretension to power was reflected in numerous speeches and in portraits showing him in martial pose, with an oversized field marshal's baton and a defiant expression. There was scarcely any domain in which Wilhelm II did not feel called to interfere with claims of superior knowledge. At a time when Friedrich Nietzsche and Henrik Ibsen had announced the death of God, public opinion – and not only in Germany – was startled by such anachronistically autocratic behaviour. Even within the Hohenzollern family it was murmured that Wilhelm II had come into the world too late; he really belonged to an earlier century. Certainly, such antediluvian notions of kingship stood in the way of his conjuring up an aura of charismatic leadership such as even the 'wooden titan' Hindenburg later managed, albeit in vastly altered circumstances[4] – not to speak of Hitler.

Under the old Kaiser, Bismarck had always been able to get his way in the end, if only by threatening to resign. With the accession of Wilhelm I's impetuous grandson, imbued with his notion of divine right and secretly influenced by ambitious generals such as Waldersee and romantic aesthetes such as Eulenburg, that was soon to change. A struggle for power with the seventy-three-year-old Reich Chancellor, Prince Otto von Bismarck, was only a matter of time.

CHAPTER 7

Bismarck's fall from power (1889–1890)

The warning signals had begun before Wilhelm's accession. A break had already occurred between the headstrong young Prince of Prussia and the Reich Chancellor in November 1887, when Wilhelm took part in a meeting at Waldersee's house in support of the Berlin City Mission led by the 'Christian-Socialist' (in other words, anti-Semitic) court preacher Adolf Stoecker. Bismarck felt obliged to reprimand him for thus identifying himself, in a manner particularly inappropriate for an heir to the imperial German throne, with the reactionary ultra-Prussian *Kreuzzeitung* faction.[1] At the same time, Wilhelm sent the Chancellor a decree addressed to 'the Princes of the German Reich', which he had drafted and which he intended to issue to each of his monarchical 'colleagues' at his accession, so that 'the old uncles' would obey him: the Kaiser by divine right. 'And jump to it they must!' Wilhelm declared in the brash jargon of the Guards lieutenant to which he had become accustomed in Potsdam, and which he used throughout his life.[2] Appalled, Bismarck urged him to burn this toxic document at once.

Even worse than this threat to the federalist basis of Bismarck's Reich was the undermining of the Chancellor's peaceful foreign policy. Since the autumn of 1887 Prince Wilhelm had become a supporter of the pro-war party that had formed around the deputy chief of the General Staff, Count Alfred von Waldersee, and had pressed for an immediate strike against France and Russia. On 17 December 1887 he went so far as to attend a 'war council' of the generals around the old Kaiser, which expressed itself in favour of a war of aggression. The Reich Chancellor complained angrily in May 1888: 'That young man wants war with Russia, and would like to draw his sword straight away if he could. I am not going along with that.' Four weeks before Wilhelm II's accession Bismarck exclaimed: 'Alas, my poor grandchildren.'[3]

Despite these gloomy forebodings Wilhelm II's relationship with the Chancellor and his family improved temporarily after his accession on 15 June 1888. In order not to 'become a burden' to the young monarch, the Chancellor withdrew to his estate of Friedrichsruh on the outskirts of Hamburg, and later to his Pomeranian property, Varzin.[4] Apart from short duty visits he did not return to Berlin until 24 January 1890. During these eighteen months the thirty-nine-year-old Count Herbert von Bismarck, whose official role was as Secretary of State at the Foreign Office, was in almost daily contact both with the monarch and, by letter and telegraph, with his father. But the flattery with which Herbert, otherwise notorious for his cynical contempt of his fellow men, sought to beguile the Kaiser betrayed the fundamental weakness of the Bismarckian system, which ultimately was entirely dependent on the 'All-Highest confidence' of the sovereign. Not a few of the Bismarcks' decisions at this time were taken against their better judgment, simply to avoid jeopardising their own position of power. Yet for how long could such tactics be used? Waldersee continued to stir up opposition to the allegedly harmful 'Russia-friendliness' of the Bismarcks and had no scruples about suggesting to Wilhelm II that Frederick II would never have become 'Frederick the Great' if he had had a minister like Bismarck telling him what to do. He would let the old man trundle on for another year or so, Wilhelm was heard to say, then he would rule himself.[5]

It was a seemingly trifling question of a public appointment that, like a distant lightning flash, announced the storm that was brewing. In May 1886, during a shoot in East Prussia, Wilhelm had met Count Philipp zu Eulenburg-Hertefeld. Twelve years the prince's senior, Eulenburg was then an insignificant diplomat at the Prussian legation in Munich and led a carefree life on the Starnberger See. Since this first meeting the friendship between the two men had deepened: Eulenburg, a poet, playwright, singer, composer, spiritualist and affectionate family man, and also an active homosexual, fell in love with the young prince, to whom he gave that unconditional devotion and admiration that Hinzpeter had once said Wilhelm would need more than any other human

11 Before the storm: Kaiser Wilhelm II with Otto von Bismarck
at Friedrichsruh in autumn 1888

being. In the autumn of 1888, soon after his accession, the Kaiser
demanded that Herbert Bismarck promote his 'best friend' 'Phili'
Eulenburg to the post of Prussian envoy in Munich. The Reich
Chancellor's consternation at the Kaiser's wish clearly demonstrates
the difference of principle between Bismarck's concept of the
state and the personal style of rule that Wilhelm II embodied
and was determined to attain. If government posts were filled
according to the monarch's wishes, Bismarck warned, government
ministers would gradually be demoted to the level of personal
royal counsellors. This was a matter of fundamental importance
over which he could not give way. If the Kaiser loved Philipp
Eulenburg more than any other human being, as Herbert had
reported, then the place for the Kaiser's friend was at court, not
in state service. It came about exactly as Bismarck had predicted:

12 Count (later Prince) Philipp zu Eulenburg-Hertefeld, the Kaiser's best friend.

in the course of the following years Kaiser Wilhelm, with Eulenburg's help, established his personal rule; the ministers and even the
Reich Chancellor were downgraded, step by step, to little more
than royal lackeys.

From May 1889 onwards conflicts accumulated between the young Kaiser and his Chancellor. Spurred on by Hinzpeter, who had retired to his home in Bielefeld, Wilhelm suddenly intervened in the miners' strike in the Ruhr district. On 12 May, 'in a very excited state', he burst into a meeting of the Prussian Ministry of State and declared that he did not agree with the Chancellor's policy, as 'the workers were His subjects whom He had to look after'.[6] Soon afterwards he received deputations from both employees and employers involved in the strike. After this worrying episode Bismarck remarked pessimistically that 'the young Master' had 'Friedrich Wilhelm I's conception of his powers' – the Prussian King Friedrich Wilhelm I was the father of Frederick the Great – and that it was imperative to set him right at once, in order to protect him from such 'overhasty actions'.[7] But that was easier said than done. The following month the Kaiser high-handedly ordered the Chancellor to abandon his plan for the conversion of Russian bonds, after Waldersee had led him to believe that a dishonest financial transaction by Gerson Bleichröder, Bismarck's Jewish banker, was involved. During the Kaiser's first Scandinavian cruise in the summer of 1889, on which Eulenburg was also present, Waldersee persuaded Wilhelm that Bismarck was completely 'Jew-ridden' and that the policy of the German Reich was being controlled by Jews! 'It is quite clear that filthy money-interests now play an important role [for Bismarck], and quite probably the only role,' the deputy chief of the General Staff claimed. 'It is truly terrible: the Jew Bleichröder has a great influence on our foreign and domestic policies. [...] The Chancellor has thrown himself completely into the arms of Herr Bleichröder.'[8] That the young Kaiser was open to such insinuations boded ill. Waldersee's paranoid delusions of a Jewish conspiracy were to play a fatal role in the final phase of the dismissal crisis, as we shall see.

Not only did Wilhelm behave with increasing self-confidence, but a secret clique of advisers formed around him, consisting of men who called into question everything the Bismarcks set out to do, whether in domestic matters or foreign policy. As well as Waldersee and Eulenburg, the clique included Wilhelm's uncle, Grand Duke Friedrich of Baden, the Badenese envoy in Berlin, Adolf Freiherr Marschall von Bieberstein, and the influential *éminence grise*, Geheimrat Friedrich von Holstein, in the Foreign Office. In the background the monarch received further encouragement from his tutor Hinzpeter and from the director of the Colonial Department of the Foreign Office, Dr Paul Kayser, an expert in social policy who had tutored Eulenburg and Bismarck's sons as students. Although Bismarck had the feeling that he was surrounded by spies, until the end he had no idea who was behind the Kaiser's campaign against him.

The perspicacious Holstein warned strongly against bringing the Chancellor crisis to a head too soon. If Bismarck with his immense prestige were to resign in anger, all the Prussian ministers would go with him. Moreover, the Reichstag election of February 1890 was not far off, and the danger of a war with Russia and France could by no means be dismissed. 'In short,' the wily privy councillor warned, 'there would be a fearful scene.' The election threatened to be catastrophic for the government, and the young Kaiser would be 'obliged to tackle an internal conflict without Bismarck [...] with France and Russia looking on'.[9] In order to avoid a chaotic state of unrest bordering on civil war, with the risk of foreign intervention and bloodshed, which would permanently discredit Wilhelm II and his budding Kaiserdom, Holstein, Eulenburg and the other secret advisers urged the young monarch to steer an ostentatiously moderate course in both domestic and foreign policy. In the Reichstag election he had to do what he could to bring about the victory of the 'state-supporting' Kartell coalition between the Conservatives, the national-conservative German Reich Party and the National Liberals. And in foreign affairs he had to insist on the maintenance of the Triple Alliance between Germany, Austria-Hungary and Italy, which Bismarck's pro-Russian policy seemed in danger of undermining.

Soon, however, the Kaiser's clandestine advisers began to suspect that Bismarck, in order to make himself indispensable and to 'drive the Kaiser to the wall', was working in precisely the opposite direction on both counts: shortly before the general election they thought he was trying to destroy the right-wing Kartell coalition and also to alienate Germany's dependable ally, Austria-Hungary, by moving yet closer to Russia. In the subsequent *Tohubawohu* ('hullabaloo', as he called it in a letter to Emperor Franz Joseph of Austria),[10] the Kaiser's hopes of gradually taking the reins into his own hands would disappear for good. In the last nine months of his Chancellorship Bismarck's every move – his tentative approach to the Centre Party to end the Kulturkampf with the Roman Catholic Church, his uncompromising attitude towards the Kartell parties over the Anti-Socialist bill, his adamant rejection of further social reforms, his flirtation with the idea of a *coup d'état*, the great military bill he planned – was interpreted by Wilhelm II and his secret advisory clique as a cunning manoeuvre to checkmate the Kaiser and establish the 'Bismarck dynasty' in permanent charge. In this endgame both sides placed high stakes on winning power: the Bismarcks – alongside egotistical motives – with a view to preventing the young Hohenzollern monarch, vain, emotionally unstable and open to uncontrollable influences as he was, from ruling in person; the clique of secret advisers in the conviction that the salvation of Prussia/Germany lay alone in the personal rule of their 'All-Highest Lord' Kaiser Wilhelm II.

When the Kaiser's proclamations on social policy, which Bismarck had bitterly contested, were promulgated on 4 February 1890 without the constitutionally prescribed countersignature of the Reich Chancellor, Kayser – who had secretly drafted them for Wilhelm at Eulenburg's bidding – was jubilant. 'Things will get better still,' he wrote; the press was 'still gazing with amazement at the mere fact, like some traveller high in the Alps when the mist clears and he is blinded by the shining landscape in the valley below'.[11] Waldersee commented gleefully on how 'the Kaiser has remained the master and overpowered the Chancellor'. Spurred on by the apparent success of his proclamations and of the international conference on workers' welfare that he had convened despite Bismarck's opposition, the Kaiser now thought he could take a more ruthless line towards Bismarck.

At the same time, however, the Reichstag election turned out so unfavourably for the government that the old Chancellor's position seemed to have become stronger again. The three Kartell parties with which the Kaiser had identified himself were beaten hands down, the mainly Catholic Centre Party acquired a decisive role in parliament by gaining 106 seats, and with almost a million and a half votes the republican/Marxist SPD (the Social Democratic Party of Germany) became the strongest party in the country in terms of its share of the poll. Was this really the right moment to sack the founder of the Reich and transfer power into the hands of an untried young Kaiser? Calls for a *coup d'état* to get rid of universal manhood suffrage made themselves heard in the imperial camp, but were quickly silenced by the realisation that such a policy of force would turn Wilhelm II's initiative on social welfare into a laughing stock. Worse still, Bismarck would become indispensable and thus emerge as victor in the conflict with the Crown after all. When the Chancellor spoke first of an even more severe Anti-Socialist bill and then of an enormous Army bill, both of which would be unacceptable to the new Reichstag, the Kaiser's friends took fright: this plan of Bismarck's was 'the most masterful move in the whole game of chess; it means checkmate for the King'.[12] As they saw it, Bismarck was pursuing a policy of provocation and confusion in order to cause *Tohuwabohu* – social unrest, the undermining of Prussia's supremacy in the Reich and jeopardising the alliance with Austria-Hungary and Italy, with the ultimate aim of permanently disempowering the monarch and perpetuating his own dictatorship as Chancellor.

On 12 March 1890 the news came as a bombshell that the Reich Chancellor had been negotiating with Ludwig Windthorst, the leader of the Centre Party, over a further dismantling of the Kulturkampf legislation against the Roman Catholic Church in Germany. Wilhelm's fury knew no bounds, especially when he learned that the meeting with Windthorst had been arranged through Gerson Bleichröder, Bismarck's banker. He saw the combination of Bismarck, Windthorst and Bleichröder as confirmation of the delusion long since implanted in him by Waldersee: that, under Bismarck, the Prusso-German Kaiserreich was being secretly ruled by Jews! In his eyes the negotiations between the Chancellor and the leader of the Centre Party represented 'collusion between the Jesuits and the rich Jews'.[13]

This was the last straw. Early in the morning of 15 March 1890 there took place one of the most highly charged scenes ever played out in Berlin's centre of government, the Wilhelmstrasse.[14] Kaiser Wilhelm II summoned the seventy-five-year-old Reich Chancellor from his bed and upbraided him for receiving Windthorst. He went on to complain that Bismarck had dug out a dusty old Cabinet Order of 1852 that prevented the monarch from receiving ministers except in the presence of the minister-president; he peremptorily demanded that the order be rescinded, which Bismarck refused to do. Wilhelm later recounted that Bismarck had become 'so violent' towards him that he was afraid the Chancellor would 'throw the inkstand at my head'.[15] After this dramatic quarrel Waldersee urged the Kaiser, in the presence of the chief of the Military Cabinet, General von Hahnke, to sack Bismarck forthwith. The present state of affairs was 'quite untenable', he argued, and moreover the Chancellor was 'too closely allied with the Jews'.[16] Wilhelm sent first Hahnke and then the chief of the Civil Cabinet, Hermann von Lucanus, to the Chancellor ordering him to hand in his resignation, which Bismarck finally did on 18 March 1890. If Waldersee, as one can safely assume, expected to take Bismarck's place he was in for a bitter disappointment. That same evening Kaiser Wilhelm II announced to the commanding generals assembled in the Berlin Schloss that 'in order to remain master of the situation' he had had to 'issue an ultimatum' to the Chancellor 'insisting that he submit'. He would accept Bismarck's letter of resignation and appoint General Georg Leo von Caprivi as Reich Chancellor in his place.[17]

The intrigue-ridden, passion-fuelled dismissal of the founder of the Reich in March 1890 was one of the most momentous decisions that Kaiser Wilhelm II was to take in his long reign. It sounded the alarm in the capitals of Europe. In Germany too the consequences were even worse than Holstein had predicted at the beginning of the crisis. Blinded by the Prussian vision of the divine monarchical principle, the Kaiser's secret advisers had underestimated the massive popular support that Bismarck enjoyed after twenty-eight years in power, both in political elites and among the educated nationalist bourgeoisie. The division of the 'state-supporting' classes into two bitterly opposed camps – the Kaiser on the one hand, the Bismarcks on the other – proved to be a burden that weighed heavily on the first years of Wilhelm II's reign.[18] Eight years later, when Prince Otto von Bismarck was dead, Wilhelm gave a telling explanation of why he had nevertheless sent away the founder of the Reich 'like a butler' and accepted the risk of a Bismarckian fronde. 'For ever & for ever,' he exulted in a letter to his mother in 1898, 'there is only *one real Emperor* in the world, & that is the *German*, regardless of his Person & qualities, but by *right* of a *thousand years tradition*. And his Chancellor has to *obey!*'[19]

CHAPTER 8

The establishment of the Kaiser's personal monarchy (1890–1897)

Just why Wilhelm II hit upon General von Caprivi as Bismarck's successor in the three highest offices – Reich Chancellor, Prussian minister-president and Prussian minister for foreign affairs – remains a mystery. The only clue we have is that Eulenburg visited the reclusive general, whom he had never met beforehand, at his regimental headquarters in Hanover on 6 March 1890.[1] Even the Kaiser's brother, Prince Heinrich, thought the news of the appointment had to be a mistake and commented that it was surely Waldersee who was to be Chancellor, while Caprivi would be chief of the General Staff.[2] The choice of this thoroughly decent, unsophisticated, non-political general gave the by no means mistaken impression that the Kaiser wanted to be his own Reich Chancellor. Caprivi had no natural supporter base at court or among the landed aristocracy, let alone in the newly elected Reichstag, where he lacked any kind of backing. Moreover, he had no experience of foreign affairs; a German diplomat spoke of his 'almost crass ignorance' in this field.[3] Caprivi's self-admitted incompetence in foreign policy became an even greater drawback when the Kaiser, after failing to persuade Herbert Bismarck to stay on, appointed as head of the Foreign Office a man who also lacked any diplomatic experience, namely Holstein's protégé Adolf Freiherr Marschall von Bieberstein, a lawyer who till then had been the representative of the south-west German grand duchy of Baden in Berlin. It is scarcely possible to imagine a more serious loss of diplomatic expertise than that constituted by the replacement of the two Bismarcks by Caprivi and Marschall.

As fate would have it, it was precisely at this chaotic transitional moment that a decision had to be reached on whether the secret Reinsurance Treaty with Russia, concluded by Bismarck in 1887 for a three-year term, should be extended. In spite of the hostility towards Russia that Waldersee had nurtured in him, Wilhelm II at first wanted to renew the treaty, but then he suddenly decided against it. In so doing he gave way to the determined opposition of Caprivi, to whom Holstein had explained the danger that the secret treaty might become public knowledge – not least through the machinations of a resentful Bismarck – which would put Germany's alliance with Austria-Hungary at risk. Thus it was that a decision of enormous significance for the future was taken in an atmosphere approaching panic – a decision that was all too soon to lead to an alliance between tsarist Russia in the east and republican France in the west, and so to conjure up the nightmare for Germany of a war on two fronts.[4]

Yet the transition from the two Bismarcks to Caprivi and Marschall amounted to far more than a change of personnel. With the fall of the almighty Prince von Bismarck the centre of power shifted from the Chancellor to the Kaiser, from the green baize tables of the Wilhelmstrasse to the Schloss, from the state to the court. As Christopher Clark has put it in his profile of the Kaiser in power, '[W]hen Wilhelm came to the throne, the office of emperor was like a house in which most of the rooms had never been occupied.' But all this was soon to change. After Bismarck's dismissal 'the throne was no longer, as under Wilhelm I, merely the seat of authority on which power depended, but a political power in its own right'.[5] The division of decision-making power between the Crown on the one hand and the machinery of state, the so-called 'responsible government', on the other, in which the possibilities open to the monarch were incomparably greater than those of the new Reich Chancellor, became more crisis-prone as a result. As German Kaiser, King of Prussia and Supreme War Lord of the armed forces, Wilhelm II was the glittering focus of a vast, magnificent court and a dominant, chiefly aristocratic and hierarchically structured elite society, both of which soon lost all trace of traditional Prussian thriftiness.[6] A visitor to the German capital would have had no difficulty in identifying the seat of power in Berlin. Between 1888 and 1910 the Prussian Civil List approved by parliament grew from 7.7 million marks per annum to 19.2 million; in addition, Wilhelm II received, in his capacity as German Kaiser, an All-Highest reserve fund of 3 million marks per annum. With over sixty castles and a gigantic private fortune, he was one of the richest men in Germany. Compared with this, Leo von Caprivi, unmarried, untitled and without private means – mocked by the East Elbian landowners as 'the Chancellor without a single acre of land' – lived in what were almost frugal conditions in the old Reich Chancellor's palace at No. 77 in the Wilhelmstrasse. The minuscule Reich Chancellery, with a mere handful of officials, served as his secretariat. The Chancellor's annual salary was fixed at a meagre 54,000 marks. In 1895 Caprivi's successor, Prince Chlodwig zu Hohenlohe-Schillingsfürst, secretly accepted a supplement to his official salary of 120,000 marks a year from the Kaiser's crown fund, which did not exactly increase his willingness to stand up to the latter.[7] Not until the Chancellorship of Prince von Bülow (1900–9) were the premises in the Reich Chancellor's palace renovated and the salary of the most senior statesman in the Reich and Prussia raised as befitted his status.[8] But, by then, imperial dominance over the machinery of state had long since been established.

A defining feature of Prussia's military monarchy was the strong army presence at court, which at Wilhelm II's accession was brought together as the 'Headquarters of His Majesty the Kaiser and King' under the command of an adjutant general. Among his martial entourage at court, Wilhelm could indulge his sense of military superiority over all civilians. There were always two energetic aides-de-camp, his *Flügeladjutanten*, on duty with the monarch, which led to an 'almost religious relationship' developing between the tall officers and the young Kaiser. Through his Military Cabinet, and the Naval Cabinet that he himself introduced in 1889, Wilhelm determined the personnel policy of both army and navy, which gave him an unparalleled influence on all the families represented in both officer corps. For any communication with the state authorities in Prussia and the Reich the monarch could call upon his Civil Cabinet, under the direction of Hermann von Lucanus. Thanks to their permanent access to the monarch, the chiefs of all three Secret Cabinets acquired an influence on the formulation of policy far beyond that of the Prussian Ministers of State and the secretaries of the Reich Offices.

In the latent power struggle between Kaiser and Chancellor that was fought out in the 1890s, the striking difference between the personalities of the protagonists must also not be overlooked. Caprivi had taken on his thorny role as Bismarck's successor with the greatest reluctance. Only rarely was he prepared, by threatening to resign, to insist on getting his way against Wilhelm II's opposition. With very few exceptions (one being the Prussian minister of war), the eight Prussian Ministers of State and the seven Secretaries of State of the Reich Offices were apolitical bureaucrats who had already been accustomed to toeing the line under Bismarck. No serious opposition to the extension of the Kaiser's power could be expected of them either. Only if they had all combined against the monarch and collectively threatened to resign could they perhaps have compelled him to withdraw a measure they considered dubious – but even so not permanently, for, as Kaiser and king, Wilhelm could gradually dismiss the recalcitrant ministers and replace them with more malleable characters. As indeed he did.

And how different from the basically servile attitude of the so-called 'responsible government' was his own self-confident, energetic, overbearing, at times almost manic personality! In asserting and extending his prerogatives Kaiser Wilhelm II showed an iron will to power. His claim to autocracy is proverbial. Even before his accession he had uttered the threat: 'Beware the time when I shall give the orders!'[9] His recently edited speeches bear testimony to his absolutist ambitions. As he announced at Düsseldorf in 1891, with the Bismarck fronde in mind, he alone was master in the Reich and he would tolerate no other.[10] '*Suprema lex regis voluntas!*' ('The will of the king is the highest law!') he inscribed in the Golden Book of the City of Munich.[11] Appalled, Wilhelm's mother wrote full of foreboding to her own mother, Queen Victoria:

I think he *can* hardly understand *what* a bévue [blunder] he is making when *he* writes such a thing!!! – A Czar, an infallible Pope, the Bourbons and our poor Charles I might have written such a sentence – but a constitutional monarch in the 19th Century!! So young a man, – the son of *his* father – & *your grandson* – not to speak of a child of mine – should neither have nor express such a maxim.[12]

Undeterred by the public outcry, the Kaiser proclaimed in a speech of 1892: 'My course is the right one, and in it I shall continue to steer. We are destined for greatness, and I shall lead you to

13 Wilhelm II with his British relations and the newly engaged couple,
Nicholas of Russia and Alix of Hesse, at Coburg in 1894.

glorious days.'[13] 'I am the sole master of German policy and my
country must follow me wherever I go,' he claimed at the turn of the
century.[14] Such assertions were so anachronistic that people seriously
wondered whether the Kaiser was mentally deranged. As early as in
1894 the historian Ludwig Quidde's pamphlet *Caligula*, in which he
levelled a barely disguised accusation of 'Caesaromania' at Wilhelm II,
had enormous success with the public. In Vienna a joke went
the rounds that Kaiser Wilhelm wanted to be the stag at every hunt,
the bride at every wedding and the corpse at every funeral!

The Chancellors, ministers and Secretaries of State of the post-Bismarck era were powerless against the relentless claims to power of their sovereign. Wilhelm tyrannised them with crass abuse. 'All of you know nothing; I alone know something, I alone decide,'[15] was the tenor of his communications, which also often found expression in unbelievably aggressive marginal comments, many of which Bismarck while still Chancellor ordered to be locked away. He even addressed the Prussian minister of war and the chief of the Military Cabinet as '[y]ou old asses'.[16] 'The Foreign Office?' he asked contemptuously. 'What do you mean? I am the Foreign Office!'[17] His diplomats had so 'filled their pants' that the whole Wilhelmstrasse stank to high heaven.[18] Of course, he reserved the right to appoint Germany's ambassadors himself. 'I shall only send to London an ambassador who enjoys *My* confidence, obeys *My* will and carries out *My* orders,' he was still insisting in 1912, when Prince Lichnowsky was appointed.[19]

In view of such a loudly proclaimed imperial appetite for power it is hardly surprising that the 'responsible government' abandoned resistance to the personal monarchy in the course of the crisis-ridden 1890s. In 1892 Caprivi resigned as Prussian minister-president and handed over this post to the arch-conservative Count Botho zu Eulenburg (a cousin of Philipp), remaining in office only as Reich Chancellor and Prussian minister for foreign affairs. The authority of the Reich Chancellor was thereby literally 'halved', especially as Wilhelm II soon appointed Botho Eulenburg to the additional post of Prussian interior minister. After the 'ninth crisis', in October 1894 he dismissed, to everyone's surprise, both Caprivi and Botho Eulenburg. Following the suggestion of his intimate friend Philipp Eulenburg, on whose estate – Liebenberg – the decision was taken, he appointed the seventy-five-year-old Bavarian Prince Chlodwig zu Hohenlohe-Schillingsfürst as Reich Chancellor and Prussian minister-president. As the Badenese Adolf Marschall von Bieberstein remained in office as Secretary of State at the Foreign Office and also played a considerable role in the Reichstag, the stage was set for a conflict between the Prussian, militaristic Hohenzollern ruler and his court on the one hand and the two more liberal 'south Germans', Hohenlohe and Marschall, in the Wilhelmstrasse on the other. Only after further violent disputes, during which the Kaiser was again advised by the 'black knight' Philipp Eulenburg at his side, did the conflict come to an end in the summer of 1897, with a clear victory for the monarch. Marschall von Bieberstein was replaced by the sleek diplomat Bernhard von Bülow – once again the candidate suggested by 'Phili' Eulenburg – who from the outset was able to play the role of a Chancellor-in-waiting. Although Hohenlohe stayed in office until October 1900 he himself admitted – as was indeed apparent to everyone – that he had sunk to becoming a mere 'straw doll' for the Kaiser.[20]

Yet, without the protection of 'ministerial clothes', as Bismarck had warned, the Crown was increasingly exposed to the storm of public criticism. In 1897 the left liberal parliamentarian Eugen Richter, to thunderous applause in the Reichstag, denounced Wilhelm II's 'personal rule' with the words:

Where are the Ministers today? Wherever you look there are only compliant courtiers who agree with every opinion from above, promoted bureaucrats, dashing Hussars turned politician, lackeys... Germany is a monarchical, constitutional country, but although it may still be possible to rule Russia according to the principles of *sic volo sic jubeo* or *regis voluntas suprema lex*, the German people will not allow themselves to be ruled like that for long.[21]

At the end of 1899 Richter and Ernst Lieber, Windthorst's successor as leader of the Centre Party, fiercely attacked the Kaiser again in the Reichstag. Thanks to his anachronistic exercise of power and his reactionary views, Wilhelm found himself on a collision course with his own people.

The enthusiasm for reform that the Kaiser had shown at his accession had long since vanished. The social policy programme inspired by Georg Hinzpeter and Paul Kayser, which had culminated in the exemplary proclamations of February 1890, soon ground to a halt when the hoped-for effect – turning the workforce against the Social Democratic Party – failed to materialise. In 1891 the Kaiser alarmed the world with a speech in Potsdam in which he told young recruits that he might one day give orders 'that you must shoot down and stab to death your own relations and brothers'.[22] From 1894 onwards, against the determined resistance of Caprivi, Marschall and Holstein, Wilhelm advocated the forcible suppression of the 'revolutionary parties' – meaning first and foremost the

Social Democrats – by means of a *coup d'état* abolishing universal suffrage. The 'Anti-Revolutionary bill' demanded by him failed miserably in the Reichstag. In 1898 Wilhelm insisted, in a speech while he was on army manoeuvres, that anyone who called a strike or prevented someone else from working had to be imprisoned with penal servitude. The 'Hard Labour bill' subsequently brought in on the Kaiser's orders, and largely drafted by him, was also rejected by parliament by a huge majority. Around the turn of the century he blustered that 'matters will not improve until the troops drag the Social Democratic leaders out of the Reichstag and gun them down'.[23] When the Berlin tram workers went on strike in 1900 the Kaiser telegraphed to the city commandant: 'I expect at least five hundred people to be shot when the troops intervene.'[24] In 1901 he warned the Alexander Regiment, garrisoned near the Schloss, that it had to 'be prepared, as it were like a bodyguard day and night, to risk life and limb for the King and his house if necessary'.[25] Two years later he threatened to 'avenge' the 1848 revolution in Berlin: he would shoot down all Social Democrats, but not until they had 'done a good job of plundering the Jews and the rich'.[26] In the Reichstag, August Bebel, the leader of the SPD, which had meanwhile grown ever larger, spoke of the 'hatred' his party felt 'towards the person of the Kaiser' and commented that every imperial speech of that sort brought the workers' party about 100,000 more votes.[27] Not a trace of the 'social Kaiserdom' of 1889 and 1890 remained. But Wilhelm also abused Catholic Germany in tirades 'spitting with rage'; Catholicism, he is said to have written in 1901, when he expelled his aunt Anna Landgravine of Hesse from the fold of the Hohenzollern family on her conversion to Rome, was 'a superstition that I have made it my life's work to root out'.[28]

When it came to educational policy and the promotion of technological innovation, however, Wilhelm II showed himself to be astonishingly progressive, in this respect true to the legacy of his grandfather Prince Albert and the influence of Hinzpeter. In his peculiar way he combined the court culture of absolutism and a class warfare approach towards millions of his subjects, on the one hand, with genuine enthusiasm for the modern world of technological progress on the other. In the background, Hinzpeter in Bielefeld

14 Wilhelm Imperator Rex: the Kaiser at the height of his personal power.

was at hand advising the Kaiser when he convened educational conferences in 1890 and 1900, which led to the reform of the public grammar schools in Prussia. Hinzpeter was succeeded as adviser on issues of educational policy by the director general of the Prussian

State Library, Adolf (von) Harnack, with whose help Wilhelm II founded the celebrated Kaiser Wilhelm Society, now the Max Planck Society, in 1911. These were certainly admirable achievements, which are constantly, and rightly, praised and emphasised by the Kaiser's apologists. Compared with the appalling deficiencies of his rule in domestic and foreign policy, however, they count for little.

CHAPTER 9

The Chancellor as courtier: the corrupt Bülow system (1897–1909)

In the summer of 1897 Wilhelm II appointed to high office two men who could hardly have been more different from each other in character, but who embodied the rift in his own personality and were to have a decisive influence on the middle years of his reign. One was the Machiavellian diplomat and courtier Bernhard von Bülow, whom the Kaiser made Secretary of State at the Foreign Office and who in 1900 (as had long been intended) was to become Reich Chancellor. The other was a 'Renaissance figure' – more the condottiere – of a different kind, the power-conscious technocrat and battlefleet fanatic with 'the Bismarck touch', Admiral Alfred von Tirpitz, who became Secretary of State at the Reich Navy Office that summer and was to remain in the post until 1916.[1]

Bülow's promotion to ambassador in Rome in 1893, Secretary of State for foreign affairs in 1897 and Reich Chancellor and minister-president of Prussia in 1900 was the work of the Kaiser's favourite, Count Philipp zu Eulenburg, whose influence on Wilhelm II in these years it is hard to overstate. Eulenburg had emerged as the clear winner from the small group of secret advisers around the Kaiser in his conflict with Bismarck. The Grand Duke of Baden withdrew from Reich politics and contented himself with issuing occasional admonitions from Karlsruhe. Waldersee was replaced by the famous Count Alfred von Schlieffen as chief of the General Staff in 1891 because he had had the nerve to criticise the Supreme War Lord's conduct of manoeuvres, and Adolf Freiherr Marschall von Bieberstein wore himself out in parliamentary battles and court intrigues. At first Eulenburg worked closely with the eccentric recluse Geheimrat Fritz von Holstein to keep the hard-pressed Caprivi afloat. Since 1894, however, the Kaiser's intimate friend (Wilhelm addressed him with the familiar *Du*) had gone his own way. Eulenburg and Holstein parted company above all in their conception of the role to which Wilhelm II was entitled in formulating German policy. The Geheimrat was appalled by Wilhelm's autocratic leanings, likening them to the disastrous ambitions of the early Stuart kings in England, and warning Eulenburg presciently in 1894 that the monarch's personal rule would result either in a dictatorship or in a republic: 'That the regime of Wilhelm II forms a transition to one of these two government systems – this is a possibility I unfortunately cannot exclude.' The Kaiser's autocratic treatment of the Chancellor and the ministers was 'an operetta government but not one that a European people at the end of the 19th century will put up with'.[2] Eulenburg, on the other hand, filled with unbounded love for Wilhelm and imbued with a mystically romantic faith in Prussia's destiny, was determined to push through the young monarch's autocracy against considerable opposition from the machinery of state, from the Reichstag and, indeed, from the entire population. 'I am convinced that the Guiding Hand of Providence lies behind this elemental and natural drive of the Kaiser's to direct the affairs of the kingdom in person. Whether it will ruin us or save us I cannot say. But I find it difficult to believe in the decline of Prussia's star.'[3]

To begin with, Eulenburg built up his own position. Thanks to the Kaiser's favour he was swiftly promoted to be Prussian envoy, first to Oldenburg in the north-west, then to Stuttgart, the capital of the kingdom of Württemberg, and in 1891 to Munich, capital of Bavaria, Prussia's main rival in the Reich. In 1894 Wilhelm appointed him to the first-rank post of Germany's ambassador to Austria-Hungary. Step by step Eulenburg brought his relations and friends into position around the Kaiser: his cousin August Count zu Eulenburg became senior marshal of the court in 1888; Wilhelm appointed August's brother Botho (as has already been mentioned) Prussian minister-president and minister of the interior in 1892; in 1893 Philipp Eulenburg succeeded in obtaining appointments for two more close friends: Kuno Graf von Moltke was appointed Flügeladjutant to the Kaiser and Axel Freiherr von Varnbüler became Württemberg's envoy in Berlin. Eulenburg congratulated the Kaiser on the choice of Moltke with the words: 'Your Majesty will become increasingly aware of what a pearl Your Majesty has acquired in this Adjutant – and I am filled with a pleasant, comforting feeling to know that *he* of all people is with my dearly beloved Kaiser.'[4] Their 'dearly beloved Kaiser' was known among Eulenburg and his friends as 'das Liebchen' ('the darling'). Such was the prevailing tone in the 'Liebenberg round table' centred on 'Phili' Eulenburg, known as 'Philine' to his friends.[5]

The most talented associate of this intimate circle around the Kaiser's favourite was Bernhard von Bülow. This cynical careerist – like Eulenburg, Moltke and Varnbüler, Bülow had homosexual tendencies – had originally backed another horse when he contracted a 'faisandé' (according to Herbert Bismarck) marriage with the divorced Countess Marie von Dönhoff, a friend of the then Crown Princess Victoria, Wilhelm's mother. After the death of Kaiser Friedrich III, however, Bülow turned towards the rising sun and offered himself to Wilhelm's most influential friend as a Reich Chancellor for the future. In unambiguous terms he put it to Eulenburg in 1893 that he (Eulenburg) was too vulnerable to assume the highest office in the Reich himself, but that he, Bülow, being like-minded and less susceptible, was able and anxious to render this service to the beloved Kaiser. 'As sisters our souls once arose from the mysterious fount of all being; only we were given distinct mortal frames and different-coloured wings,' wrote Bülow, when Eulenburg affectionately suggested they use the more intimate *Du* form of address.[6] Putting his confidence in this false friend, Eulenburg continued to work behind the scenes on his master plan to guide Bülow into the highest office in as crisis-free a manner as possible. Bülow's eventual rise to Reich Chancellor in October 1900 made him the only Chancellor in Wilhelm II's thirty-year reign whose appointment was planned well in advance and carried through without a hitch.[7]

Bülow, of course, knew exactly on what conditions the Kaiser and his intimate friend had chosen him. In a now famous letter of 23 July 1896 he put himself forward with the revealing words:

I would be a different kind of Chancellor from my predecessors. Bismarck was a power in his own right, a Pepin, a Richelieu. Caprivi and Hohenlohe regarded or regard themselves as the representatives of the 'Government' and to a certain extent of the Parliament in relation to His Majesty. I would regard myself as the executive tool of His Majesty, so to speak his political Chief of Staff. With me personal rule – in the good sense – would really begin.

15 The statesman as courtier: Bernhard von Bülow, foreign secretary
1897–1900, Reich Chancellor 1900–1909.

Prophetically, the Chancellor-in-waiting added: '[I]f this attempt at a real personal rule were to fail, things would look black for our beloved Kaiser!'[8]

In July 1897, when Bülow met his patron Eulenburg at Frankfurt railway station on his way from Rome to take over the Foreign Office, Wilhelm's closest friend pressed a note into his hand, reminding him that he was the Kaiser's 'last card'. Eulenburg's note carried this telling advice:

Wilhelm II takes everything personally. Only personal arguments make any impression on him. He likes to give advice to others but is unwilling to take it himself. He cannot stand boredom; ponderous, stiff, excessively thorough people get on his nerves and cannot get anywhere with him. Wilhelm II wants to shine and to do and decide everything himself. What he wants to do himself unfortunately often goes wrong. He loves glory, he is ambitious and jealous. To get him to accept an idea one has to pretend that the idea came from him. [. . .] Never forget that H.M. needs praise from time to time. He is the sort of person who becomes sullen unless he is given recognition from time to time by someone of importance. You will always accomplish whatever you wish so long as you do not omit to express your appreciation when H.M. deserves it. He is grateful for it like a good, clever child. If one remains silent when he deserves recognition, he eventually sees malevolence in it. We two will always carefully observe the boundaries of flattery.[9]

This, then, was the basis on which, seven years after Bismarck's fall, the 'Bülow system' began. At best characterised as a dubious compromise between Kaiser and Chancellor, the risk inherent in it of appalling errors of judgment and scandals was unmistakable.

In essence, the Bülow system was the institutionalised continuation of Philipp Eulenburg's fawning backstairs crisis management. 'Unless I maintain constant (verbal and written) contact with H.M.,' Bülow admitted soon after moving to the Wilhelmstrasse, 'the status quo which was so painstakingly glued together will fall apart.'[10] In his daily dealings with the monarch, Bülow observed the 'boundaries of flattery' as little as Eulenburg before him. Not only by the standards of today but also in the eyes of contemporaries the obsequious sycophancy in which the new Reich Chancellor indulged was utterly repulsive. A senior court official observed with disgust how Bülow made notes on the cuffs of his shirt so as to be sure not to forget His Majesty's All-Highest orders. Ten years after Bismarck's fall the German Chancellor had in fact been reduced to the level of a courtier.

16 The Kaiser making his 'Hun speech' in Bremerhaven on 27 July 1900.

Bülow, of course, calculated that by playing the sycophantic courtier and keeping on terms of amusing banter with him he would win over the Kaiser to his own policy. He also assumed that close contact with the volatile monarch would enable him to prevent further damaging gaffes. In this he was by no means always successful, as Wilhelm's bloodthirsty speech of July 1900 was to demonstrate, when he exhorted his marine troops bound for China to conduct themselves 'like the Huns under their King Attila a thousand years ago', so that 'no Chinaman will ever again dare so much as to look askance at a German. [. . .] Pardon will not be given, prisoners will not be taken. Whoever falls into your hands will fall to your sword.'[11] Bülow had to take care to avoid anything that could have jeopardised the 'All-Highest confidence' in him, however. 'I cannot consider it useful to make suggestions to His Majesty the Kaiser which have no prospect of actual success and would only make the All-Highest annoyed with me,' he declared in a letter of 1899 to Holstein, thus giving away his entire system.[12] Between the domineering Kaiser, who insisted on determining the guidelines of domestic and foreign policy himself, and his 'Bülowchen' (as Wilhelm called him) there emerged a symbiotic relationship that makes it well-nigh impossible to establish in retrospect who persuaded whom to take which decision, and how often the Chancellor had to give way, against his better judgment, in order not to endanger the mutual harmony. What is clear is that a system so based on unctuous insincerity was unworthy of the German people, and in no way appropriate to cope with the demands of the tension-ridden world situation at the beginning of the twentieth century.

PART III

1896–1908: The Egregious Expansionist

CHAPTER 10

The challenge to Europe: Weltmachtpolitik and the battlefleet

Very soon after the establishment of the German Reich Bismarck had been compelled to acknowledge that with his three wars of unification, against Denmark in 1864, Austria in 1866 and France in 1870–1, the empire had reached the boundaries of what the European states system could tolerate. He had therefore set his face against demands for a further war against Austria or France and entered the race for overseas colonies with great reluctance. Instead, he encouraged the other European great powers (Great Britain, France, Austria-Hungary and Russia) to indulge in imperial expansion, thereby succeeding to a certain extent in diverting their rivalries away from Germany and out to the periphery, where they found themselves in conflict with each other.[1] Such self-imposed restraint was utterly foreign to the young, hot-headed Wilhelm II, eager for action and craving recognition. His veneration for his dynastic forebears – above all the Great Elector, the 'Sergeant King', Frederick the Great and his own grandfather Kaiser Wilhelm I – expressed itself not only in his determination to reassert the rights of the Crown after Bismarck's long quasi-dictatorship as Chancellor; his identification with the warlike Hohenzollern heroes of yore also convinced him that he had a duty to lead Prussia/Germany to new greatness. On 22 March 1897, the centenary of his grandfather's birth, he made a speech asserting that Prince von Bismarck and Field Marshal Count Helmuth von Moltke had been nothing but 'lackeys and pygmies' of his grandfather; it was not they but 'Kaiser Wilhelm the Great' who had enlarged Prussia and made it the centre of the German Reich – and in the same way he aimed to make the German Reich the centre of a united European continent.[2]

Fired by a poisonous brew of ancestor worship, absolutist notions of divine right, militarism, navalism and racism, Wilhelm II held tenaciously to the idea that he had been called as the instrument of God to lead the German people – the salt of the earth – into a glorious new era. In human history, he maintained, the divine will showed itself in the rise and fall of peoples led by their crowned heads. The 'feminine' Latin and Slav races had become degenerate; the future belonged to the 'masculine' Protestant-Christian Germanic races. On 22 March 1905 – his grandfather's birthday again – at the dedication of a monument to his father in Bremen, he declared:

The *Weltreich* [world empire] that I have founded for Myself [sic!] shall consist in the fact that, above all, the newly created German Reich shall enjoy the complete trust of all parties, as a quiet, honest, peaceful neighbour, and that if history should perhaps one day speak of a German *Weltreich* or of a *Hohenzollernweltherrschaft* [a Hohenzollern world supremacy], it shall not have been founded on conquests by the sword, but through mutual trust between nations aspiring to the same goals.[3]

This apparently peaceful 'German mission' was an idea that he had in fact confided to his friend Eulenburg soon after coming to the throne, saying: 'I hope that Europe will gradually see the underlying purpose of my policy: leadership in the peaceful sense – a sort of Napoleonic supremacy – [but] in the peaceful sense.'[4] Similarly, Wilhelm announced at a meeting of the Prussian Ministry of State in February 1894: 'Our supremacy must be demonstrated to Europe not only by our Army, but also through commercial policy.'[5] And in July 1895 he assured the Crown Prince of Sweden and Norway: 'All my ideas and endeavours and all my policies are directed towards bringing the Germanic peoples in the world, especially in Europe, closer together and forging a stronger relationship between them.'[6]

However erratic the 'zigzag course' of Wilhelmine foreign policy seems in retrospect, Wilhelm II's guiding principle remained the same throughout: the unification of the monarchical states of the European continent under German leadership. But whether this German supremacy in Europe could be achieved by peaceful means was more than questionable, for not only Russia and France, allied to each other since 1894, but in the final analysis also the oceanic world power, Great Britain, would most certainly resist German hegemony and unite to defend their independence and, indeed, existence.

Misjudging the danger of encirclement that Bismarck had foreseen so clearly, Wilhelm II encroached on the other great powers' spheres of influence, both in Europe and abroad. Taking as his watchword that the German Reich was now a *Weltreich*, on 3 January 1896 he turned up unannounced at the Reich Chancellor's palace in the Wilhelmstrasse accompanied by three admirals and demanded dramatic action to help the Boers against the British in the wake of the Jameson Raid. The foreign secretary, Adolf Marschall von Bieberstein, recorded the confrontation in his diary in unforgettable terms:

H.M. developed some weird and wonderful plans. Protectorate over the Transvaal, which I at once talked him out of. Mobilisation of the marines. The sending of troops to the Transvaal. And on the objection of the Chancellor [Prince Hohenlohe]: 'That would mean war with England,' H.M. says: 'Yes, but only on land.' [. . .] Finally at my suggestion, His Majesty sent a congratulatory telegram to President Kruger.[7]

It is hard to imagine a more damning example of the Kaiser's militaristic browbeating of his supposedly 'responsible' civilian advisers. The notorious 'Kruger telegram' that was eventually decided on was indeed the foreign secretary's idea, as his diary makes clear, and the telegram itself, congratulating the Boer president on preserving the 'independence' of his country against foreign aggression without resorting to outside help, was actually drafted by Paul Kayser, hastily summoned from the Colonial Department next door for the purpose. But there can be no doubt who the real author of this disastrous démarche was.[8] As for the historians who have pointed to the immense damage done to Anglo-German relations by the telegram, Christopher Clark complains of their 'perplexing tendency. . .to see things from the Westminster point of view'.[9] It seems important therefore to point out that, in German political circles also, the Kruger dispatch became a byword for the monarch's disastrous intervention in foreign affairs, marking the beginning of the deterioration in public attitudes that was to overshadow Anglo-German relations for the next fifty years and beyond.[10] British outrage at the Kaiser's support for the Boers was fuelled not just by oversensitivity in view of the precarious situation in southern Africa; the even greater danger to Britain lay in the perceived threat, which was by no means unfounded, that Wilhelm was bidding to put himself at the head of the wave of anglophobia then sweeping Europe with the aim of forming a continental league.[11]

If the Kruger telegram of January 1896 outraged public opinion in Britain, another initiative of the Kaiser's in the following year was perceived as a challenge primarily to Russia in the Far East. In November 1897 Wilhelm II informed the Reich Chancellor and his Foreign Office, who had nervously warned of the dangers of infringing Russian interests in China:

I am now quite determined to give up our excessively cautious policy, which is already regarded as weak throughout east Asia, and to use all severity and if necessary the most brutal ruthlessness towards the Chinese, to show at long last that the German Kaiser is not to be trifled with, and that it is a bad thing to have him as an enemy.[12]

On the Kaiser's orders, in December 1897 Germany annexed the Bay of Kiaochow in north-eastern China along with 150,000 square miles of hinterland and its more than 33 million inhabitants.[13] In 1900 he insisted that Field Marshal Count von Waldersee, mocked as *Weltmarschall,* be appointed commander-in-chief of the international expeditionary force sent to put down the Boxer rebellion in China.[14] There could hardly have been a more demonstrative indication that Imperial Germany had abandoned Bismarck's policy of restraint and was now claiming a leading role on the world stage.

A high point of Wilhelm II's *Weltmachtpolitik* at the turn of the century, and another alarming demonstration of the extent to which he had strayed from Bismarck's famous dictum that the entire Orient was not worth risking the life of a single Pomeranian grenadier, was his spectacular journey to Constantinople, Haifa, Jerusalem, Beirut and Damascus in the autumn of 1898. Then as now the Middle East was one of the most dangerous trouble spots on earth, where not only the interests of the great powers but also those of the three world religions – Judaism, Christianity and Islam – collide. His triumphal entry into Jerusalem on 29 October 1898 for the consecration of the Church of the Redeemer, on horseback, clad in the uniform of a Prussian field marshal beneath a tropical helmet, must have made a worrying impression, and not only on the ever-suspicious sultan, Abdulhamid II, whose city this was. In Jerusalem he received a Zionist delegation led by Theodor Herzl and expressed himself favourably towards their wish that he proclaim a German protectorate over a Jewish homeland in Palestine. He telegraphed to the Pope declaring his willingness to take over the protectorate of the Catholics in the Holy Land. At the same time, he took on the protectorate of the German Lutheran-Evangelical Christmas Church in Bethlehem. Nor was Islam to be deprived of the favour of the German sovereign. In Damascus he praised Saladin as 'one of the most chivalrous rulers of all time' and announced: 'May the Sultan and the 300 million Mahomedans who live scattered throughout the world and who revere him as their Caliph, rest assured that the German Kaiser will be their friend for all time!'[15] Bülow, who was accompanying him, realised at once what a disastrous effect this speech would inevitably have in Paris, London and St Petersburg, since all three governments ruled over countless millions of restless Muslim subjects. But he was powerless to prevent its publication; Wilhelm had already wired the text of his speech to Constantinople.

The devious ulterior motive that led the Kaiser to make this theatrical appearance in the Middle East came out in the autograph letter that he sent – as always without informing the Reich Chancellor – to Tsar Nicholas II from Constantinople on 20 October 1898. With the aim of stirring up Russian hostility towards Britain, he told the tsar that he should never forget 'that the Mahometans [are] a tremendous card in our game in case you or I were suddenly confronted by a war with the certain meddlesome Power [i.e. Britain]!'.[16] The idea that he could incite the Islamic world to mobilise against Germany's enemies, preferably under the command of a Prussian general, retained its appeal for Wilhelm II well into the First World War, as we shall see.

For the 'belated nation' of Germany at the beginning of the twentieth century, plenty of territory seemed still available to develop its own overseas empire. In 1899 Bülow, announcing to the Kaiser the acquisition of two Samoan islands in the South Pacific, described this as a glorious success for the German navy and nation and assured him, his unctuous grandiloquence revealing what he thought the monarch wanted to hear:

These islands, where Germans have worked so long and so diligently, and which serve as a base for our trade in the Pacific Ocean with Polynesia, Australia and Western America, have great commercial value. Greater still is their maritime significance for our inter-oceanic shipping, in view of the future Panama Canal and the projected German world cable link. But the place which the islands occupy in the nation's heart is of even higher value. [...] Ineradicable memories and the blood of dear ones have long since formed a bond between these islands, which Your Majesty has now won, and Germany. Neither the Navy nor the people would ever have recovered from their loss; their gain will inspire both to follow Your Majesty further on the path towards world power, greatness and everlasting glory.[17]

Above all, the great land bridge from the shores of the eastern Mediterranean via Mesopotamia, Persia and India to China held great allure as a long-term aim: Mesopotamia (present-day Iraq) had been in his mind as a colonial territory 'for years', Wilhelm declared in a memorable meeting with Cecil Rhodes at the turn of the century, as he pressed energetically ahead with the building of the Baghdad Railway – 'My railway!', as he proudly called it.[18] In Africa he set his sights on bringing together a central African bloc of German colonies – *Mittelafrika* – by acquiring the Belgian Congo. The Caribbean, with the Dutch and Danish islands and beyond them the whole of Latin America, offered the Imperial Navy and German emigrants and businessmen ample room for expansion. When the US president Theodore Roosevelt put it to the Kaiser in 1903 that he really ought to expand in eastern Europe rather than in the Western Hemisphere, Wilhelm II commented mockingly in a marginal note in English: 'Prosit! That's where the Russians are. No, South America is our goal, old boy!'[19] Gradually the danger inherent in the unbridled Wilhelmine *Weltmachtpolitik* became clear to Washington too, and the United States built up its Atlantic fleet. This did not prevent the Kaiser from periodically suggesting to the Americans (as, for example, in an interview with the journalist William Bayard Hale in 1908, which is cited below) that the United States and Germany should divide up the British Empire between them![20]

Around the turn of the century the German Admiralty Staff, with the lively participation of Wilhelm II as Supreme War Lord, worked out fantastic operational plans for a possible war against the increasingly powerful North American republic. The German fleet was to attack Puerto Rico and thereby provoke the US Navy into a pitched battle in the Caribbean. This would be followed by the shelling of New York City from Long Island. At the same time, an army of considerable size would land on the coast of New England and march on Baltimore and Washington. These absurd plans were not cancelled until Schlieffen made it clear in 1903 that, in order to ship 100,000 men across the North Atlantic, Germany would first have to be absolutely safe from an attack in Europe.[21] Nothing demonstrates the strategic dilemma of German *Weltmachtpolitik* as clearly as this devastating judgment by Schlieffen: in order to become a global world power on a par with the British, Russian or French Empires, the German Reich would have to free itself from the vice-like grip of the Franco-Russian alliance and neutralise Great Britain's might as guarantor of the balance of power on the European continent. But how?

From the turn of the century Kaiser Wilhelm and his paladins pursued two grand strategies against the two European flanking powers – Great Britain to the west, tsarist Russia to the east – with the aim of cutting the Gordian knot. The Tirpitz Plan, initiated in 1897 with the appointment of Alfred Tirpitz as Secretary of State at the Reich Navy Office, provided for the construction of sixty ships of the line by 1920 – and then some. They were all to be stationed under one command in the North Sea and the Baltic, ready for action.[22] Building a battlefleet on this scale constituted an existential challenge to Great Britain that – Tirpitz calculated – she would in the end be unable to meet, for, in order to maintain her supremacy at sea and fulfil her worldwide commitments, Britain would need to lay down at least three warships to every two built by Germany. And for that, in the long run, she lacked both the economic resources and the manpower. The ultimate aim of the Tirpitz Plan was to put an end to Britain's dominant position in the world, either through a well-timed, decisive battle against the Royal Navy in the North Sea, or through a political capitulation by London whereby the Kaiserreich's dominant status worldwide (and, most directly, its hegemony over Europe) would be guaranteed by treaty. For all the admiral's careful calculations, however, his stratagem contained serious errors and was based on a massive underestimation both of Britain's resolve and of her ability to find allies or support from the dominions. Thanks to the alliance concluded with Japan in 1902 and the Entente Cordiale

17 Admiral Alfred von Tirpitz, Secretary of State at the Reich Navy Office 1897–1916.

with France in 1904, Britain was able to bring home her ships from the Far East and the Mediterranean. With that Tirpitz's calculations were already out of kilter, for the German navy did not stand a chance against the combined naval powers of Britain, Japan and France – and, after the formation of the Triple Entente in 1907, of Russia too. Nevertheless, Kaiser Wilhelm insisted on maintaining the accelerated shipbuilding plan and openly threatened the British with war if they continued, in their 'incredible…impertinence', to demand a reduction in the rate of construction. 'No! No, no and no again!' he exclaimed.[23] For Bülow, as the statesman with direct responsibility for German foreign policy, the construction of the battlefleet acted as an iron straitjacket that drastically limited his freedom of manoeuvre, but even had he wished to do so he would never have dared call the Kaiser's favourite plaything into question.

18 Kaiser Wilhelm II in England after the funeral of his grandmother, Queen Victoria, in February 1901, resplendent in his new uniform as a field marshal of the British army.

The greatest danger for Wilhelm II's grandiose battlefleet plans lay in the ever-present possibility that the British would sink the Imperial Navy in a preventive strike before it reached a critical strength, much as they had destroyed the Danish fleet in 1807 to prevent it from falling into Napoleon's hands.[24] While passing through this 'danger zone' the Kaiser went out of his way to stress his love for Britain and his close relationship with the British royal family as Queen Victoria's eldest grandchild – true to the motto that he cynically liked to cite, that blood is thicker than water. 'I am the only one who is still holding the English back, otherwise they will break out too soon and my fleet is not ready,' he declared in a marginal note on a report from London in 1902, giving away his entire plan.[25]

But what did Wilhelm and his admirals propose to do if the British really did 'break out too soon'? In the first few years of the twentieth century the German Admiralty Staff, with the Supreme War Lord's express approval, worked on a plan to occupy Denmark and besiege Copenhagen. They calculated that British public opinion would not tolerate the violation of this helpless small neutral state. The Royal Navy would feel compelled to detach a squadron to relieve the Danish capital, where it would be sunk by the German High Seas Fleet waiting at the Belts and in the Sound. Then the Imperial Navy would take on the remaining units of the British fleet in the North Sea. This absurd plan was not abandoned until February 1905, when the General Staff under Schlieffen – again – pointed out that the two army corps that the Admiralty had designated for the invasion of Denmark would be needed for an offensive war against France. After the Entente Cordiale between London and Paris a war 'against England alone' was out of the question, and the plans to invade Denmark were dropped.[26]

CHAPTER II

The Russo-Japanese War and the meeting of the emperors on Björkö (1904–1905)

Without a solution to the strategic dilemma in the west, Wilhelm II's ambition to achieve German hegemony in Europe and a large colonial empire overseas remained a very distant prospect for the time being. Yet the alliance concluded between Britain and Japan in 1902 marked a shift in the international states system that seemed to hold out the promise of a dramatic triumph over his Russian relatives in the east. He had worked to bring about the marriage between Tsar Nicholas II and his (Wilhelm's) cousin Alicky of Hesse and the Rhine, now the Tsarina Alexandra, and his brother Heinrich was married to Alexandra's younger sister, Irène. Since 'Nicky's' accession in 1894, mostly without the knowledge of the Reich Chancellor or the Foreign Office, 'Willy' had kept up a highly political correspondence in English with him, which shocked the world when it was published by the Bolsheviks in 1918.[1] The 'Willy–Nicky correspondence' reached a new intensity in 1902. From then on, Wilhelm II openly pursued the goal of entangling the tsar in a war with Japan, by assuring him of German backing. If this succeeded, he calculated, Russia would be tied up in the Far East for a long time, France would therefore be isolated and Germany's pre-eminence over the entire Eurasian continent would be as good as assured.

Never had the chances of a breakthrough to world power seemed within closer reach than in the years from 1902 to 1905. In his letters and telegrams to the infantile Nicholas II and in their meetings at Gdansk (then called Danzig), Tallinn (then called Reval), Wiesbaden and Darmstadt, Wilhelm urged the tsar to turn away from Europe, annex Manchuria and Korea and threaten the British in India, Afghanistan and Persia. As he had done with the notorious drawing 'Nations of Europe, protect your holiest possessions!', which he had sent to the tsar

19 The Admiral of the Atlantic meets the Admiral of the Pacific in the Baltic.

in 1895,[2] Wilhelm put pressure on Nicholas, telling him that his God-given role was the defence of Christendom and the white race against the heathen 'Yellow peril', and that he could regard himself as 'Admiral of the Pacific', while he, Wilhelm, would play his part as 'Admiral of the Atlantic'. Then the *five* great powers of the European continent – that is to say, including France – would be able to form a Holy Alliance against the democratic wind blowing from the Atlantic. The aim of this personal diplomacy was nothing less than, as Bülow put it, 'to detach France from England and push her towards us and Russia'.[3] In his elation, Wilhelm described to the tsar what the new Europe would look like once Germany and Russia had come together:

The smaller nations, Holland, Belgium, Danmark [sic], Sweden, Norway will all be attracted to this new great centre of gravity, by quite natural laws of the attraction of smaller bodies by the larger and compacter ones. They will revolve in the orbit of the great block of powers (Russia, Germany, France, Austria, Italy). [. . .] The dual Alliance combining with the Triple Alliance gives a Quintupel [sic] Alliance, well able to hold all unruly neighbours in order, and to impose peace even by force.[4]

On two occasions, in December 1904 and then again during his celebrated meeting with Nicholas II on the island of Björkö in the

Gulf of Finland in July 1905, the Kaiser believed he had pulled off the greatest coup of his life, through which he hoped to be able to unhinge the existing European states system and establish Germany's hegemony. So his disappointment at seeing his house of cards collapse was all the more bitter. It is not without irony that the influence of the Russian ministers on their apparently 'absolute' ruler, the tsar, turned out to be greater than that of the 'responsible' Reich Chancellor on the supposedly constitutional German Kaiser. On the insistence of his advisers Nicholas withdrew his consent to the Treaty of Björkö, which both emperors had already signed, unless France freely agreed to it – which, of course, was out of the question. Wilhelm was utterly dismayed. This, he exclaimed after the initial setback in December 1904, was 'the first failure that I have personally experienced'.[5]

Now, however, even Bülow recognised the danger lurking in the solo forays made by his sovereign into the field of high politics. As a protest against the alteration of a clause in the Treaty of Björkö that Wilhelm had made on his own initiative, Bülow handed in a letter of resignation on 3 August 1905 after consulting Holstein. The Chancellor's letter provoked a nervous breakdown in the Kaiser.

You will perhaps excuse me, my dear Bülow, from describing my state of mind to you. To be treated in such a way by the best, closest friend I have…was such a fearful blow to me that I broke down completely and cannot help fearing I may fall victim to a severe nervous disorder!

Piteously he begged the Chancellor to withdraw his threat to resign; otherwise he would take his own life. 'For if a letter of resignation arrived from you, the next morning *would find the Kaiser no longer alive!* Think of my poor wife and children!'[6] It was a moving but at the same time shocking admission of the helplessness and dependence of the outwardly boastful autocrat, militarist and racist who occupied the most powerful throne in the world.

CHAPTER 12

War in the west? The landing in Tangier and the fiasco of Algeciras (1905–1906)

When the Russo-Japanese war for which Wihelm had longed began in February 1904 with the Japanese attack on Port Arthur, the Kaiser found himself confronted with a crucial question: should he seize the moment to make a lightning attack on France? The temptation to risk striking out to the west while Imperial Russia was tied down in the Far East became more alluring still when the Russian forces suffered unexpected defeats on land and at sea and revolution broke out in 1905. Wilhelm had always had nothing but contempt for the 'Gauls', as he called the French; they were a 'feminine' race, a race of regicides and atheists. In comparison with a population of 38 million the other side of the Rhine, he pointed out to the tsar, Germany already had 56 million inhabitants and could therefore field 3 million more soldiers than France.[1] He told an American guest (no doubt as a joke) that Germany had such a population surplus that one day he might well have to ask the French to move aside to make room for Germans to resettle in northern and eastern France.

In January 1904 Wilhelm – again without the knowledge of the 'responsible' Chancellor – gave away his General Staff's intention of attacking France through neutral Belgium in the event of a conflict in the west. During a banquet for King Leopold II of the Belgians he claimed boastfully that he was of the school of Frederick the Great and Napoleon I, and, just as Frederick had invaded Saxony without warning in 1740 at the beginning of the First Silesian War, so he would strike like lightning against France. He was not to be trifled with, he told the astonished king: 'Whoever is not on my side in a European war is against me.'[2] He bluntly confronted Leopold with the question of 'what attitude he, the King, intended to adopt in case an armed conflict should break out between Germany and France or

Germany and England'. As the German chargé d'affaires in Brussels discovered (albeit not until a year later), on this occasion the Kaiser demanded categorically of his guest that he should give him

a written declaration now in time of peace to the effect that in case of conflict Belgium would take her stand on our side, and that to this end the King should amongst other things guarantee to us the use of Belgian railways and fortified places. If the King of the Belgians did not do so, he – His Majesty the Kaiser – would not be able to give a guarantee for either his territory or the dynasty. We would then, if the case arose, immediately invade Belgium. [. . .] If on the other hand the King were to make the desired declaration at this stage, he – His Majesty the Kaiser – felt inclined, though he did not like doing so, to give him not only a guarantee regarding the continued existence of the Kingdom of Belgium in its present form, but also to enlarge Belgium by granting it territory in Northern France – His Majesty at this point also used the term 'Old Burgundy'.[3]

King Leopold was so shocked by this ultimatum that when he stood up he put on his helmet the wrong way round, with the eagle facing backwards. News of the extraordinary incident naturally spread like wildfire.[4] In Paris and London conclusions were drawn, confirming the need to stand together. The Entente Cordiale between France and Britain was signed in the spring of 1904.

What the Kaiser's offer to King Leopold was actually worth is clear from the telegram that Wilhelm II sent to Bülow on 30 July 1905, immediately after signing the Treaty of Björkö, which had secured, or so he believed, the alliance with Russia. Informing the Chancellor of his intention to replace Count Schlieffen as chief of the General Staff with his Flügeladjutant Helmuth (nicknamed Julius) von Moltke, the Kaiser waxed lyrical at the prospect of continental domination opened up by the alliance with Russia but also showed himself fully aware of the danger of conflict the diplomatic revolution had brought about in the west:

I have. . .talked over all the eventualities with Julius von Moltke. [. . .] The result is as follows: [. . .] If England starts a war with us in some way or other, two dispatches must immediately be sent by Your Excellency to Brussels and Paris demanding that they declare within six hours whether they are for or against us. We must march into Belgium at once, however she declares herself. In the case of France it depends whether she remains neutral – which I should like to think is not entirely out of the question,

20 The fraught ride through the streets of Tangier on 31 March 1905; the Kaiser's saddle is held by Adjutant General von Plessen, just to be sure.

even if the probability is slight –; then the Russian *casus foederis* [Russia's commitment to stand by France] can be discounted. If she [i.e. France] mobilises, then that is a threat of war against us in favour of England, and in that case Russian regiments must march with us. I believe that to rape and pillage in beautiful Gaul would be a pleasant enough prospect to lure the Russians. It might be worth considering whether France could be offered a rounding-off at Belgium's expense as bait for good behaviour towards us, as a substitute for the lost Reich lands [of Alsace and Lorraine]. [...] We cannot count on active Russian help in the near future, as war and revolution is [sic] keeping the army busy and the fleet is no longer in existence. But it leaves us free to the rear! Very good passive help![5]

Not content with threatening King Leopold of the Belgians with the obliteration of his country and dynasty in January 1904, just a few days later Kaiser Wilhelm II outraged the government of the Netherlands by secretly informing Queen Wilhelmina that in the event of a war against France he intended to occupy the entire Dutch coast in order to prevent a British landing there.[6]

In an atmosphere so charged with tension it is understandable that the sudden arrival of the German Kaiser at the international port of Tangier on the Moroccan side of the Straits of Gibraltar on 31 March 1905 was regarded by the rest of the world as a deliberate provocation. The visit caused a serious international crisis, which for the first time brought the powers to the brink of a major war. King Edward VII was convinced that Wilhelm's theatrical procession on horseback through Tangier was indeed intended to provoke a war, and from then on he regarded his nephew as Britain's most dangerous enemy. To Prince Louis of Battenberg he wrote on 1 April 1905:

I consider that the Tangiers incident was one of the most mischievous & uncalled for events which H.M. G[erman] E[mperor] has ever undertaken. It was a gratuitous insult to 2 Countries [...] & would make me laugh were the matter not a serious one. [...] I suppose G[erman] E[mperor] will never find out as he will never be told how ridiculous he makes himself. [...] I have tried to get on with him & shall nominally do my best till the end – but trust him – *never*. He is utterly false & the bitterest foe that E[ngland] possesses![7]

Who was behind the Kaiser's dramatic landing at Tangier, and what was it meant to achieve? Even today nobody quite knows, as the documentary sources are sketchy. At the time puzzled German diplomats accused the members of Wilhelm's military entourage of pushing him towards a point that was close to war. Others blamed Bülow, and above all Geheimrat von Holstein, for persuading a reluctant Kaiser to take such a provocative step. What is clear is that Holstein, with cover from Bülow and in close contact with Schlieffen, was indeed the actual architect of German policy in the First Morocco Crisis. Even if he was not aiming directly at a war in western Europe in the supposedly favourable conditions resulting from Russia's troubles, the guileful privy councillor pursued an intransigent course that deliberately took into account the possibility, if not the probability, of a war with France (and if necessary Britain too). France was to be confronted with a stark choice: either she could abandon the Entente Cordiale with Britain and submit herself to an alliance with Germany or she could face the prospect of invasion by the Prussian/German army. The goal was not territorial or commercial gain in north Africa but the forcible separation of France from her new Entente partner. As the French Republic would be without the support of her ally Russia for the foreseeable future, capitulation to the German threat of war would be tantamount to

de facto recognition of German supremacy on the Continent.[8]
Obviously, this staggeringly risky strategy would succeed only if
the threat of war were real, and sustained convincingly to the end.
And it was precisely in this regard that Holstein's game of hazard
contained an unpredictable element: the Kaiser.

However aggressive and belligerent Wilhelm's attitude had been
after the outbreak of the Russo-Japanese War, he was far from
underestimating the dangers of a war with the two great powers in
the west. Neither the army nor – in particular – the navy was ready
for war, and, as he also realised, his own people would rebel against a
war perceived to be one of aggression. In addition, the Prussian
minister of war, General Karl von Einem, warned him as Supreme
War Lord that the German field artillery was at that moment inferior
to the French. The Kaiser panicked when Sir Arthur Lee, Civil Lord
of the British Admiralty, threatened to sink the still very incomplete
German battlefleet.[9] He reacted with fury to press reports that on
the outbreak of war the British intended to land an expeditionary
force of 100,000 men on the Continent.[10] He complained that it was
still anything but clear what attitude Germany's allies and the neutral
states would adopt in a conflict in western Europe. Furthermore, the
idea he cherished of bringing the Islamic world under his command
was very far from realisation. And finally, to add to all this, the Reich
Chancellor pointed out to him that Schlieffen was too old to conduct
a major war. Privately, as a contemporary observer remarked,
'Bülow's heart sank into his boots, saying war is impossible with *this*
Kaiser'.[11]

What proved decisive was the discussion that Wilhelm II held
on 28 December 1905 at the Neues Palais in Potsdam with the
British South African diamond millionaire Sir Alfred Beit, whom
he thought to be a close friend of King Edward VII. Beit left him in
no doubt that Britain was determined to stand by France precisely
with regard to the Moroccan question, which was, after all, at the
heart of the Entente Cordiale. Three days after this meeting
Wilhelm wrote his *Silvesterbrief* (his New Year's Eve letter) – one
of the most notorious letters of his entire reign – in which he
gave Bülow a list of arguments against unleashing a 'world war'
(the Kaiser actually used the word '*Weltkrieg*') – for the time being.
He wrote:

To do England the favour of taking on the odium of attacking France on account of Morocco, so that the English at last have the desired opportunity to set upon us in the fine guise of 'protecting the weak against aggression', is not in our interest, nor is it a programme likely to inspire the enthusiasm of our people. [. . .] If you, my dear Bülow, are reckoning on the prospect of a possible war. . .you ought to be very active in seeking out our allies. It would be absolutely essential to call upon them for help, for their existence would then also be at stake since it would be a world war. But above all an alliance ought to be concluded with the Sultan [Abdulhamid] at once, coute qui coute [sic], which would place the Mohammedan forces to the furthest possible extent – under Prussian leadership – at my disposal, and likewise with all Arab rulers. For on our own we are not in a position to wage war against an alliance of Gaul and England. Next year is particularly unpropitious, as we are in the process of re-arming our artillery with a new (recoil) gun, which will take a year to complete. The infantry is also in the process of being re-equipped and is receiving new rifles and new ammunition. Around Metz there are still unfinished forts and batteries everywhere, which are the first to be attacked. Thus in technical military terms we are not at a stage at which I as Supreme War Lord would happily agree to send our Army into action without further ado.

At sea Germany was 'well-nigh powerless', because the Reichstag had refused for years to strengthen the fleet, the Kaiser continued, writing: 'We are absolutely defenceless against a comb[ination] of France and England's navy.' Then he concluded:

So I would very strongly advise that matters should be arranged so that as far as is at all possible, we are spared the necessity of deciding to go to war for the time being. Furthermore, at a moment like this when the Socialists are preaching and preparing open rebellion, I cannot take a single man out of the country without the greatest danger to the life and property of its citizens. First [we must] shoot down the Socialists, behead them and render them harmless – if necessary by a bloodbath – and then [fight a] war against the foreign foe! But not beforehand and not *a tempo*.[12]

The Kaiser's decision against war ruined Holstein's plans. To be sure, Germany's heavyweight tactics had succeeded in forcing the resignation of the French foreign minister, Théophile Delcassé, the architect of the Entente Cordiale with Britain, and in causing an international conference on the future of Morocco to be convened in Algeciras. But where was this supposed to lead? The German delegation received no instructions from a deadlocked Berlin, while the other delegates (from Austria-Hungary, France, Britain, Spain, Italy,

Portugal, the Netherlands, Belgium, Sweden, Norway and the United States) spent months in the small southern Spanish port puzzling over what the Kaiserreich actually hoped to achieve by the whole operation. Eventually, on 7 March 1906, Bülow passed on to the principal German negotiator in Algeciras, Joseph Maria von Radowitz, the Kaiser's orders to come to a compromise.[13] Far from having fulfilled its purpose of breaking up the Anglo-French Entente, Imperial Germany's belligerent stance had led to still closer solidarity between the two west European imperial powers. Worse still, apart from Austria-Hungary all the other participating states, including the nascent new superpower, the United States, had taken sides against Germany. The restless Kaiserreich, with its egregious and unpredictable emperor, found itself caught in a cul-de-sac of isolation.

CHAPTER 13

The intensification of the Anglo-German conflict

At the beginning of 1904 Wilhelm II had announced his intention of appointing his Flügeladjutant and close friend Helmuth ('Julius') von Moltke, nephew of the celebrated field marshal, to be Count Alfred von Schlieffen's successor as chief of the Great General Staff. If the pliable Bülow owed his appointment to the promptings of Philipp Eulenburg, and Tirpitz his to the influence of the anglo-phobic chief of the Kaiser's Naval Cabinet Admiral Freiherr Gustav von Senden-Bibran, the choice of Moltke to head the General Staff was entirely the Supreme War Lord's own decision; indeed, it was a truly alarming example of personal rule at its most extreme. As the bearer of a historic name and as one of the *Lange Kerls* whom Wilhelm had gathered around him in conscious imitation of his seventeenth-century forebear, the brutal 'Sergeant King', Friedrich Wilhelm I of Prussia,[1] Moltke had from the beginning played a certain part at court and in the Kaiser's personal diplomacy; it was he who had taken Wilhelm's 'Nations of Europe!' drawing aimed against the 'Yellow peril' to Tsar Nicholas II in 1895.[2] But chief of the General Staff?! The appointment of this courtly general to the most influential post in the Prussian/German army was decided by the Kaiser against the advice of the chief of the Military Cabinet and almost all the generals in the army. Field Marshal Count von Waldersee commented, despairingly, 'I do not believe there could be a greater humiliation for the General Staff.'[3] No one was more convinced of his unsuitability for the highly responsible post than Moltke himself, melancholy and fatalistic by nature and, under the influence of his wife, susceptible to the occultism of Rudolf Steiner. Yet Wilhelm insisted on his promotion, remarking ominously that 'he did not need a General Staff, he will do everything alone with his Flügeladjutanten'. In the Kaiser 'the sense of greatness is growing in a way that is becoming positively frightening', Waldersee, now on his deathbed, observed.[4]

Moltke's appointment as chief of the General Staff in January 1906 brought onto the scene in Berlin yet another figure who would work closely with Wilhelm II to shape the course of German policy right up to the outbreak of war in 1914. If Bülow, as the so-called 'responsible' Reich Chancellor, had already lacked the courage to challenge what he gradually realised to be the disastrous plans made by the Kaiser for the battlefleet, now he was even less inclined to encroach on the hallowed ground of Prussian military command, forbidden to him as a civilian in any case, by daring to question the plans that the Supreme War Lord was hatching in close collaboration with his new chief of the General Staff. The Chancellor was as good as powerless against the combination of the Kaiser and Tirpitz on naval policy and the Kaiser and Moltke where the army was concerned. As a result his room for manoeuvre was reduced still further, especially as, after the humiliation of Algeciras, Kaiser Wilhelm II was more inclined than ever to take personal charge of policy towards Britain.

It may seem surprising at first that Moltke did not suggest that Russia, paralysed by the defeats she had suffered in the war with Japan, should be considered as a potential target for attack, as was to be the case after 1912. Like Wilhelm II and Tirpitz, however, he too continued to regard the two western powers, and above all Britain, as the enemies that needed to be fought if Germany were to gain dominance on the Continent. Although the Treaty of Björkö had in effect been shelved by both the Russian and the German governments, the Kaiser and the chief of the General Staff still pinned their hopes on Russian neutrality in the event of a European conflict.

Thus, just as he had ordered Bülow immediately after the signing of the Björkö Treaty in July 1905 to ensure that in any future war Britain would appear as the aggressor (see above, pp. 87–8), so again three years later, in July 1908, the Supreme War Lord sent a telegraph to the Chancellor – once more after discussions with Moltke on board the imperial yacht *Hohenzollern* – insisting that, if it came to war in the west, its outbreak had to be engineered in such a way 'that England must attack us and if she gets France to join in, France must also declare war on us [so that] we are the ones being attacked', and Russia would no longer be bound by treaty to stand by her ally France. The Chancellor therefore had to,

in the event of serious complications, organise our tactics in such a way that England and France attack us, so that we are the victims. . . In that situation Moltke and I can cheerfully face even the heaviest trials with complete calm and confidence, trusting in God.[5]

With Moltke as head of the General Staff the 'provoked defensive war', on the model of Bismarck's manipulated Ems Telegram of 1870, became a central element of German war planning. At the same time the Kaiser ordained that the Tirpitz battlefleet plan would be 'fulfilled down to the last iota; whether it suits the British or not is of no consequence! If they want war, let *them start* it; we are not afraid of it!'[6]

As far as Britain was concerned, Kaiser Wilhelm considered himself infinitely superior to his ministers and diplomats because of his close relationship to the British royal family. On the basis of his repeatedly expressed conviction that the British understood nothing but brutal frankness, in 1908 he took a series of initiatives of such monumental tactlessness that Bülow was not alone in wondering in horror whether his sovereign was still in his right mind. In February 1908, without consulting the Chancellor, the Secretary of State for foreign affairs or Admiral von Tirpitz, the Kaiser sent Lord Tweedmouth, the First Lord of the British Admiralty, a letter riddled with untruths obviously calculated to gain time for his battlefleet construction programme. It was one of the worst blunders he ever made, which caused a serious international crisis and which Maximilian Harden described as 'far, far worse than the Kruger Telegram'. Tirpitz threatened to resign and had to be placated with a seat in the upper house of the Prussian parliament. Bülow and the foreign secretary, Wilhelm von Schoen, hurried to the British embassy to find out whether the rumours about the Kaiser's letter were true. When the ambassador, Sir Frank Lascelles, said 'it was in fact true, Bülow fell back into his armchair with his head thrown back and his face so red Lascelles thought the Chancellor was going to have a fit on the spot'.[7] Princess Marie Radziwill expressed doubts about the mental health of a monarch who had acted so autocratically and irresponsibly on such a dangerous question.

Never has such unparalleled imprudence, lack of tact, and abysmal forget-fulness of the position of the Head of State been seen before. I am beginning to be absolutely convinced our Sovereign isn't well and that his brain is no longer quite normal. [...] This time it's really worse than a bloomer. [...] For a long time now his character has been becoming more and more autocratic, liking to give advice when it is not wanted and wishing to dominate everything.[8]

But worse was to come.

On 11 August 1908, at Schloss Friedrichshof in Kronberg in the Taunus Mountains above Frankfurt, Wilhelm II had an argument in the presence of his uncle Edward VII with the British permanent under-secretary for foreign affairs, Sir Charles Hardinge, about the murderous naval arms race between Britain and Germany. By the Kaiser's own account, he reacted to Hardinge's demand for a reduc-tion in the pace of German battlefleet building by declaring: '*Then we shall fight for it is a question of national honour and dignity.*' Evidently proud of his diplomatic skills, the Kaiser reported to his Chancellor: 'The frank discussion with me, when I showed my teeth in no uncertain terms, had its effect. That is how one always has to behave with the English.'[9] Bülow was appalled, and had the impres-sion that Wilhelm had tried to turn the confrontation in Kronberg into a kind of 'world-historic scene' similar to 'the one that had been played out between Wilhelm I and Benedetti at Ems in July 1870'.[10]

During his Scandinavian cruise that summer Kaiser Wilhelm II gave the *New York Times* journalist the Reverend Dr William Bayard Hale an interview, the content of which again spread like wildfire from government to government and caused immense damage. Hale was shocked and telegraphed the Kaiser's explosive comments to New York with the warning that 'Germany is expecting to fight England, and, in my judgment, the Emperor does not care how quickly. He poured a steady stream of insults upon the English for two hours.' Throughout the interview, Hale reported, the Kaiser had expressed his bitter hatred of Britain and emphasised

that Germany was ready for war at any moment with her and the sooner it came the better. He claimed that Great Britain looked upon Germany as her enemy because it was the most dominant force on the continent of Europe and it had always been England's way to attack the strongest Power. France and Russia were now out of the running, he said, and she was friendly with them, so everything was directed against Germany. The Emperor said that Great Britain had been degenerating ever since the Boer war which was a war against God and for that she would be punished as all nations have been who have done wrong to a weaker Power that was in the right. He believed that a war would come, and he was aching for the fight, not for the sake of war, but as something that was unpleasant and inevitable, and the sooner the better.

Hale understood from the Kaiser that 'his ambition was to take Egypt from the British and later the Holyland [sic] from Turkey thereby emulating the deeds of the Crusaders in taking the land of Christ from the Infidels. He appeared to be very bitter against his Uncle King Edward and accused him of trying to set the other powers against Germany. As to France and Russia he said they were not worth talking about from a military or naval point of view.' As he spoke, Hale reported to the editors of *The New York Times*, 'the Emperor walked the floor and spoke forcefully and earnestly. [...] He seemed to be full of electricity, and his eyes snapped when he spoke of England, his bitterness was so intent.'[11] Bülow only just succeeded in preventing the publication of this disastrous interview. Had the text become public knowledge in November 1908, namely at the same time as the Kaiser's notorious interview in *The Daily Telegraph*, Wilhelm II would almost certainly have been forced to abdicate, so outrageous were his documented remarks to the American journalist.

Behind Wilhelm's elemental fury against Britain lay the irreconcilable conflict between two European states systems: the balance of power versus hegemony. For centuries the maintenance of the balance of power on the Continent had been the guiding principle of British policy on Europe. Whether against Philip II's Spain or the France of the 'Sun King' and Napoleon, Britain had sought to safeguard her interests, and ultimately her national existence, by always throwing her weight behind the weaker power groupings on the Continent in order to prevent any single great power achieving supremacy.[12] At the turn of the century the government in London and influential British public opinion both identified the highly

21 Uncle and nephew: Edward VII and Wilhelm II in Kiel in June 1904.

successful German Reich, with its irritating, ambitious and yet so unpredictable Kaiser, as the greatest threat to the balance of power. It was therefore no accident that, when Britain decided to abandon her 'splendid isolation' after the Boer War, she did not (as Wilhelm had at first hoped) ally herself with Germany but sought a rapprochement with the French Republic, itself under threat from Germany and allied since 1894 to the absolutist Russian Empire. Neither their constitutional differences nor their rivalries overseas weighed heavily enough to prevent these three imperialist powers from throwing in their lot together against the perceived more immediate threat in the heart of Europe. The political rationale that compelled Britain to take a stand alongside France and Russia against the increasingly powerful German Reich was summed up by King Edward VII in 1909, when he stated that, if the British Empire stood aside in a continental war, 'Germany would have the power of demolishing her enemies, one by one, with us sitting by with folded arms, & she would then probably proceed to attack us'.[13]

From Wilhelm's point of view, however, the Triple Entente, concluded between 1904 and 1907, amounted to an utterly unacceptable 'encirclement' of his Reich that wrecked his hopes of German supremacy on the Continent. He held his uncle Edward principally responsible for thwarting his ambitions. 'He is a Satan; it is quite unbelievable what a Satan he is,' he exclaimed in his frustration.[14] From 1905 the international isolation of the German Reich could no longer be ignored, and it generated both in Wilhelm II and in German public opinion a panicky nervousness that expressed itself, in classic fashion, in the form of scandals.

PART IV

1906–1909: *The Scandal-Ridden Sovereign*

CHAPTER 14

The Eulenburg affair (1906–1909)

Shortly before his dismissal Prince Bismarck had had to confront the truth of a fundamental flaw in the structure the Reich he had created: that a monarch without the protection of ministerial clothing was in danger of being exposed to merciless public scrutiny and criticism. Never was that danger greater than in the system of personal monarchy as practised by Wilhelm II under Bülow's chancellorship. The conflict between the Kaiser's anachronistic notions of divine right and the byzantine attitudes this engendered in the statesmen and the military, on the one hand, and the highly literate mass culture of Germany's burgeoning cities on the other was, by the turn of the century, producing an unstable compound that needed only a spark for it to explode and rock the monarchy to its foundations. The frustration and humiliation increasingly felt by all segments of society at the obvious setbacks in the country's foreign standing since Bismarck's fall were well expressed in the letter the great sociologist Max Weber wrote in December 1906 to the liberal parliamentarian Friedrich Naumann:

The amount of contempt which we as a nation receive abroad (Italy, America, everywhere!) – *rightly*, that is the crucial thing – *because* we 'put up with' *this* rule by *this* man, really has now become a factor of first-rate 'world political' importance for us. [. . .] We are becoming 'isolated' because this man rules us in this way and we tolerate and find excuses for it.[1]

From late 1906 the widely felt bitterness with Wilhelm's personal rule discharged itself in a long series of court scandals at the centre of which stood the Kaiser's best friend, Philipp Eulenburg, and the so-called Liebenberg round table.

As has been seen, Count (later Prince) Philipp zu Eulenburg-Hertefeld, the 'black knight who was at the side of the Imperial Wanderer when he chose the false path', as Holstein once called him,[2] had advised the young monarch throughout the chancellorship crises of the 1890s and had finally managed, with the appointment of Bülow first as foreign secretary in 1897 and then as Reich Chancellor in 1900, to push through Wilhelm II's personal monarchy against the resistance of the officially 'responsible' statesmen in the Wilhelmstrasse.[3] As a practising homosexual, however, 'Phili' Eulenburg had put himself in extreme danger. To be sure, as a diplomat he had been able to avoid being posted to countries in which certain homosexual acts were more severely punished than in Germany, but even in the relatively tolerant Bavaria where he had acted as Prussian envoy until 1894 his excesses were common knowledge. As German ambassador in Vienna from 1894 to 1902 he was shadowed by the secret police, not in order to incriminate him but to keep blackmailers away from him. Nevertheless, he fell victim to a Viennese bathhouse attendant, who demanded and received 60,000 marks for his silence. Reich Chancellor Prince Hohenlohe was enraged when Eulenburg had the nerve to use a pretext to ask for a refund of this sum from the public purse.

In 1897 a decision by Wilhelm II to make Eulenburg happy by sending Count Kuno von Moltke to be his military attaché at the embassy in Vienna had disastrous consequences. Shortly beforehand 'Tütü' Moltke, probably as a 'beard' for his homosexuality, had made the mistake of marrying the young Lili von Kruse, who as his newly wedded wife insisted on moving to Vienna with him, where she became the witness of the infatuated relationship between her husband and Eulenburg. When she pressed for divorce and threatened to make public what she had seen, she narrowly escaped being marched off into a madhouse. She divulged her experiences to the society doctor Professor Ernst Schweninger, whose illustrious patients famously included Prince Bismarck and the Kaiser's sister, Hereditary Princess Charlotte of Saxe-Meiningen, as well as that 'truth fanatic', the journalist Maximilian Harden. Rumours quickly got around, and, by the time Harden began his press campaign against the 'Liebenberg round table' in his journal *Die Zukunft* in November 1906, the homosexuality of Eulenburg and Moltke was already the talk of the town.[4]

22 Philipp Eulenburg being carried on a stretcher from his hospital bed to the courtroom.

Eulenburg had had to resign from his post as ambassador to Austria-Hungary in 1902 for fear of unwelcome revelations and had promised to keep away from the Kaiser, but from then onwards he was on treacherous ground. In April 1906 Friedrich von Holstein, bitter at his own dismissal in the wake of the First Morocco Crisis, expressed astonishment 'that somebody who had as much dirt sticking to him as Philipp Eulenburg, who is open to attack from any side you care to choose, should turn to threats. But such characters occasionally have moments of hysterical over-excitement.'[5] Incredibly, the seventy-year-old and half-blind Holstein challenged the Kaiser's closest friend to a duel with an insulting letter whose message was only too clear. 'My Phili!' the letter ran. 'This greeting is not a mark of esteem, for "Phili" to-day among contemporaries signifies – nothing good. [. . .] I am now free, I need exercise no restraint and can treat you as one treats any contemptible person with your characteristics.'[6] A fatal shoot-out was only just prevented through the mediation of the Württemberg envoy Axel Freiherr von Varnbüler, whom Eulenburg had asked to act as his second.[7]

But Holstein's challenge was only the prelude to a series of sensational trials that shook the monarchy to its very foundations. When Harden's hints of Eulenburg's and Moltke's homosexuality in *Die Zukunft* became increasingly unambiguous and the young Crown Prince finally felt compelled to show the articles to his reportedly 'thunderstruck' father on 2 May 1907, Harden wrote to Holstein saying that his contacts in the gay community were claiming that 'H.M. knows nothing about this subject, treats it like a crime and has never heard of the mass of medical literature about it'.[8] But can this really be true?[9] As far as is known, Wilhelm II never indulged in any homosexual acts, but he had often shared a room with Eulenburg on hunting expeditions, gone out in a rowing boat with him and the chief witness for the prosecution, Jakob Ernst, on the Starnberger See and kept a portrait of Eulenburg in his cabin in the *Hohenzollern*. Is it credible that the Kaiser, whom the Liebenberg circle called *das Liebchen* – 'the darling' – had no inkling of the homosexual orientation of his closest friends until this very moment? Eulenburg boasted in court that he had had no secrets from His Majesty, and such trustfulness in a close friendship lasting twenty years seems to have been reciprocal. On one occasion, in a 'painful outpouring of his feelings', the Kaiser unburdened himself to Eulenburg about the Kaiserin, asking tearfully: 'What am I to do? These crises and scenes are killing me. I cannot stand it.'[10] In such moments did they not also discuss the Liebenberg circle's affairs of the heart? When Varnbüler heard from Eulenburg about their mutual friend, Kuno Moltke's, marital catastrophe in 1898 he hastened to assure the latter (they called each other by the nickname 'Dachs' – badger) that Wilhelm II would surely understand his problems.

And also the One, my Dachs – I'm sure I am not mistaken in thinking that your pain is sharpened because you cannot hide, keep at bay, all this ugliness from him, from the *Liebchen*. But do not torment yourself unnecessarily about this – he is man enough to put a stop to nasty gossip – and he knows and loves you too well in your peculiarity [*Eigenart*] to allow even the shadow of blame to fall upon you.[11]

The homoerotic character of this male club is unmistakable, but the attraction of the Liebenberg circle for Wilhelm II, we would like to think, was not primarily sexual. In this versatile group of men around Philipp Eulenburg he found artistic talent, uninhibited high spirits and childish tomfoolery, spiritualist hocus-pocus and seemingly self-less advice on the endless political crises, which were often too much for him. But, above all, in the friendship of the gentle Eulenburg Wilhelm found that unconditional love and admiration that had been withheld from him in his childhood. It was precisely this 'sycophantic' idolisation of the monarch that Harden denounced and blamed for Germany's setbacks.

Although his tone in the course of the series of trials that ensued became increasingly homophobic, Harden's campaign against the 'Liebenberg round table' was not directed against homosexuality as such but against the traits of character that he thought he discerned, particularly in the 'soft' Eulenburg: his rapturous, infatuated, wholly uncritical behaviour towards the Kaiser; his penchant for mysticism, spiritualism and faith healing; the cliquishness of the Liebenbergers, which supposedly shielded the Kaiser from harsh reality; and, not least, Eulenburg's limp, pacifist attitude to foreign policy, in collaboration with homosexual foreigners who (Harden believed) were endangering the national security of the Reich. The news that Eulenburg had brought the loquacious Kaiser together with the notoriously homosexual French diplomat Raymond Lecomte in an intimate house party at Schloss Liebenberg at the height of the First Morocco Crisis was the last straw for Harden, and it was this that sparked off his crusade in November 1906.[12]

The attacks on the Liebenberg round table created a perilous dilemma for Prince (as he now was) Bernhard von Bülow as Reich Chancellor, which he tried to solve with characteristic duplicity. On the one hand, the Liebenberg clique, trusting in its influence on Wilhelm, really was planning to bring down the supposedly worn-out Bülow and seize power for itself: the newly appointed chief of the General Staff, Helmuth von Moltke, was to become Chancellor with Varnbüler as either foreign secretary or ambassador in St Petersburg. It was natural, therefore, for Bülow to try to protect himself, and leaking damaging information to Harden was the obvious way of doing so. On the other hand, Bülow was himself so compromised by his own homosexual past that he was in danger of being dragged into the whirlpool of scandal at any moment. He had Eulenburg to thank for his rapid rise in the Kaiser's favour; moreover, Eulenburg was in possession of countless letters from Bülow teeming with declarations of love for him and the 'dearly beloved Kaiser', some suggesting that, though they may not actually have been lovers, they had had intimate moments with a third man.[13] In the gay world Bülow's homosexual inclinations were anything but unknown, especially as he had appointed Max Scheefer, his long-time partner in Rome, as his private secretary in the Reich Chancellery. Indeed, when Harden began his campaign against the Liebenberg circle Adolf Brand, an early advocate of homosexual rights, went so far as to try to 'out' the Chancellor, for which he was sentenced to eighteen months in prison, which broke his health.[14]

Bülow rightly saw that the only possibility of preventing a disastrous scandal that would do incalculable harm to the monarchy, the reputation of the Reich and not least himself was for Eulenburg to disappear quietly abroad. The Chancellor summoned Varnbüler and, 'amid the usual protestations of friendship for Phili', drew attention to the overwhelming quantity of incriminating evidence against Eulenburg 'in secret reports from the political and moral police in Vienna, Munich and Berlin' that lay in the safes of the Auswärtiges Amt.[15] In spite of this warning Eulenburg refused to take the proffered escape route, and relied on bluff instead. He vehemently denied any 'perverse inclination' or 'filthiness', even under oath, and as a result found himself caught, like Kuno Moltke, in a disastrous series of sensational trials that shook the Hohenzollern throne. When Eulenburg finally stumbled into the trap that Harden and his ingenious lawyer Max Bernstein had set for him in a trumped-up libel case in Munich in 1908 he was, as Varnbüler remarked bitterly, 'a hopelessly lost cause'. In Varnbüler's opinion, suicide was the only course left for Eulenburg; he should sacrifice himself to save the honour of his family name.[16]

In May 1907 Wilhelm II had impulsively broken off all contact with his two closest friends, so in effect condemning them in the public eye. Although from time to time he was hopeful of an acquittal and sometimes even spoke of rehabilitation, he was clearly shaken by the lurid details of their relationship, which were revealed daily in the courts and touted in the international press. During the first Moltke–Harden trial he suffered a fainting fit, caused, as he maintained, by the 'dreadful bouts of mental depression' brought on by the case. He told Bülow:

I was so unwell yesterday I had a sudden fainting fit and would have fallen to the ground had I not grasped the back of a chair as I fell, which threw me onto the sofa; I was brought round with champagne by the Kaiserin who rushed in by chance. [. . .] I shall do everything I can to regain my strength through exercise in the fresh air, riding etc. and hope for the best; but I have had a hard knock and influenza is probably partly to blame.[17]

The fall of his closest friends Philipp Eulenburg and Kuno Moltke, whom Wilhelm never again received, left a void in his life that was all the more marked because other members of the Liebenberg circle (such as his childhood friend the sculptor Emil Count von Görtz) also thought it advisable to stay away from him. In their place the Kaiser chose the Badenese *grand seigneur* Max Egon II Prince zu Fürstenberg, who with his close family ties across the border was to bring him into contact with the leading lights of the Austrian high aristocracy around Archduke Franz Ferdinand at his castle of Donaueschingen in the Black Forest. It was there that Wilhelm was staying for a fox shoot when the full impact of the next great catastrophe of his reign hit him.

CHAPTER 15

Bülow's betrayal of the Kaiser: the Daily Telegraph *crisis (1908–1909)*

On 28 October 1908 there appeared in the London *Daily Telegraph*, with the express permission of Kaiser Wilhelm II, an interview that he had given to an unnamed English 'diplomat'. The storm of indignation it aroused in Germany was so massive that the Kaiser was almost swept from the throne. Like the vast majority of Germans, Baroness Hildegard von Spitzemberg, Axel Varnbüler's sister, thought the interview was 'the most shaming, despicable, indiscreet and dangerous thing that the Kaiser has ever done! [...] The Kaiser is ruining our political position and making us the laughing-stock of the world...!! It makes one despair and wonder if one is in a madhouse!' People all over Germany felt a sense of misery and anger, she recorded, just as if a battle had been lost. 'There is something so unmanly and childish in this talkativeness that seems positively contemptible in ordinary mortals.'[1] Maximilian Harden saw the newspaper interview as confirmation of his very worst fears. In a letter to Holstein he expressed the stark alternatives Germany faced, in his view: 'To clear ourselves of shame and ridicule, we will *have* to go to war, soon, or face the sad necessity of making a change of imperial personnel on our own account, even if the strongest personal pressure had to be brought to bear.'[2] In many towns angry crowds demanded the Kaiser's abdication; in an extraordinary debate in the Reichstag on 10 and 11 November deputies from all parties castigated Wilhelm II's 'personal rule'. The government bench looked on helplessly. 'One more day like that and we shall have a republic,' the future Reich Chancellor Theobald von Bethmann Hollweg, who was reportedly 'in a state of collapse', declared after the tumultuous parliamentary session.[3]

Only gradually did Wilhelm himself grasp the severity of the constitutional crisis provoked by his interview. He had been on a visit to Archduke Franz Ferdinand in Bohemia before going on to Donaueschingen to shoot foxes. It was not until 11 November 1908 that Prince Fürstenberg, the chief of the Military Cabinet, General Count Dietrich von Hülsen-Haeseler, and the chief of the Civil Cabinet, Rudolf von Valentini, informed the monarch – who was 'completely floored' by the news – of the strength of the reaction to his interview. 'Tears of anger and disappointment' rose to his eyes. 'Tell me, what is really happening? What does all this mean?' he asked in bewilderment as the party set out for the shoot. After all, he had discussed everything with the Chancellor as the constitution required, had sent him the text of the interview and asked him to check it over personally. He could not understand 'how his good intentions had been so misunderstood, and how his political activity could be judged so harshly and disparagingly'.[4] How had it come to this constitutional crisis, the most serious of Wilhelm II's reign, and what role did Reich Chancellor Prince von Bülow really play in it?

The 'November storm' of 1908 had in fact been brewing for a long time. One year earlier, on 11 November 1907, the very day on which the latest German Navy bill had been published, Kaiser Wilhelm arrived in London for a state visit. Not least because of the shock of the revelations about the homosexuality of his closest friends, he decided to take a three-week holiday to recover at Highcliffe Castle in Hampshire, on the south coast of England. In his speeches in London and Windsor, and, curiously, also in an 'interview' he was supposed to have given to the *Daily Dispatch*, a regional Manchester newspaper, Wilhelm sought to allay British fears about Germany's naval shipbuilding programme and her possible plans for conquests on the Continent.[5] It was at Highcliffe that he first set out for his host, Colonel Edward James Stuart Wortley, the 'proofs' of his loyal attitude towards Britain, which the gullible colonel, at Wilhelm's request, then had published in the form of an interview in *The Daily Telegraph* a year later. According to these preposterous assertions, the German fleet was being built not against Britain but for the joint struggle with the Royal Navy against the 'Yellow peril' – Japan and China – in the Pacific; the majority of the German people were anti-British, to be sure, he admitted, but he, the Kaiser, always did everything he could to stand up for the interests of Great Britain; and he, after all, determined the country's policy. Why, in the Boer War he had even sent his grandmother Queen Victoria the plan of campaign with which Field Marshal Lord Roberts had secured victory in South Africa; and, when Russia and France approached him at that difficult time with a plan for a continental league aimed at humiliating Britain 'into the dust', he had not only rejected this idea out of hand but immediately informed London of the perfidy of Russia and France – now *nota bene* Britain's partners in the Triple Entente.[6] After his return to Germany Wilhelm II repeated these *horrenda* (as Bülow was later to call them) so insistently to influential Englishmen that one gets the impression that he actually believed his protestations of friendship.

As with his earlier letter to Lord Tweedmouth, Wilhelm II intended these assurances to convince the British that the German fleet-building programme was a harmless affair. On 10 September 1908 he summoned Eddy Stuart Wortley, who had meanwhile been promoted to brigadier general and whom Wilhelm had invited to the German army's manoeuvres in Lorraine, to come and see him. In a ploughed field, on horseback, he repeated the 'proofs' of his friendship for Britain that he had expounded at Highcliffe the previous December. He asked the ingenuous Englishmen to have the main points of their conversation published in an English newspaper. In high delight, Wilhelm wrote to Chancellor Bülow saying that Stuart Wortley had told him his compatriots were as 'mad as March hares' if they believed Germany was planning an attack.[7] Six weeks later these remarks were to appear, word for word, in *The Daily Telegraph*.

On 23 September 1908 Stuart Wortley sent the Kaiser the text of his article for his approval. The original, which still survives, consists of ten typescript pages. In itself this is already proof that Bülow was telling an outright lie when he claimed not to have read what he described as an illegible, handwritten English scribble on flimsy paper. In addition, further copies were made in the Berlin Foreign Office, so that no fewer than three versions were available to the Reich Chancellor at one and the same time. It was neither out of ignorance of the Kaiser's claims nor – as his 'pro-Kaiser' enemies later alleged – in order to expose the monarch and increase his own power that Bülow gave his consent to publication, but because he agreed with Wilhelm's motivation for the interview. Accepting Wilhelm II's high-handed actions had in any case long since become a systematic reaction for him.

The officials at the Auswärtiges Amt to whom Bülow entrusted the checking of the article were out of their depth. They assumed that the Chancellor himself would take responsibility for the over-arching decision on whether publication was politically opportune. As far as the ultimate aims of Tirpitz's battlefleet programme were concerned, these civilians were as little in the know as the members of the Reichstag who approved the funds for it. With regard to the Boer War, in December 1899 and February 1900 Wilhelm had indeed sent unsolicited memoranda entitled 'Notes on the War in the Transvaal' to the British court, but they had caused offence and had no influence at all on the conduct of the war in South Africa. Particularly embarrassing was Wilhelm's claim to have repudiated a Franco-Russian proposal to form a continental league against Britain, since the officials knew perfectly well that the Kaiser had been aiming at just such an alliance as long ago as in 1896, when he sent the Kruger Telegram, and that it had continued to be the main goal of his continental policy ever since. What sparked off the explosion of fury against him was not any particular comment in the interview, however, but, rather, the fact that he had spoken out at all to a foreigner about German policy.

The target of universal anger that exploded in the *Daily Telegraph* crisis of November 1908 was the personal rule exercised by Wilhelm II since 1890. Yet, although the almost revolutionary mood that swept the country and the tumultuous debate in the Reichstag would have provided the ideal opportunity for fundamental constitutional reform, the chance was missed. True, Bülow managed to extract a declaration from the deflated monarch on 17 November 1908 that in future he would guarantee 'the stability of Reich policy while observ-ing constitutional responsibilities',[8] but insiders knew only too well that little had changed with this compromise. With justification, the Kaiser's sister Charlotte commented gloomily that 'H.M. thinks himself infallible, Bül[ow] carries on juggling and I...cannot stop being deeply pessimistic about the future of our German political, dynastic and governmental affairs'.[9] With his 'treachery to the Crown', moreover, Bülow had forfeited the 'All-Highest confidence' once and for all, and his dismissal was henceforth only a matter of time.

After the Eulenburg scandal, the Tweedmouth letter, the Hale interview and the *Daily Telegraph* affair, state leaders in London and Paris, Washington, St Petersburg and Tokyo wondered more anxiously than ever whether the Kaiser, who commanded the most perfect war machine on earth, was still in his right mind. Their fears were not ungrounded. After the bizarre death in Donaueschingen of General Count Dietrich von Hülsen-Haeseler, dressed as a ballerina,[10] and the partial publication of Wilhelm's rabid comments to Hale, he suffered another nervous breakdown.

For weeks the All-Highest withdrew from public life, sulking and plotting revenge. He developed the wildest conspiracy theories to explain the debacle of the *Daily Telegraph* crisis. Neither he himself nor his personal manner of ruling was to blame for the events of November, he maintained; no, it was Bülow, the elderly Geheimrat Friedrich von Holstein and the Jew Maximilian Harden who had conspired against him on behalf of international Jewry in order to deprive him of power! In December 1908 he complained in a letter to Fürstenberg:

I have really been under a great deal of strain! In 1907 Kuno Moltke and [Count] Hohenau [forced to leave the country after another homosexuality scandal], and throughout the year the Eulenburg affair which went on into the spring of 1908. Then in 1908 the events we know well! It really has been a bit too much for a sensitive disposition! [...] Holstein has a firm agreement with Harden; they hunt as a pair. Holstein has fully recovered his old influence over Bülow and is the irresponsible controller of our policy... It is this choice circle which – the impulsive unconstitutional Kaiser having been excluded – runs the German Reich indirectly through Bülow, under Holstein's direction.[11]

Some days later, in another bitter missive to Fürstenberg, the Kaiser wrote:

The Golden International has our Fatherland in its grip and plays ball with our holiest possessions through the press which it controls! One is gradually turning into a convinced anti-Semite. If the German *Volk* ever wakes from the torpor of the hypnosis induced by the Jewish press and becomes seeing, we could be in for a nice surprise![12]

An alarming loss of grasp on reality combined with a personal decision-making power that had survived virtually intact did not bode well for the maintenance of world peace, which needed cool-headed crisis management more urgently than ever.

CHAPTER 16

From Bülow to Bethmann Hollweg: the Chancellor merry-go-round (1909)

After his 'treachery' in the *Daily Telegraph* affair Bülow's days as Reich Chancellor were clearly numbered. Encouraged by Max Fürstenberg and other 'pro-Kaiser loyalists', Wilhelm II allowed himself to be carried away by the idea that the interview in the London newspaper had been a trap deliberately set for him by Bülow in order to bring universal disgrace on him and seize power for himself. He complained bitterly that the affair had

brought months of attacks of the vilest and rudest kind upon me, buried the Crown in a deep layer of filth, greatly harmed the Old Prussian Kingdom and the prestige of the German Imperial Crown, undermined our reputation abroad, brought boundless shame and disgrace on the House of Hohenzollern and unspeakable suffering and sorrow on myself and the Kaiserin.[1]

At first he showed little of his change of attitude towards the Chancellor, but the intimate trust that had formed the basis of their close relationship since 1897 had been completely destroyed. When the Reichstag rejected the Finance Reform bill on 24 June 1909 and Bülow handed in his resignation, Wilhelm immediately accepted it, in spite of the obvious danger that sacking the Chancellor after a defeat in parliament might give the appearance that the Reich was sliding towards parliamentary forms. The irresponsible manner in which the new Reich Chancellor and Prussian minister-president was appointed shows very plainly, however, that the power of the Crown was wholly undiminished in this decisive respect.

Since the 'November storm' unleashed by the *Daily Telegraph* interview Wilhelm had had seven months in which to consider whom he should call on to take up the highest office in the land.

For a time he thought of appointing his Flügeladjutant, General Alfred von Loewenfeld, then the Bavarian envoy Count Hugo von Lerchenfeld-Köfering, and later the ambassador in Paris, Prince Hugo Radolin. In April 1909, on his way to Corfu, he promised Count Anton Monts, the ambassador in Rome, that he would be made Chancellor, but in his final audience Bülow talked the monarch out of this idea with the strange argument that in the coming years the most difficult problems would be those of domestic policy, and that Bethmann Hollweg, the then Secretary of State in the Reich Office of the Interior, would be a more appropriate choice than a diplomat. Yet when Valentini, the chief of the Civil Cabinet, put forward Bethmann Hollweg's name on 3 July 1909 on board the *Hohenzollern* at Kiel, the Kaiser, impatient to set off on his annual cruise along the coast of Norway, rejected this choice with the telling remark: 'I know exactly what he is like. He is an arrogant, pig-headed schoolmaster; I can't work with him.'[2]

The Kaiserin was equally averse to Bethmann, whom she described as 'too philosophical, unworldly and ponderous'.[3] Three further candidates, the brothers August and Botho zu Eulenburg and the Statthalter of Alsace-Lorraine, General Count Carl von Wedel, turned down the Reich Chancellorship, whereupon the Prussian finance minister, Freiherr Georg von Rheinbaben, came under discussion. When Valentini came aboard the *Hohenzollern* on 7 July 1909 with this latter suggestion, however, Wilhelm had himself hit upon the idea of appointing the fearsome Field Marshal Colmar Freiherr von der Goltz, then back in Constantinople reorganising the Ottoman army – whose choice as Reich Chancellor, as his recent biographer makes clear, would have been tantamount to war![4] The Kaiser actually ordered the Civil Cabinet chief 'to take the Orient Express to Constantinople at once!' and offer the chancellorship to Goltz. While Valentini was consulting the railway timetable the valet called him back again to see the Kaiser in his cabin.

In the meantime His Majesty had changed into tennis clothes and he received me on his way out of the door. He had thought the matter over again, he said; it would be unfair to the Turks to take away the General [von der Goltz] now, when he had an important mission to fulfil there; he was willing to have Bethmann, and I should now make all the necessary arrangements quickly!

With that the Kaiser was at last free, after his game of tennis, to set off on his Scandinavian cruise.[5] On 14 July 1909 Bethmann Hollweg, having been 'chosen' in this farcical way, accepted the highest and most challenging office in the German Reich and Prussia. To this man, utterly inexperienced in international politics, was to fall the lot of plunging the world into the catastrophe of the Great War in the summer of 1914.

PART V

1908–1914: *The Bellicose Supreme War Lord*

CHAPTER 17

The Bosnian annexation crisis (1908–1909)

The all too trustful relationship that Wilhelm II developed in the wake of the Eulenburg scandal with Prince Max Egon zu Fürstenberg and other members of the Austrian high aristocracy around Archduke Franz Ferdinand was soon to lead to serious political consequences. In the course of the Young Turk revolution, which to the Kaiser's indignation imposed a constitution along British lines on Sultan Abdulhamid II throughout the Ottoman Empire, the Austro-Hungarian foreign minister, Alois Freiherr Lexa von Aehrenthal, on 5 October 1908 announced the formal annexation of the provinces of Bosnia and Herzegovina, which had been administered from Vienna since 1878. This move by his ally was a severe setback to the Kaiser's dizzying ambition to win over the entire Muslim world in order to counter the increasing isolation of the German Reich. Back in 1905 he had declared: '[I]n the present very tense circumstances, when we stand almost *alone* in the face of great coalitions which are being formed against us, our *last trump card* is *Islam* and the *Mohammedan world*.'[1] In the rebellion of the Young Turk officers, whom he at first considered 'lackeys of England', he saw his Turkish policy, 'laboriously built up over 20 years, go up in smoke'.[2] 'We are now finally thrown out of the Near East and can pack up,' he complained in October 1908.[3]

Aehrenthal's reckless plan to ensure the lasting supremacy of the Habsburg Empire in the Balkans at the expense of Russian interests by annexing the two Turkish provinces of Bosnia and Herzegovina had received the express support of Chancellor Prince von Bülow and the Reich's foreign secretary, Wilhelm von Schoen. The Kaiser, on the other hand, was completely surprised by the coup, which plunged him into a conflict of loyalties between Vienna and

Constantinople. 'I am personally most deeply hurt in my sentiments as an ally that H.M. [Emperor Franz Joseph] did not in the slightest take me into his confidence beforehand!' he commented.[4] Bülow succeeded in winning the Kaiser round, however, in a conversation in the garden of the Reich Chancellor's palace in the Wilhelmstrasse on 12 October 1908. From then onwards Kaiser Wilhelm ardently supported his ally's initiative and, as usual, overshot the mark in his martial enthusiasm. When the possibility of war between Austria-Hungary and Serbia loomed, he exclaimed: 'If only it would start!'[5] He was fully aware of the danger that Germany could be drawn into a war against Russia and France by a Balkan conflict.

Thirteen years earlier, in November 1895, Wilhelm II had assured the Austro-Hungarian ambassador, Count Ladislaus von Szögyény-Marich, 'quite plainly' that he would

stand at Austria-Hungary's side with all the forces at my disposal, without any further enquiry as to whether the *casus foederis* existed in accordance with our treaty of alliance. [. . .] Your All-Highest Sovereign [Franz Joseph] may be quite sure that if at any moment the position of the Austro-Hungarian monarchy is at issue. . .my entire fighting forces will be immediately and unconditionally at his disposal.[6]

This fatal promise, leaving the decision over war and peace to the emperor and statesmen in Vienna, Kaiser Wilhelm now repeated 'very forcefully' when he met Count Szögyény on 21 October 1908. Emperor Franz Joseph was indeed 'a Prussian Field Marshal, and so only has to give the order and the whole Prussian army will obey his command', the German Kaiser assured him.[7] Breathtakingly, with this display of unquestioning loyalty Wilhelm anticipated the notorious 'blank cheque' that he was to give (once again, to none other than Szögyény) on 5 July 1914. The comparison is all the more uncanny because, at precisely this time in the autumn of 1908, Wilhelm met the Austrian diplomat Alexander Hoyos, who was to travel to Berlin at the beginning of July 1914 with Franz Joseph's letter asking for German support in the event of war with Russia.[8]

A week after the assurance given to Szögyény on 21 October 1908 the *Daily Telegraph* crisis broke, but even during the 'November storm' Wilhelm II continued to pledge his loyal support to Austria-Hungary. After his dramatic visit to Donaueschingen he wrote to his

Badenese-Austrian friend Max Fürstenberg: 'Yes, Austria can count on me, and I stand by you through thick and thin!'[9] From the military standpoint, he commented in mid-December 1908, this was in any case 'the best moment to settle accounts with the Russians'. Germany had to 'definitely yes, take preventive action, as Fred[erick] the Great did in his day'.[10] Again, at the end of the year Wilhelm wrote to the heir to the Austrian throne, Franz Ferdinand, saying that he was keeping his powder dry and was on guard. 'That you can count on us, you know, and whether our army is worth anything you are best able to judge.'[11] Such promises by the German Kaiser were all the more dangerous because the chief of the General Staff, Helmuth von Moltke, was also telling his Austrian counterpart, Franz Conrad von Hötzendorf, that 'an Austrian invasion of Serbia might lead Russia to intervene actively. With this, the casus foederis [the obligation to enter the war on her ally's side] would arise for Germany', which would probably, if it came to war, begin the offensive with an attack on France in the west.[12]

Once again in eerie anticipation of the way in which the wheels of the alliances could be set in motion, and in July 1914 actually were to lead from a Balkan conflict to world war, in February 1909 Wilhelm II and von Moltke considered in detail how France should be handled if there were an imminent threat of war, in order to clarify the situation for the German army. In a comment on a report by Heinrich von Tschirschky und Bögendorff, Germany's ambassador in Vienna, on 24 February 1909 Kaiser Wilhelm ordered:

It must be made clear to France that in the event of Russia's intervening against Austria, the *casus foederis* arises for us immediately, i.e. mobilisation. France must be forced to make a binding and clear declaration that it will in this case *not go to war with us at all*. Not at the start of the war, nor later. A declaration of neutrality is not sufficient. If France refuses to make this declaration, that is to be taken by us as a casus belli, and the Reichstag and the world informed, that France, despite our invitation to tread together with us the only possible path to maintain the peace of Europe, has refused and has therefore *willed the war*. This clarification, in this form, is necessary so that we can start our mobilisation in the first instance against France and finish her off. In no case can the army get into the position where one half is engaged against Russia and the other half standing guard against an unreliable France. We must throw everything against the West or everything against the East.[13]

In 1909 a great war was avoided only because Imperial Russia, still shaken by her defeat in the war with Japan and the revolution within her own borders, backed down. There can be no doubt, however, about Wilhelm II's willingness to go to war throughout the whole Bosnian annexation crisis of 1908–9. On the contrary, until the very end the Supreme War Lord eagerly advocated an Austrian attack on Serbia, with exhortations such as 'So forward and invade!'[14] or 'Well then, let him get in there!'.[15] After Russia had given way Wilhelm concluded that this success was proof that strong collaboration between Germany and Austria-Hungary was the right course to pursue – indeed, that it had been 'a wonderful trial-run for the event of a showdown'.[16] Not the least of the consequences of Russia's humiliation in this crisis was that Wilhelm acquired the fateful conviction that Great Britain would neither choose, nor be able, to intervene in a European war arising out of a conflict in the Balkans.[17]

However striking the similarities between the two crises, it would be wrong, despite the 'trial-run' significance that Wilhelm imputed to German–Austrian solidarity in 1908–9, to construct a direct causal link between the Bosnian annexation crisis and the July crisis of 1914. Germany's willingness to go to war side by side with her ally Austria-Hungary against Russia and France was undoubtedly a given, but the *will* to bring about such a war was still absent in Berlin in 1908–9. This developed only after further serious clashes with the two western powers under Bülow's successor Bethmann Hollweg and the rumbustious new foreign secretary, Alfred von Kiderlen-Wächter.

CHAPTER 18

The 'leap of the Panther' to Agadir (1911)

With the death of his uncle King Edward VII on 6 May 1910 Wilhelm II's hopes were revived for a rapprochement between Germany and Britain that would at last enable the German Reich to achieve the world status marked out for it by 'Providence'. In that year the Kaiser explained his racial vision for the future to David J. Hill, the American ambassador in Berlin: the English, he claimed, were already on the downhill road while his own empire was advancing.

We do not want their colonies nor the dominion of the sea, we only want to have our rights respected. Germany is now almost as rich as England. [. . .] What we want is an equal chance. They have tried to hold us up as a menace to Europe, but we have menaced no one. They have tried to array Europe against us, but their entente is weakening. As for the Latins, they have had their day. I do not believe the Slavs are to be the leaders of the future. Providence has designs, and it would not be a compliment to Providence to believe that it is to the Slavs and not to the Germanic race that Providence looks for the civilization of the future. No, it is the Germanic race, – we here in Germany, the English and the Americans, – who are to lead the civilization of the world.[1]

In eager anticipation of the forthcoming visit of the former US president Theodore Roosevelt to Germany, Wilhelm went into raptures about a 'coming together of the Teutonic-Anglo-Saxon countries'.[2] 'The Germanic + Anglo Saxon Races combined will keep the world in order!' he wrote enthusiastically to Roosevelt after the visit, sending him photographs of the two of them together on manoeuvres.[3]

Not only were Wilhelm's overblown aspirations met with scepticism on the part of the Americans, but they were principally thwarted by the refusal of the British to break off their ententes with France and Russia in order to allow Germany a hegemonic position on the Continent. During the funeral ceremonies for his uncle, King Edward VII, in London in May 1910, and again at the unveiling of the memorial to his grandmother, Queen Victoria, a year later, the Kaiser played on the charm of his personality in the belief that he could win over the English and above all his cousin, King George V, to an agreement with Germany. In actual fact, during this visit to England (it was to be his last) Wilhelm delivered himself of one of the most disastrous tirades of his reign, which proved to have a fateful effect on British policy. On 20 May 1911 he told Prince Louis of Battenberg on board the *Hohenzollern*, anchored on the Thames, that he earnestly wished to establish the friendliest relations with England, but added that 'you must not preface every conversation with the condition that you cannot come to an agreement with us on this or that subject if it were to affect the interests of France or Russia'. He vehemently rejected Battenberg's argument that Britain's good relationship with these two countries was 'the natural & necessary counterpoise to the Triple Alliance'. According to the prince, 'The Emperor fired up & proceeded with more & more warmth, not to say heat, to ridicule this conception of the balance of power in Europe.' Wilhelm exclaimed: 'You must be brought to understand in England that Germany is the sole arbiter of peace or war on the Continent.' 'If we wish to fight,' he added, 'we will do so with or without your leave.'[4]

Battenberg sent his record of the conversation to the king, who forwarded it immediately to the prime minister, Herbert Henry Asquith. He in turn showed it to the foreign secretary, Sir Edward Grey. All three were appalled and seriously wondered whether the German emperor was in his right mind. As Asquith put it: 'One is almost tempted to discern in some of the things he said to Prince Louis the workings of a disordered brain; but (even if that is so) they are none the less dangerous.'[5] The Foreign Office was more firmly convinced than ever that Germany was seeking 'hegemony in Europe'.[6] At any rate, the Kaiser's threats influenced the British government's decision to stand by France when the Second Morocco Crisis precipitated the next great trial of strength over German supremacy in Europe.

It was not Kaiser Wilhelm but, rather, a brash, bibulous, self-assured Swabian, Alfred von Kiderlen-Wächter, who hit upon the bold plan of responding to the French occupation of the Moroccan city of Fez in 1911 by sending the gunboat *Panther* to Agadir, in order to exact compensation for Germany under threat of war.[7] Kiderlen's ultimate aim was not the annexation of southern Morocco but the establishment of a gigantic German *Mittelafrika* that would in the end embrace German South-West Africa, German East Africa, the Belgian Congo, the French Congo, the Cameroons and Togo, and the Portuguese colonies of Angola and Mozambique. By stoking up hopes of Moroccan territorial gains in German nationalist and industrialist circles in order to strengthen his bargaining position vis-à-vis France, however, Kiderlen also put the Kaiser dangerously under pressure. For, when the reckless plan threatened to turn into a fiasco, the Kaiser was abused as 'Wilhelm the Peaceful' in those very circles. People talked of a new 'Olmütz' – Prussia's humiliation at the hands of Austria in 1850 – and asked what had become of the old Prussia: 'Have we become a race of women?'[8]

However little enthusiasm the Kaiser had for the acquisition of more colonies in Africa, it is clear that Wilhelm had known about Kiderlen's objectives since the beginning of May 1911 and had also formally approved the foreign secretary's provocative action several times, most recently at Kiel on 26 June 1911. On 5 July Wilhelm set off on his annual cruise along the Norwegian coast. In spite of the tension the voyage began in the usual carefree atmosphere. The chief of the Naval Cabinet noted in his diary: 'A lot of tomfoolery at gymnastics this morning. His Majesty cut through [Adjutant General] von Scholl's braces with a penknife.'[9] Far from expressing any doubts about Kiderlen's action, Wilhelm grew impatient with the snail's pace of the negotiations, through which France was to be forced to cede the whole of her colony on the Congo to Germany. Kiderlen should speed up the talks and, above all, insist on the cession of the French Congo, he grumbled. For his part, Kiderlen, no doubt mindful of the sudden retreat by the Kaiser in the First Morocco Crisis in 1905, threatened to resign if the monarch withdrew his 'All-Highest confidence' from him at the decisive moment. 'I do not believe that the French will take up the gauntlet,' he wrote, 'but they must be made to feel that we are prepared to go to the utmost extreme.'[10]

For the Kaiser, the Chancellor and nationalist public opinion in Germany, the warning uttered by the British Chancellor of the Exchequer, David Lloyd George, on 21 July 1911 – that Britain would stand by her Entente partner if it came to war between Germany and France – felt like a 'box on the ears'. Once again Europe stood on the brink of a major war. When the *Hohenzollern* returned to Swinemünde at the end of July Kiderlen made a 'brash speech' to the Kaiser in which he conceded, as Admiral von Müller noted, 'War with France very inopportune at the moment, as England certainly on the side of France and then our allies more or less worthless. H.M. very quiet. In agreement, however.'[11] Baroness Spitzemberg, on the other hand, heard that in Swinemünde the Kaiser had been 'by no means limp, but even more aggressive than his ministers!'.[12] Wilhelm raged about the 'colossal piece of impudence on the part of the French' that was out of keeping with 'the dignity of the German Reich and People'.[13] 'The French must clear the ditch somehow or other, or feel our spurs,' he declared.[14] And, if the British were to land troops on the French or Belgian coast, then Germany had 'submarines!'.[15] The chief of the General Staff, von Moltke, likewise complained bitterly: 'If we once again emerge from this affair with our tail between our legs, if we cannot bring ourselves to make energetic demands which we would be ready to force through with the sword, then I despair of the future of the German Reich.'[16] The Prussian minister of war, General Josias von Heeringen, stated that the army had been 'absolutely prepared for the event of war with France' without actually wishing for it, as the younger officers and the Pan-German League had.[17]

Kaiser Wilhelm II had not been the initiator of the disastrous 'leap of the *Panther*' to Agadir, nor did he take much pleasure in the 275,000 square kilometres of infested swamp that Kiderlen ended up by extracting from the French. The Kaiser's aim was not primarily colonial acquisitions but a global power shift in favour of the German Reich. Thus, following the Reich's belligerent confrontation with Russia over Bosnia and its reckless threatening of France over Morocco, when during the Agadir crisis British sea power had yet again proved to be the guarantor of the status quo – the so-called balance of power – in Europe, Wilhelmine *Weltmachtpolitik* came to set its sights once again on the British Empire as its principal opponent.

CHAPTER 19

The battlefleet and the growing risk of war with Britain (1911–1912)

While Bethmann Hollweg intensified his efforts to come to an agreement with Britain, the Kaiser and Tirpitz insisted on a massive acceleration of the battleship-building programme, despite the danger that the British would respond with a preventive strike to sink the German fleet. Even Tirpitz acknowledged that, as yet, his fleet would hardly stand a chance in a battle with the Royal Navy. The present moment was 'as unfavourable as possible', he conceded; every additional year would be advantageous. He listed the measures that would have to be taken to improve the situation: 'Heligoland, [Kaiser Wilhelm] Canal, Dreadnoughts, U-Boats etc.'[1] Inside the Admiralty, as distinct from the Reich Navy Office, which Tirpitz controlled, influential voices advocated delaying the confrontation with the British Empire at least until the Kaiser Wilhelm Canal (now Kiel Canal) linking the Baltic and North Seas was navigable for big battleships of the *Dreadnought* class – that is to say, until the autumn of 1914. Yet Wilhelm II categorically insisted that three battleships and three large cruisers should be built per annum, whatever it cost. The expansion of the fleet he demanded was 'not merely a matter of life and death for the future development of the *Navy*, but for the future foreign policy of *the Reich*'.[2] Paradoxically, the aim of this highly risky naval policy was not to bring about a war with Britain but, on the contrary, to achieve the breakthrough to world power without war. Indeed, to force Britain into an alliance that would permanently guarantee German supremacy in Europe and overseas would be, as one of Tirpitz's closest associates put it, 'the keystone of our naval policy'.[3]

Bethmann Hollweg, Kiderlen-Wächter and Adolf Wermuth, the Secretary of State of the Reich Treasury, stubbornly resisted the

23 The gathering storm: Winston Churchill with Wilhelm II at the 'Kaiser manoeuvres' of the German army in 1909.

Kaiser's policy, which they considered far too dangerous, and they found allies in both the navy and the army, and especially in the diplomatic corps. A decision between Tirpitz and Bethmann – a perfect example of what has been called the kingship mechanism – became inevitable, but the Kaiser prevaricated, unwilling to risk the resignation of either. In mid-October 1911 he complained that the Reich Chancellor, as Müller recorded, was

full of doubts and is completely dominated by fear of England. But I shall not let England dictate to me what I should and should not do. I have told the R[eich] C[hancellor] he should remember that I am descended from the Gr[eat] Elector and Fred[erick] the Gr[eat], who did not hesitate to act when they thought the time right. I also told the Reich Chancellor that he must take Divine Providence into account, which will certainly see to it that a people that has so much to answer for as the English will also be brought low some day.[4]

The crisis dragged on throughout the winter. In January 1912 Wilhelm again complained 'in the sharpest terms of the feebleness and timidity' of Bethmann and the civilians in the Wilhelmstrasse. When a retired ambassador also spoke out against the forced pace of dreadnought building, the Kaiser retorted: 'I will tell you something, you diplomats have filled your pants, the entire Wilhelmstrasse stinks of. . .'[5] In the end the Chancellor succeeded in reducing by half the *Novelle* for the fleet demanded by the Kaiser and Tirpitz, but, even so, the acceleration of the battlefleet-building programme was seen by London as a provocation. In response, the newly appointed First Lord of the Admiralty, Winston Churchill, doubled the Royal Navy's budget and transferred ships stationed in the Mediterranean to the North Sea. General Henry Wilson, director of military operations at the War Office in London, began to hold regular meetings with his French counterparts to discuss the landing of a British expeditionary force on the Franco-Belgian border.[6] At the end of 1911 Admiral Lord Fisher predicted that the decisive battle would begin 'in September 1914', not least because the Kaiser Wilhelm Canal would then be navigable for large battleships.[7] Already both countries and their allies were teetering on the brink of a world war.

CHAPTER 20

Doomed to failure: the Haldane Mission (1912)

The fundamental reasons for the antagonism between Germany and Great Britain became clear in the course of the negotiations that the British minister of war, Lord Haldane, held with the Reich Chancellor, Grand Admiral von Tirpitz and Kaiser Wilhelm in Berlin in February 1912. The initiative for the meeting had come from the director of the Hamburg shipping line Hapag, Albert Ballin, in Germany and, in England, from the Anglo-German financier Sir Ernest Cassel. When the British indicated that they were ready to enter into discussions Wilhelm II saw this as confirmation of his belief that London had come round purely out of fear of his battlefleet programme. His greatest hopes seemed about to be fulfilled. On 10 January 1912 Bethmann Hollweg told him that an agreement with Great Britain would bring the German Reich 'a great colonial empire', with the Portuguese and Dutch colonies and the Belgian Congo. Not only that but an Anglo-German agreement would 'drive a wedge into the Triple Entente' and thus ensure German pre-eminence on the Continent.[1] The Kaiser was jubilant and saw himself, as Müller noted on 7 February, 'already as leader of the United States of Europe, and a German colonial empire stretching right across Central Africa'.[2] Wilhelm told Walther Rathenau that his plan was to create a 'United States of Europe against America. [...] Five states (incl. France) could do something.'[3] Tirpitz, on the other hand, scented nothing behind Albion's surprising approach but a perfidious attempt to torpedo his battlefleet plans – plans that he saw as the only means of forcing Britain permanently to accept 'equal rights' throughout the world for Germany. Once again the Kaiser found himself in the extremely uncomfortable position of having to mediate between Bethmann Hollweg and the grand admiral.

Feverishly Wilhelm drafted in his own hand the document that was to serve as the basis of the negotiations with Haldane. Full of distrust for Bethmann and the Wilhelmstrasse, he pointed out that, while the British government was a committee, 'the government here, by contrast, is directed by *one man*, the Kaiser, i.e. the Chancellor speaks in his name', so that the latter was not in a position to make any binding agreements.[4] Nor was Wilhelm prepared to allow anyone else but himself to play the leading role in the decisive negotiations between Haldane and Tirpitz. Basically, in return for a reduction in the tempo of Germany's battlefleet-building programme, the British were to enter into a political agreement with the Kaiserreich, intended to last twenty years, by which they would be contractually bound to remain neutral in *any* European war however it arose and, moreover, to assist Germany in acquiring colonies overseas. But a forced settlement of this kind, based on blackmail, was wholly unacceptable to Great Britain. It would have given the Kaiserreich a free hand to attack France at will; or, now that France would no longer have the protection of the Royal Navy, to force her into a continental league with the central European powers and Russia. The British Empire would then be under threat not only in the North Sea and the Atlantic but also in the Mediterranean, Persia, India and the Far East.[5]

When it became clear that Britain would refuse to agree to German demands for unconditional neutrality in a continental war, Wilhelm II's bitterness knew no bounds. 'My patience and that of the German people is at an end!' he declared.[6] More than ever he considered himself superior to his Chancellor and ministers, who had 'fallen for' the English bluff.

I hope that my diplomats will draw the lesson from this, to pay more attention to their master and his commands and wishes in future than hitherto, especially when it is a matter of doing anything with England, whom they do not know how to handle; while I know England well![7]

The chief of the Naval Cabinet, Admiral von Müller, was shocked by the Kaiser's 'incredibly coarse language' in his dispatches to the Chancellor and the ambassador in London, Count Paul von Metternich, and assumed that it was intended to provoke both men to resign.[8] Indeed, in protest at the bellicose line that the Kaiser was pursuing with total disregard for his 'responsible' advisers, Bethmann Hollweg handed in his resignation on 6 March 1912. He remained in office, however, and worked with the leadership of the army to redirect strategic planning on the basis of war with the land powers of France and Russia rather than, as hitherto, with the two western powers. Enormous sums were to be demanded from the Reichstag to enlarge the army at the expense of Tirpitz's battlefleet programme. But Great Britain's role in such a conflict between the Central Powers and the Franco-Russian Dual Alliance was, of course, still in the lap of the gods.

CHAPTER 21

Turmoil in the Balkans and a first decision for war (November 1912)

The focus of trouble in Europe was in any case shifting from west to east as a result of the rapid decline of the Ottoman Empire. The Young Turk revolution of 1908, the Bosnian annexation crisis of 1908–9, the removal of Sultan Abdulhamid II in 1909 and the Italian attack on Tripoli (Libya) in 1911 had aroused hopes of territorial expansion among the smaller Balkan states. In late September 1912 the First Balkan War broke out when Montenegro, Serbia, Bulgaria and Greece attacked Turkey. Kaiser Wilhelm II welcomed the Balkan countries' advance, and in his characteristic style mocked the diplomats trying to restore peace as 'eunuchs'. He declared scornfully that 'civilians' could not judge the situation, as 'that is a matter for the military'.[1] On 4 October 1912 he ominously exclaimed: 'The Eastern Question must be resolved by blood and iron! But at a time that suits us! That is now.'[2]

It was the Kaiser's dream that the four Christian states in the Balkans would combine in a '4-Power League', which would then be taken into the 'European Concert' as 'a 7th Great Power', and would in fact be 'aligned with Austria and the Triple Alliance!'. Austria, he demanded, had to

give the construction of a 'United States of the Balkans'...her energetic support. For in such a formation the Balkan states will soon get themselves into opposition to Russia, and will then quite naturally have need of Austria and hence of the Triple Alliance, for which they will provide a very desirable reinforcement and an offensive flank against Russia.[3]

When on 1 December 1912, while in Donaueschingen, the news reached him that Bulgaria had offered to enter into an alliance with Turkey, Wilhelm once again saw himself as the ruler of a powerful worldwide empire, this time based on the Middle East. On that day he sent the following staggering telegram to his Foreign Office:

Austria must enter a military alliance with Turco-Bulgaria, and we must cooperate in strengthening and regenerating both states. Such a power combination will drive Greece and even Serbia helplessly towards Austria. Thus, Austria will become the predominant Power in the Balkans and the Eastern Mediterranean, and together with Italy and a regenerated or newly constructed Turco-Bulgarian fleet, will be a powerful counterweight to England, whose communications with Alexandria could be threatened. Russia will then be finished in the Balkans and Odessa threatened. Then the Triple Alliance Powers will be preponderant in the Mediterranean, and have control of the Caliph and thereby of the whole Mohammedan world! (India).[4]

The Kaiser's extraordinary flight of fancy was not shared by the Austrians, who viewed the expansion of Serbia with growing anxiety, nor by his own General Staff or the Wilhelmstrasse, who saw in the tense relationship between Austria-Hungary and Serbia an opportunity for a showdown with Russia and her ally France before the moribund multinational monarchy on the Danube became incapable of taking action. On 9 November 1912, at his hunting lodge at Letzlingen near Magdeburg, the Kaiser resisted the pressure of both his military and his civilian advisers to give the Austrians a pledge of German support in the event that their planned attack on Serbia – as in the Bosnian crisis of 1908–9 – should provoke conflict with Russia (and possibly also France). He sent a revealing telegram to Kiderlen-Wächter saying that he had 'distinctly' told the Reich Chancellor at Letzlingen that 'that *under no circumstances* will I *march against Paris and Moscow*' in order to halt the Serbian advance to the Adriatic.[5] Yet in the course of that same day the Kaiser made a complete about-turn. Evidently persuaded by someone in his entourage that public opinion in Europe would now consider an Austro-Hungarian attack on Serbia as justified, Wilhelm suddenly gave his approval to the policy of war-readiness that Moltke, Bethmann Hollweg and Kiderlen-Wächter had been urging on him. On 19 November 1912 the foreign secretary was able to convey to the Austrians, through the back channel of Wilhelm's friend Fürstenberg, the assurance that, if complications arose, the German Reich 'would not hesitate for a moment to fulfil our alliance obligations'.[6] Two days later Wilhelm

24 'I'll stand by you through thick and thin!': Wilhelm II and his friend Archduke
Franz Ferdinand at their crucial meeting at Springe in November 1912.

himself promised the Austrian military attaché, Karl Freiherr von
Bienerth, 'that Austria-Hungary could count unconditionally on the
support of the German Reich'. As the Kaiser put it, 'Germany's
sword is already loose in its scabbard, you can count on us.'[7] This
was 'a moment of profoundest seriousness' for Germany too, the
Kaiser wrote on a report from Vienna. He recognised full well what it
could mean: 'It can turn into the Europ[ean] War and for us possibly
a struggle for existence against 3 Great Powers.'[8]

On 22 November 1912 Field Marshal Blasius Schemua, who had
temporarily replaced General Conrad von Hötzendorf as chief of the
Austro-Hungarian General Staff, arrived in Berlin for secret discussions with the Kaiser and Moltke. Once again the Supreme War
Lord and the chief of the German General Staff promised that the
Austrians 'could count absolutely on Germany if Russia threatened
us, and that it was also an eminent interest of Germany's too that we

[the Austrians] should not be weakened'. The Russian army was very far from being ready for war, Schemua was assured, while the French were in a peaceable mood and the Italians (so King Victor Emmanuel had promised the German Crown Prince while chamois hunting in the Alps, as the Kaiser informed the visitor from Vienna) were willing to fulfil their obligations under the Triple Alliance and join in the fray. Helmuth von Moltke explained to his Austrian colleague that

the seriousness of the situation was clear to him. German mobilisation would automatically entail that of France, and to have two mobilised armies standing alongside each other was an untenable situation which was bound to lead to a clash. But then the first consideration, naturally, must be to crush the enemy in the West first – which he hoped to do in 4 to 5 weeks – and then to transfer the spare capacity in forces to the East.[9]

Following the fateful meeting with the Austrian field marshal Kaiser Wilhelm II travelled to Springe (outside Hanover) to go shooting with Archduke Franz Ferdinand. Moltke, Tirpitz and Bethmann Hollweg were also present. On 2 December 1912 the latter made a speech in the Reichstag, the crucial passages having been dictated to him by Moltke, in which he solemnly announced Germany's 'firm and unflinching' support for Austria-Hungary in a conflict with Serbia.[10] A European war seemed to be in the immediate offing. But how would Britain react?

CHAPTER 22

War postponed: the 'war council' of 8 December 1912

In the belief that a continental war was imminent, on 21 November 1912 the Kaiser ordered 'that the ambassadors in *Paris* and *London* must be ordered *at once* to ascertain *with absolute clarity* and to report to me, whether in such circumstances *Paris* would definitely go along with Russia immediately, and what side England will take'.[1] At the same time Wilhelm asked his brother, Prince Heinrich of Prussia, who was about to pay a visit to England, to find out what line Britain would take in a war arising out of the tumult in the Balkans. In London on 4 December 1912 Heinrich asked his brother-in-law, the First Sea Lord, Prince Louis of Battenberg, point-blank whether Britain would remain neutral in such an eventuality. Alarmed, Battenberg immediately wrote to his cousin, King George V, saying that Heinrich and Wilhelm evidently did not understand that, 'if War were to break out between Germany & Austria v[ersus] Russia & France, we here cannot permit either of the two latter countries, especially France, to be crippled – consequently we *cannot* stand out in certain circumstances'.[2] The king gave the Prussian prince the same reply, almost word for word, when Heinrich asked him the same crucial question at Sandringham on 6 December 1912. Later he told the foreign secretary, Edward Grey, that Heinrich had asked him 'whether, in the event of Germany and Austria going to war with Russia and France, England would come to the assistance of the two latter Powers. I answered "undoubtedly, Yes – under certain circumstances." [. . .] Of course Germany must know that we would not allow either of our friends to be crippled.'[3] In a presumably well-meaning but highly irresponsible manner, Heinrich gave his brother the Kaiser a distorted version of this clear statement by the king: England was peaceable, he said, and wished to avoid any conflict with Germany.[4]

25 The cousins Wilhelm II and George V at Potsdam for the wedding
of Princess Viktoria Luise, the Kaiser's daughter, on 24 May 1913,
Queen Victoria's birthday.

Wilhelm might have continued to pursue his belligerent policy of
support for Austria-Hungary in the winter of 1912 had not the newly
appointed ambassador in London, Prince Karl Max von Lichnowsky,
told him the truth in a report of 3 December; for, unlike Prince
Heinrich, Lichnowsky made it clear that Lord Haldane – in all
probability in response to Bethmann Hollweg's Reichstag speech of
the previous day – had told him in no uncertain terms that 'in a general
European conflict that might arise from an Austrian invasion of Serbia'
it was 'hardly likely that Great Britain would be able to remain a
passive observer'. The principle of the balance of power was simply 'an
axiom' of British foreign policy and had led the United Kingdom to
align itself with France and Russia. 'England could therefore under no
circumstances tolerate the crushing of the French. [...] England
cannot be, and is not willing, to be confronted afterwards by a united
continent under the leadership of one Power.'[5]

Wilhelm II received Lichnowsky's report on the morning of
Sunday 8 December 1912, on his return to Berlin after a shoot in
Bückeburg. The violent marginal comments he wrote on it expressed

his rage at the British balance of power policy, which would, he said, make 'England our enemy for ever'. Obsessed with racialist delusions, he predicted that in the forthcoming 'final struggle between Slavs and Teutons. . .the Anglo-Saxons' would find themselves 'on the side of the Slavs and Gauls' as 'loyal supporters of the Gallo-Slavs against the Teutons!'.[6] He told the Bavarian envoy, Count Lerchenfeld, that it would be 'a case of all or nothing for Germany soon, perhaps very soon. Threatened on three sides, we must be prepared for everything and must leave nothing undone to strengthen the army and navy.' If the Reich Chancellor made difficulties for him, Bethmann would simply have to go. As well as increasing expenditure on the army and navy, Germany had to 'look for alliances everywhere'.[7] In the same excitable state the Kaiser wrote to Albert Ballin, who had engineered Haldane's mission earlier in the year, declaring that the conflict between Austria and Serbia was a matter of 'a *racial struggle*. . .between the Germans and the overweening Slavs', and thus 'a *question of life and death* for the *Teutons* on the continent. [. . .] As now, however, war with Russia means immediate war with *France*, it was of interest to know whether in this – purely *continental* case – England could not quite well declare the neutrality she had proposed to us in February.' But instead Haldane had now declared that, 'if Germany were involved in a war with Russia and France, England will *not* stay *neutral*, but *immediately* fly to the assistance of France. The reason for this was: England cannot and will *not ever* allow us to establish a predominant position on the continent that would allow it to unite.'[8]

These furious outbursts from the Kaiser in December 1912, which could be quoted for pages more, are the most telling sources we have about his strategic expectations on the eve of the First World War.[9] A conflict between Austria-Hungary and Serbia in the Balkans would be the trigger for the '*racial struggle*' against Russia and France that would seal the German Reich's predominant position on the European continent for ever. And that was not all: in spite of the experiences of the two Moroccan crises and the failure of the Haldane Mission, until that Sunday morning Wilhelm II laboured under the illusion that Great Britain would be prepared to leave both her Entente partners in the lurch and tacitly accept German hegemony. His bitter disappointment at the news that the balance of power was regarded as axiomatic to British foreign policy was a reflection of the completely unrealistic expectation of British neutrality that he had cherished up to this point, according to which Britain – not least out of respect for his battlefleet – would simply watch the forcible overthrow of the European states system, and in particular the conquest of Belgium and France, without lifting a finger. Astounding as this imperial hallucination in the winter of 1912 might seem, the pipe dream of British neutrality was to form the basis of his policy a year and a half later, when the world really did stumble towards catastrophe over an Austro-Serbian conflict.

As things stood in December 1912, however, Wilhelm found himself compelled, in the light of Lichnowsky's report, to withdraw the support he had already promised on the evening of 9 November for an Austrian attack on Serbia. The notorious 'war council' that he summoned on 8 December 1912 was for a long time at the heart of the second phase of the international 'Fischer controversy', as possibly the moment at which the Kaiser and his 'loyal paladins from the army and navy' had decided to launch a major war in about a year and a half's time. This interpretation is by no means wrong.[10] But, if one assumes that in Vienna and Berlin the decision to go to war *immediately* had already been taken in mid-November 1912, the military conference in the Berlin Schloss on that Sunday morning looks more like a tactical retreat: in view of the imminent danger of British intervention, the war that had already been decided on was put off for a year or two until the army had been enlarged, the Kaiser Wilhelm Canal widened and deepened to take dreadnought-class battleships, the U-boat harbour on Heligoland fortified and better relations with Britain established. In the meantime, in accordance with the Kaiser's orders, new allies were to be sought out and a propaganda campaign launched to prepare the German people for war. First, however, the Austrians had to be dissuaded from carrying out their plan to attack Serbia – a thorny task that, as can be demonstrated, Prince Heinrich, the chief of the General Staff, von Moltke, and Reich Chancellor Bethmann Hollweg took on.[11]

CHAPTER 23

The postponed war draws nearer (1913–1914)

Wilhelm II, still very much the key figure in German foreign policy, also left no room for doubt in Vienna that continental war had only been postponed, not cancelled. Although he urged Archduke Franz Ferdinand to give way to Russia in February 1913 (it was said that in 'postponing the great decision' he was influenced not only by 'fear of England' but also by the desire to celebrate the twenty-five-year jubilee of his reign in peace[1]) by April of that year he had already reverted to a martial tone when a new conflict between Austria and Serbia over the Albanian town of Scutari was in the offing. For Austria to achieve success against Serbia, Germany 'must help Vienna coute qui coute [sic] – even with weapon in hand!',[2] Wilhelm exclaimed, albeit on the assumption that Britain would also be ready to take action 'against Asiatic Slavs and Tartars!'.[3] He and the Wilhelmstrasse shared the crucial but ill-judged conviction that Britain would stay out of a European war provided that Russia put herself into the wrong. 'It is very important for us to have the role of provoked party as I think that England would then – and only then – be able to stay neutral,'[4] declared the foreign secretary, Gottlieb von Jagow, in April 1913, echoing his sovereign's thoughts. In Berlin there was another war council on 5 May 1913, at which the outbreak of a major war came within a hair's breadth. Once again Moltke assured the Austrian military attaché that the diplomatic solution of the Scutari question had been 'only a postponement',[5] and Kaiser Wilhelm expressed himself with his customary brashness about the racial war that he regarded as imminent: 'The struggle betw[een] Slavs and Germans can no longer be avoided and will surely come. When? We shall see.'[6]

On 24 May 1913, Queen Victoria's birthday, the royal families of Germany, Britain, Russia and Denmark met for what was to be the last time for the wedding in Berlin of the Kaiser's daughter Viktoria Luise to Ernst August Duke of Brunswick. Wilhelm used the occasion to regale Lord Stamfordham, King George V's private secretary, with dire warnings of how the current war in the Balkans could spiral into a general war between the great powers. He told the dumbfounded Englishman:

This [Balkan] war has upset the whole of the East & it will some day raise a question not British, or Russian but international, for it will be racial. – The Slavs have now become unrestful & will want to attack Austria. Germany is bound to stand by her ally. – Russia and France will join in & then England – fighting against the Anglo-Saxons & the Culture of the world. He cannot understand how we wish to join the Latin Races in preference to the Teutons. 'I know this, that you are engaged to help the French.'

When Stamfordham pointed out 'that only an unprovoked attack would involve us', the Kaiser mockingly replied:

And will you tell me what an unprovoked attack is – Is it enough to knock your cap off or must I kick your shins. Look at that Morocco business: I know that [Sir John] French was over in France or your Staff Officers were & you promised to send 100,000 troops & *that's what made us so sore.* I am a man of peace – but now I have to arm my Country so that whoever falls on me I can crush – & crush them I will.

Wilhelm went on to say he had given the tsar clearly to understand 'that if Austria is attacked, he would be absolutely obliged to support her: he could not desert the old Emperor Franz Joseph, with all his past defeats, his sorrows etc.' 'How could I do anything other than stand by him?' he cried. The English, the Kaiser said, 'talk a good deal about the balance of power & that to maintain it you joined the *Entente*: but *Germany* holds the balance of power'. 'He must arm every man available, especially considering the combination against him.' Over and above that, the course of events would be determined by Providence. 'I am always telling people that in their calculations they forget Providence but I do not.' Stamfordham was so flabbergasted by the Kaiser's outbursts that he made numerous attempts to capture their nuances exactly.[7] That Wilhelm's remarks were not simply mindless babble but intended to serve the serious purpose of persuading Britain to stay out of the 'inevitable' war against 'the Slavs' to get 'elbow room' for Germany on the

Continent is evidenced by the fact that Jagow felt compelled to back up his sovereign's admonitions in very similar terms.[8]

As the measures to strengthen the German army decided upon in December 1912 advanced, and as the enlargement of the Kaiser Wilhelm Canal neared completion, so the demands made by Wilhelm and Moltke for energetic action by Vienna became ever more pressing. During the manoeuvres in Silesia in September 1913 the Kaiser expressed his annoyance to Franz Conrad von Hötzendorf, now back in office as chief of the Austrian General Staff, that he had not yet invaded Serbia. 'Why did this not happen?' he asked. 'Nobody was stopping you!'[9] Moltke assured his opposite number that 'the present oppressive atmosphere is building up for a storm. [. . .] I only know this, that if it comes to fighting, the Triple Alliance will do its duty.'[10] Again he warned Conrad, however, that Germany, 'if it came to a war, would attack France with her main forces and could only turn east after that.' It was true that he had 113 divisions at his disposal, but 'we have to think of the English, who will certainly be on France's side'.[11] When Austria sent an ultimatum to Serbia in October 1913 demanding that her troops besieging Scutari be withdrawn from Albania within eight days, Vienna, having received what amounted to a blank cheque from Berlin, was able to count on unconditional support from the German Reich. 'His Majesty the Kaiser and King [Wilhelm II] has received the news that Austria-Hungary is this time firmly determined not to give way to Serbia with great satisfaction,' Count von Wedel, the representative of the Foreign Office in Wilhelm's suite, was able to report.[12]

At the end of October 1913 the Kaiser met the Austro-Hungarian foreign minister, Count Leopold Berchtold, in Vienna and told him in no uncertain terms (as Berchtold recorded) that, if the Serbs refused to accept subordination to Kaiser Franz Joseph,

'Belgrade will be bombarded and occupied until His Majesty's [Franz Joseph's] will has been fulfilled. And of this you can be sure, that I [Kaiser Wilhelm II] stand behind you and am ready to draw the sword whenever your actions make it necessary.' (His Majesty accompanied these words by moving his hand to his sabre.) [. . .] Whenever during our talk, which lasted an hour and a quarter, the opportunity arose to touch on our alliance relationship, His Majesty ostentatiously seized the opportunity to assure me that we could count on him fully and entirely. That was

26 Kaiser Wilhelm II with the advocates of war, Grand Admiral Alfred von Tirpitz
and the chief of the General Staff, Helmuth von Moltke.

the red thread that ran through the Highest Lord's words, and when on departing I alluded to this and thanked him, His Majesty deigned to assure me that whatever came from the Vienna foreign office was for Him a command.[13]

In a report to Bethmann Hollweg the German ambassador in Vienna, Heinrich von Tschirschky, confirmed that the Kaiser had very distinctly given Berchtold to understand that the Dual Monarchy had to '*incorporate* Serbia somehow, *come what may*, especially in the military field, so as at least to have a guarantee that *in the event of war with Russia* it will have the Serbian army, not against it, but on its side'.[14] The Kaiser could not have spoken more clearly; and when the Austrians asked for German backing a mere eight months later, in case their intended attack on Serbia escalated into a continental war, they could not have been in any doubt what the answer would be.

In the west too preparations for the great European war were advancing by giant strides. In November 1913 King Albert of the Belgians had discussions with Kaiser Wilhelm II and General von Moltke at the Neues Palais in Potsdam, which left him in no doubt

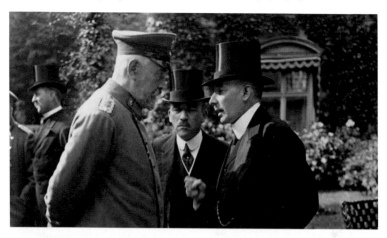

27 Reich Chancellor Theobald von Bethmann Hollweg, in military uniform, with the foreign secretary, Gottlieb von Jagow, and Karl Helfferich of Deutsche Bank.

of their resolve to attack his country and France in the near future. Using the same threatening tactics as he had with Albert's predecessor, King Leopold II, in January 1904 Wilhelm told the new king that war with France was both inevitable and imminent; given the overwhelming superiority of her army, Germany was sure of victory, and the king would do well not to resist its advance. In striking agreement with his sovereign, Moltke confirmed that war with France was close. 'Your Majesty [King Albert] can surely imagine how the whole German people will be swept along in irresistable enthusiasm on that day. [...] There will be no resisting the *furor teutonicus* once it is unleashed.' Like the Kaiser, the chief of the General Staff threatened that the outcome would be dire for Belgium if she tried to impede the German attack. 'The small states would be very well advised to go along with us, as the consequences will be hard for those who are against us.'[15] Once again, the German threats spread like wildfire around the world; they were even to play a role in the formulation of the notorious war guilt paragraph of the Versailles treaty. The fact that they were serious is borne out by the mass of belligerent marginal notes that Wilhelm II scribbled at this time expressing hostility to France: 'Just let them come! Then we will *finally*, with God's help, *settle accounts* with them!';[16] and: 'It is a question of our standing in the world, which is under attack from all sides! So head held high and hand on sword-hilt.'[17]

Although the vital question of how Britain would behave in a European conflict was still unclear, Wilhelm II was supremely confident that the power-political lever exerted by his battlefleet-building programme was working its wonders. 'England is *drawing towards us* not despite, but *because of My Imperial Navy!!*' he exulted in October 1913.[18] Precisely at this moment Tirpitz told his closest colleagues in the Reich Navy Office that he would use his influence to bring about a war soon, even without having reached the ultimate goal of his naval policy.

The question…of whether Germany should fight against England, if necessary, for her world position – with the enormous effort that such a struggle would involve – or confine herself in advance to the position of a European continental Power of the second rank, this question is in the last resort a matter of political conviction. In the end it would seem more worthy of a great nation to fight for the highest objective and perhaps to perish with honour, than ignobly to renounce the future.[19]

By throwing his immense weight behind the generals with this irresponsible do-or-die attitude, Grand Admiral von Tirpitz ensured that the momentum for war had become almost unstoppable. Who could now have opposed the war party within the Berlin leadership, even if they had wanted to? Not, in the long term, the civilian Chancellor von Bethmann Hollweg or the diplomats in the Wilhelmstrasse. The one man with the authority to prevent the looming catastrophe was Germany's Supreme War Lord. But did he have the desire, and if so the courage, to oppose his loyal paladins of the army and navy?

In July 1914 Wilhelm found himself facing the gravest test of his entire long reign. And this time the gentle Eulenburg, confined to Liebenberg for fear of provoking a reopening of his trial, was not at his side to guide him.

CHAPTER 24

The Kaiser in the July crisis of 1914

Three weeks *before* the assassination of Archduke Franz Ferdinand in Sarajevo on 28 June 1914 Kaiser Wilhelm II had prophesied: 'We shall soon be coming to the 3rd chapter of the Balkan Wars, in which we shall all be taking part.'[1] Exactly as in November 1912, when the German decision for war was taken the first time, the monarch now ordered the Reich leadership to 'clarify the position in relation to England!'.[2] Accordingly, Bethmann Hollweg once again addressed the crucial question to Prince Lichnowsky in London on 16 June – two weeks *before* the Sarajevo assassination: how would Britain behave in the event that 'any sort of clash of interests, even quite a minor one, between Russia and Austria-Hungary' should 'ignite the torch of war'?[3] That very day the quartermaster general on the German General Staff, Georg Count von Waldersee, who, like Moltke, had very recently spoken out in favour of bringing about a war against France and Russia while the going was good,[4] summoned the military representatives of the three non-Prussian kingdoms – Bavaria, Württemberg and Saxony – and asked them not to send any written reports to their ministers of war until further notice; officers of the General Staff, he added, were on their way to Munich, Stuttgart and Dresden to explain the need for silence.[5] In line with this, in late May 1914 Moltke asked Gottlieb von Jagow, the Secretary of State for foreign affairs, 'to conduct our policy with a view to bringing about an early war'.[6] Thus there are indications that the leadership of the Reich – that is to say, about twenty military officers and the civilian statesmen Bethmann Hollweg, Jagow and undersecretary Arthur Zimmermann – had already decided in favour of war with France and Russia before the atrocity at Sarajevo took place.

That Wilhelm II was under considerable pressure especially from the military is beyond doubt.[7] An unpublished document in the archives in Karlsruhe bears witness to the incredulity with which the Kaiser's unwillingness to wage war in what were considered to be most advantageous circumstances was met by Germany's decision-making elite. On 11 March 1914 the representative of the Grand Duchy of Baden in Berlin, Count Sigismund von Berckheim, reported that on the previous day he and his Saxon colleague had been treated to a thirty-minute monologue by the monarch in which Wilhelm had seemed to list all the grounds for an early war: the Home Rule crisis at Westminster and the threat of a religious civil war in Ulster would keep Britain from supporting her Entente partners on the Continent; France was being racked by financial crisis and would be unable to sustain the three-year military service on which she had embarked; and, although the Russian General Staff was coordinating its mobilisation and campaign plans closely with its French ally, the Russian army would not be ready to fight for many a year, and in any case the tsar knew very well that a war could spell the end of the monarchy. 'However, whatever the case may be,' Berckheim quoted him as insisting, '*he, the Kaiser, would never wage a preventive war.*' The Baden envoy, a civilian, could not believe his ears at what to him was an irresponsible non sequitur. He determined to have a word about these 'All-Highest utterances', as he sarcastically called them, with the foreign secretary, von Jagow, and at a dinner that same evening he confronted Moriz von Lyncker, as head of the Kaiser's Military Cabinet one of the two or three most influential generals in the land, about the monarch's pusillanimity. With evident relief at finding his views shared by powerful figures in the imperial entourage, Berckheim concluded his report to Karlsruhe with the words: 'Freiherr von Lyncker confirmed to me – albeit with regret – this reluctance of His Majesty to use the present moment which in the eyes of the military is still favourable to unleash the unavoidable conflict.'[8] Like Moltke, Falkenhayn and his colleague in the Naval Cabinet, Admiral von Müller, all advocates of continental war, General von Lyncker knew that the Supreme War Lord's soft spot was his veneration for the old Emperor Franz Joseph in Vienna and his detestation of the regicides in Belgrade.

The opportunity provided by the Sarajevo assassination to provoke a war against France and Russia via the Austro-Serbian conflict must have seemed irresistible to the German General Staff. At the memorial service for Franz Ferdinand at St Hedwig's Church in Berlin on 3 July 1914 the military plenipotentiary of the kingdom of Saxony, General von Leuckart, learned that Moltke, Waldersee and the other leading generals were convinced 'that we might become involved in a war from one day to the next'. Although the Kaiser himself was 'said to have pronounced in favour of maintaining peace', Leuckart reported in a handwritten letter to his minister in Dresden, the Great General Staff 'would regard it with favour if war were to come about now. Conditions and prospects would never become better for us.'[9] Tellingly, as with several other key documents indicating the German army's intentions in 1914, this vital piece of evidence is omitted from Christopher Clark's influential book *The Sleepwalkers*, which insists that there was no such plot to start a war.

As Kaiser, King and Supreme War Lord, Wilhelm II had the last word in the decision for peace or war, but how firm was his decision for war in July 1914? He certainly tried to remove any doubt about his resolve by declaring 'This time I shall not topple over!',[10] and yet, in view of his notorious erraticism, and in particular of his surprising statement of 10 March 1914, he was seen by the others in the know as an unreliable element – and not without reason. His assent was imperative in order to set the juggernaut of war into motion, but after that he needed to be calmed down as much as possible and sent away until the last stage of the crisis, when he would have to be brought back to Berlin to sign the mobilisation order. In this manipulation by his advisers we can perhaps see the first sign of Kaiser Wilhelm's loss of power, which set in dramatically soon after the beginning of hostilities.[11]

When the news of the assassination of his friend 'Franzi' reached him, Wilhelm II was yachting at Kiel Week. His first reaction, when Admiral von Müller broke the news to him on board the *Meteor*, was outwardly calm. He agreed to allow the regatta to continue, spent the night on the imperial yacht *Hohenzollern* and returned with the Kaiserin to Potsdam the next morning by train.[12] His intentions at this initial point in the crisis are unclear, and the situation is not helped by some obfuscation of what little evidence we have. Several historians, notably Christopher Clark, quote Wilhelm (or perhaps

Admiral von Müller) as saying that he wanted to return to Berlin to 'take the situation in hand and preserve the peace of Europe', but where does this statement come from and how reliable is it? It is not in any letter of the Kaiser's, nor is it to be found in Müller's diary. In Clark's biography of Wilhelm II, the Kaiser's purported statement, though set in quotation marks as if it were an authentic source, actually only repeats a paraphrase by Lamar Cecil, the Kaiser's American biographer, of a letter written in December 1919 – after Germany's defeat and the promulgation the Treaty of Versailles, when Wilhelm was being sought as a war criminal. The author of that letter of 1919 was none other than Admiral Johannes von Karpf, the commander of the imperial yacht *Hohenzollern*, an intimate friend of Wilhelm and his sons and, in the circumstances, hardly an impartial witness. In Clark's *The Sleepwalkers*, Lamar Cecil's words 'to take things in hand and preserve the peace of Europe' are again quoted in inverted commas as if from an original source, except that on this occasion Clark does not attribute the quotation to Cecil's biography but says he is 'citing' it from David Fromkin's *Europe's Last Summer*, a book published in 2005. There, however, the words purporting to show the Kaiser's intention 'to preserve the peace of Europe', though printed in double inverted commas, are cited without attribution to any source at all. In this way a loose paraphrase of a letter written by the Kaiser's close friend, the commander of the imperial yacht, in December 1919 has acquired the status – even more so in German translation – of authentic contemporary testimony.[13]

It is true that, back in Potsdam, the Kaiser gave no indication at first of a decision to go to war. He planned to travel to Vienna with his brother Heinrich for Franz Ferdinand's funeral and abandoned this idea only when the danger of an assassination attempt against him was spelled out to him.[14] As late as 3 July he spoke of his intention of visiting Romania in the autumn, and yet later that same night he repeated his marginal comment of October 1913, which is now generally accepted to have given the signal for the beginning of the Austrian–Serbian war, with all the consequences that that might entail. 'Now or never' the Serbs had to be 'sorted out', he declared, '*and* that means *soon*.'[15] What exactly the Kaiser aimed to achieve by this comment – whether he really wanted to bring about a continental war, as his generals undoubtedly did, or was merely accepting the risk that such a war could arise from the planned Austrian attack on Serbia – remains obscure, however. Nor do we know what influences were at work on him in these first days of the crisis.

On 5 July 1914 Kaiser Wilhelm received the Austrian ambassador, Count Szögyény, at the Neues Palais in Potsdam. After reading the two documents that Alexander Hoyos had brought with him from Vienna,[16] he expressed his satisfaction at the Austrian decision to eliminate Serbia as a power in the Balkans. He pressed for swift action. At the same time the ambiguity of his position – shifting between being simply prepared for war and actually wanting war – was clearly in evidence. Szögyény wrote: 'Russia's attitude will inevitably be hostile, but he had been prepared for this for years [the Kaiser said], and if it should come to war between Austria-Hungary and Russia, we [Austrians] could be confident that Germany will, as usual, stand by our side as a loyal ally.'[17] Once again, as in 1895 and in 1908 and on numerous occasions subsequently, the German Kaiser had given the Austrian leaders a blank cheque to do as they wished.

That same day Wilhelm summoned the Reich Chancellor, the undersecretary at the Foreign Office, Arthur Zimmermann, the Prussian war minister, General Erich von Falkenhayn, the chief of the Military Cabinet, General Moriz Freiherr von Lyncker, Adjutant General Hans von Plessen and a representative of the Admiralty Staff to see him at Potsdam. The generals assured him that the army was prepared for all eventualities.[18] The next morning he gave orders to Admiral Eduard von Capelle, who reported to him as representative of the Reich Navy Office while Tirpitz was on leave, secretly 'to prepare to mobilise the fleet'.[19] On balance, however, he seems to have been counting on a climbdown by Serbia, because, as he said – as always besotted with notions of the divine right of kings – 'the Tsar would not support regicides and because Russia was currently not entirely ready for war militarily and financially'.[20]

On 6 July, at the request of Bethmann Hollweg, Wilhelm set out on his customary cruise along the coast of Norway. This was a ruse by which the Chancellor sought to make it appear that Germany had no inkling of Vienna's intention of attacking Serbia.[21] No doubt Bethmann was also influenced by the desire to keep his unpredictable sovereign away from Berlin until the decisive moment. That the voyage was only a pretence is evident from the simple fact that this time the *Hohenzollern*, instead of sailing to the North Cape as usual, dropped anchor at Balholm (Bålen) in the Sognefjord, only about eighty miles north of Bergen. From there the Kaiser could be in Cuxhaven within twenty-two hours or at Kiel in two days to sign the mobilisation orders, as the head of the Military Cabinet informed his wife from on board the imperial yacht on 21 July 1914.[22]

Far from being excluded from the unfolding drama, at Balholm the Kaiser received dozens of dispatches from Berlin, which not only kept him in touch with what was going on but enabled him to intervene actively in the course of events. Prompted by the Chancellor, Wilhelm ordered his son to hold his tongue when the impetuous Crown Prince threatened to arouse suspicion about German intentions with his aggressive utterances.[23] From the Sognefjord Wilhelm also made active efforts to forge alliances with Turkey, Bulgaria, Romania and Greece and to involve Italy in the expected conflict with Russia and France.

Supposedly neither the German government nor the Kaiser and his entourage at Balholm had prior knowledge of the Austrian ultimatum, yet four days *before* it was delivered Kaiser Wilhelm suggested that his Foreign Office should confidentially inform the Hapag and Norddeutsche Lloyd shipping lines of the imminent danger of war. As early as 19 July Admiral von Müller noted in his diary on board the *Hohenzollern*: 'His Majesty greatly excited about the consequences of the ultimatum that Austria is to present to Serbia on the 23rd.'[24] When news of the deliberately unacceptable text of the ultimatum reached him, the Kaiser was exultant: 'That is indeed a strong note for once, what?'[25] And when a climbdown by Serbia seemed to be in the offing, he exclaimed: 'Bravo! One wouldn't have thought the Viennese could do it! [. . .] The proud Slavs! How hollow the whole so-called Great Serbian state now looks, and so it is with all Slav states! Just stamp firmly on the rabble's toes!'[26] That this marginal comment cannot be seen as an expression of relief at the avoidance of a major war is shown by the order the Supreme War Lord gave that very day to the commander of the High Seas Fleet, Admiral Friedrich von Ingenohl, whose flagship had anchored at Balholm: he was to begin the war with Russia with the destruction of the naval bases of Reval (now Tallinn, the capital of Estonia) and Libau (Liepaja in Latvia). Ingenohl ignored the command and succeeded in postponing the bombardment of the Russian naval ports.[27]

At this moment Kaiser Wilhelm's desire for war was stronger than that of the Chancellor or the diplomats in the Wilhelmstrasse. On 25 July Bethmann Hollweg asked despairingly: 'What does this puffed-up lieutenant (W.II) intend to do with the world?'[28] As the German High Seas Fleet was conducting manoeuvres off southern Norway while the Royal Navy was assembled off Southampton for a grand naval review, Bethmann was most anxious that the dispersal of the British ships planned for 27 July should not be disturbed by a premature recall of the Imperial Navy to base. But his calculations were thwarted by the excitable state of the Supreme War Lord, who on the morning of 25 July gave orders for the immediate return home of his fleet. The Reich Chancellor's plea that such a step would put the British navy on the alert too soon and therefore had to be avoided provoked a furious tirade from Wilhelm II. The '*Civilian* Chancellor's' telegram was 'unheard of!' and 'incredibly impertinent!', he raged. The Serbian mobilisation

can lead to Russia's mobilisation and *will* lead to Austria's mobilisation! In that event I must have my fighting forces *together* on land and sea. There is not a single ship in the Baltic!! [...] If Russia mobilises, my Fleet must already be in the Baltic, hence it is coming home!'[29]

And indeed, just as Bethmann had feared, the Royal Navy, on the orders of Winston Churchill, sailed by night and without lights from the Channel northwards into Scottish waters.

Not only the Imperial High Seas Fleet; the Kaiser himself, fearing capture by the Royal Navy, as he said, decided on 25 July to return to Germany.[30] On the journey home Wilhelm showed himself as determined as ever to bring about a major shift of power 'in the Balkans and in Europe' in favour of the Central Powers. 'Austria must become preponderant in the Balkans *vis à vis* the other smaller states, at Russia's expense; otherwise we shall have no peace,' he wrote.[31] He brushed aside suggestions of mediation, and when the Russian foreign minister, Sergei Sazonov, warned of war if Austria marched into Serbia, Wilhelm shrugged it off with the remark: 'Well then, go ahead!'[32]

As he sailed towards Kiel the Kaiser still seemed to be expecting a continental war. The members of his suite were therefore all the more surprised when on the evening of 26 July he telegraphed to the Kaiserin saying he hoped to be able to come and join her at

Wilhelmshöhe soon for their summer holiday together.[33] Altogether, the following days were to be characterised by wavering uncertainty, the main reason for which, as we shall see, lay in the attitude Germany's leaders thought Great Britain would adopt towards the events unfolding on the Continent.[34]

When the *Hohenzollern* berthed at Kiel on 27 July the Kaiser was still in such a belligerent mood that even the admirals shook their heads. His order to blockade the eastern Baltic was greeted by Tirpitz and Capelle as 'militarily nonsensical' and 'pathological'. 'Now he is playing at soldiers!' they exclaimed in horror. For his part, Wilhelm was indignant at the Chancellor's request that he should go to Potsdam rather than Berlin, as the demonstrations that were to be expected when he appeared in the capital might be interpreted as showing Germany seeking war, whereas his (Bethmann's) policy was aimed at putting Russia 'come what may. . .in the wrong in the eyes of the world'.[35] 'It gets crazier all the time,' the Kaiser complained, uncomprehendingly. 'Now the man is telling me that I may not show myself to my people.'[36] During his audiences with Bethmann Hollweg, Moltke and the chief of the Admiralty Staff, Hugo von Pohl, on his arrival at the Neues Palais he took an aggressive line: it was still too early to send the tsar one of the dispatches drafted in the Foreign Office, he said; the Austrians ought to make a generous offer of compensation to the Italians to persuade them to enter the war too; the British proposal for an international conference must be rejected. Müller summed up the outcome of the audiences with the words 'staying calm, letting Russia put herself in the wrong, but then not shrinking from war'.[37] The war minister, Erich von Falkenhayn, heard privately that it had been decided to fight the matter out, 'whatever it might cost'.[38]

Until this point in time the Kaiser had proceeded on the assumption that Britain – provided Russia could be cast in the role of the troublemaker – would keep out of the war. In order to maintain this illusion, the Chancellor had given Wilhelm a watered-down version of Lichnowsky's warning dispatches. But on 27 July a report arrived from London that was so serious that it could not be withheld from the Supreme War Lord: Sir Edward Grey, Lichnowsky stated, considered the Serbian reply to the ultimatum to be so conciliatory that Austria and Germany would put themselves in the wrong if they did not enter into negotiations with Belgrade.[39] Lichnowsky's dispatch was shown to the Kaiser on the morning of 28 July. For the first time he began to have doubts about the course on which he had embarked.

In view of the Serbian near-compliance, Wilhelm now declared, there was no longer any reason for Austria-Hungary to go to war with Serbia. Instead, Austria should occupy Belgrade as security until her demands were completely fulfilled.[40] In the belief that this had brought the international crisis to an end he even tried to resume his plans for a holiday. He complained in aggrieved tones that Vienna had kept him in the dark about its intentions for weeks. But he failed to see through the machinations of his own government. Bethmann conveyed his sovereign's 'halt in Belgrade' proposal to Vienna in a distorted form and too late to prevent the Austrian declaration of war on Serbia and the bombardment of Belgrade. In addition, the Chancellor made it clear in his instructions to the German ambassador in Vienna, Tschirschky, that Germany had no desire to hold Austria back in any circumstances.[41] Thus the Kaiser's attempt at mediation came to nothing, especially as the generals soon managed to win him over to their war policy again. On the evening of 28 July, on a visit to the Neues Palais, Falkenhayn found Wilhelm still at a loss. 'He makes confused speeches, from which the only clear thing that emerges is that he does not want war any more and to this end is even determined to leave Austria in the lurch.' The war minister, as he recorded, pointed out to the Kaiser that 'he is no longer in control of the matter'. To his satisfaction, it soon became plain that Wilhelm had once again concluded that 'the ball which has started to roll cannot be stopped'.[42]

Why? What had happened to put the Kaiser into a warlike frame of mind again? On the morning of 29 July he received a letter from Prince Heinrich, who – just as in December 1912 – had been to London to sound out George V about British intentions. During an extremely brief meeting at Buckingham Palace on the morning of Sunday 26 July 1914, when the king was on his way to church, Heinrich believed he had been given an assurance of British neutrality by his cousin. He told his brother that 'Georgie' had promised: 'We shall try & keep out of it, we shall probably remain neutral.'[43] Suddenly Wilhelm again believed in the possibility of waging war

28 Prince Heinrich of Prussia (standing, second from the left) at Maresfield in
Sussex on Sunday 26 July 1914.

against Russia and France without having to fear British participation. He told Tirpitz: 'I have the word of a king, and that is enough
for me.'[44]

The celebrated exchange of telegrams between the Kaiser and Tsar
Nicholas II in the last days of the July crisis was nothing but a charade
the aim of which, as Bethmann said, was to 'expose Russia's guilt in
the most glaring light'.[45] Unlike the telegrams to the tsar, which the
Auswärtiges Amt simply submitted to him for his signature, Wilhelm
personally drafted the dispatches that he and Heinrich sent to King
George V in the hope that he, the British monarch, would decide
Britain's stance. The illusion of neutrality that Heinrich's meeting at
Buckingham Palace had fostered was shattered several times over on
30 July by telegrams from London, however, according to which Grey
was said to have declared that England could not remain neutral in
a war between Germany and France, but would send her fleet into
action at once. 'That was the hardest blow in these days,' wrote
Admiral von Müller; the Kaiser was 'greatly taken aback'.[46] Gripped
by panic that seemed to presage a nervous breakdown, Wilhelm hit
out wildly about him: neither he nor his ally Austria but the others and
especially the British were to blame for the impending disaster.[47]

Nevertheless, Wilhelm made a final attempt to stop the machinery of war that had been set in motion. Shortly before midnight on 30 July a telegram from George V to Prince Heinrich arrived at the Neues Palais, in which the king welcomed the Kaiser's 'halt in Belgrade' proposal and promised to do whatever he could on his side to avert a catastrophe.[48] Wilhelm ordered his brother to hurry immediately to Berlin with the telegram and show it to the Reich Chancellor, who should send it on to Vienna. At the same time the Chancellor should inform London that Austria would be satisfied with a pledge of security and was ready to renounce all territorial demands on Serbia. Heinrich handed Bethmann Hollweg the king's dispatch at 1.15 a.m. and returned to Potsdam at half past two.[49] When he got up the next morning Wilhelm repeated his order to the Chancellor to submit draft replies to the king and the tsar 'about England's and Vienna's proposals that are almost identical to mine'.[50] Potentially, the Kaiser's brother's nocturnal ride to the Reichkanzlerpalais could have marked the start of negotiations. But Bethmann Hollweg ignored his sovereign's order. In truth, neither the German nor the Austrian government was prepared to respond to Wilhelm's peace initiative.

Put into an optimistic mood by the conciliatory tone of his English cousin's dispatch, in the last phase of the July crisis Wilhelm II showed himself once again eager for war, convinced that victory over France and Russia was within reach. The Kaiser was decidedly on the side of the chief of the General Staff, von Moltke, and the Prussian war minister, von Falkenhayn, the Bavarian General von Wenninger reported on 30 July.[51] He was 'determined to settle accounts with France', Wilhelm told the Austrian ambassador.[52] His aim was 'to free the Balkans from Russia for ever!'.[53] He was encouraged in this attitude by his six sons and his brother Heinrich, who (as Valentini remarked) were 'all eager for war [*alle voller Kriegslust*]'.[54] The Kaiserin too helped steady her husband's resolve.

Moltke and Falkenhayn pressed for the proclamation of a state of 'imminent danger of war' as a first step towards mobilisation, but Bethmann held back in the hope that there was still a chance Russia would put herself in the wrong by declaring mobilisation first. They agreed to wait until noon on 31 July, and when news of Russia's general mobilisation arrived twenty minutes before the expiry of the deadline there was jubilation in Berlin.[55] 'Beaming faces everywhere,' Wenninger reported after a visit to the War Ministry.[56] Wilhelm gave the instruction for the declaration of 'imminent danger of war' and moved with his brother and sons from Potsdam to Berlin. In the Sternensaal that afternoon he addressed the assembled generals, according to Falkenhayn, with 'an exposé of the situation and pushes all the blame onto Russia. His bearing and language are worthy of a German Emperor! Worthy of a King of Prussia!'[57] Wilhelm instructed the Reich Chancellor to send an ultimatum to Russia and then to France too. At the signing of the mobilisation order on 1 August 1914 the Kaiser and the war minister had tears of emotion in their eyes. The Supreme War Lord made a speech from the balcony of the Schloss that had the desired effect of stirring up popular enthusiasm. 'The mood is brilliant,' Müller noted in his diary. 'The government has succeeded very well in making us appear as the attacked.'[58] Bethmann Hollweg and his closest advisers too were euphoric at the warlike mood their policy had engendered in the country.[59] Wilhelm sent a telegram to Emperor Franz Joseph that described the war with Serbia as 'completely peripheral'; now Austria had to 'commit her main forces against Russia' and not divide them by a simultaneous offensive against Serbia.[60] He wrote letters to the Kings of Italy, Greece and Romania, as well as to the governments in Sofia and Constantinople, calling upon them all to fight with Germany against the common enemy.

On that day, 1 August 1914, there also occurred what is probably the best-known episode of the whole crisis. After Moltke and Falkenhayn had left the Schloss to begin 'the bloodiest enterprise that the world has ever witnessed' (Falkenhayn),[61] they were called back and confronted with the news that, in another telegram from London, Lichnowsky had held out the prospect of British neutrality if Germany attacked only Russia and not France; indeed, in such an event, Britain would vouch for France's neutrality. To the horror of Moltke, the Supreme War Lord exclaimed: 'Therefore we simply march east with the whole army!'[62] When the chief of the General Staff pointed out the impossibility of redeploying an army of millions from the western to the eastern front, the Kaiser became 'very angry' with him and retorted: 'Your uncle would have given me a different answer!'[63] Through Adjutant General Hans von Plessen he ordered

29 'Today we are all German brothers': the Kaiser proclaims the outbreak of war from the balcony of the Berlin Schloss on 1 August 1914.

telegrams to be sent halting the attack on Luxembourg and Belgium. Moltke had a nervous breakdown, turned red and blue in the face and wept tears of despair. As if stunned, all he could utter was the lament: 'I am happy to wage war against the French and the Russians, but not against such a Kaiser.'[64]

Although one can well understand his frustration, Moltke's reaction to the (admittedly bizarre) news from London was not shared by the other generals and statesmen present; they all considered the Kaiser's order to stop the advance in the west as sensible, since Grey's apparent offer seemed to give Germany the chance to conduct the war against Russia in almost ideal conditions. The mood of jubilation in the Schloss increased when at half past eight in the evening a further telegram from Lichnowsky held out the prospect of war against Russia *and* France without British intervention. In a 'very elated mood' the Kaiser called for champagne;[65] the goal of his hegemonic policy, for which he had striven so long, seemed to have been reached.

The illusion did not last the night. Astonished by the joyful telegram that the Kaiser had sent him following Lichnowsky's first dispatch, George V summoned the foreign secretary to Buckingham Palace. Grey drafted the king's telegram declaring Lichnowsky's report to be a misunderstanding; nothing had changed in Britain's stance. At 11 o'clock at night Moltke was summoned back to the Schloss. The Kaiser was already in bed and received the chief of the General Staff in his dressing gown, in a 'very agitated' state. 'Now you can do what you like,' he said.[66] Thus the lightning attack on Liège and the invasion of Luxembourg were set in motion again, and the die was cast for war. The Kaiser went to bed for days. Moltke's nervous system was 'badly affected'.[67] When the American ambassador arrived at the German embassy in Carlton House Terrace to take over its affairs he found Prince Lichnowsky wandering through the rooms in his pyjamas in mid-afternoon like a broken man. Princess Mechtild Lichnowsky swept the portrait of Kaiser Wilhelm off her husband's desk, crying: 'That is the swine that did this.'[68]

Such condemnation, expressed in a moment of despair, is perhaps rather too harsh. Wilhelm II was by no means acting on his own; he was not even the principal advocate of war, and during the July crisis his advisers had at times pulled the wool over his eyes, notably when he seemed in danger of 'toppling over'. He had personally chosen all these advisers, however, because he considered them forceful or adaptable, and kept them in office because they followed the guidelines of his policy. The personal rule he had exercised throughout two decades had produced, in the Prussian-German state apparatus and partly also in the officer corps, a dysfunctional polyarchy and a courtier culture in which cautious men such as the ambassadors in London, Count Metternich or Prince Lichnowsky, could not make themselves heard. The more the heroic-militaristic personal monarchy of Wilhelm II came into conflict with the overwhelming majority of the German people, the more threatened the Supreme War Lord and his paladins in the army and navy felt at home. Their determination grew to break out of domestic and foreign encirclement before it was too late, and to do it by the Bismarckian means of provoking a 'defensive' war. The Kaiser may occasionally have procrastinated when the situation became acute towards the end of the July 1914 crisis, for, despite years of relentless naval expansion, he saw more clearly than his army chiefs and diplomats the danger that British participation in a continental war represented for the German Reich. Nonetheless, in his dealings with Archduke Franz Ferdinand and his close friend Max Fürstenberg he steered deliberately towards a continental war, trusting in his feigned attachment to the British royal family and in particular in the myth that he had been Queen Victoria's favourite grandchild, whom he had held in his arms as she lay dying, to keep Britain out of the conflict. So he does bear a heavy responsibility – perhaps the heaviest overall – for having brought about Europe's great catastrophe. As chief witness for the decisive longer-term role that Wilhelm II played on the eve of the world war, Austria-Hungary's long-serving ambassador in Berlin, Szögyény, is worth citing. In August 1913 he assured his foreign minister, Count Berchtold, 'If I ask myself the question who now really directs German foreign policy I can only come to one answer, and that is that neither Herr von Bethmann Hollweg nor Herr von Jagow but Kaiser Wilhelm himself has his hands on the controls of foreign policy, and that in this regard the Reich Chancellor and the Foreign Secretary are not in a position to exercise any significant influence on His Majesty.'[69]

PART VI

1914–1918: The Champion of God's Germanic Cause

CHAPTER 25

The Kaiser's war aims

For Wilhelm II and his entourage the bloody conflict that broke out between the nations of Europe in August 1914 was, not least, also a worldwide struggle between the divine principle of monarchy and the diabolical notion of democracy. 'If you do not want to see God's hand in everythng, even in the most unbearable, you are lost,' wrote the head of his Military Cabinet, General von Lyncker, in his diary after losing two of his sons.[1] The Kaiser's absolutist convictions came vividly to light in conversations he had with the American ambassador, James Gerard, in late 1915, after the war had been raging for eighteen months. As Colonel Edward House noted,

the Kaiser talked of peace and how it should be made and by whom, declaring that 'I and my cousins, George and Nicholas, will make peace when the time comes'. Gerard says to hear him talk one would think that the German, English, and Russian peoples were so many pawns on a chessboard. He made it clear that mere democracies like France and the United States could never take part in such a conference. His whole attitude was that war was a royal sport, to be indulged in by hereditary monarchs and concluded at their will.

Not surprisingly, Colonel House wondered whether the Kaiser 'was crazy or whether he was merely posing'.[2] On another occasion Wilhelm announced that the 'pointless bloodletting' had to be 'brought to an end through an agreement between the monarchs', since 'in the other countries a conscienceless lawyer class without any sense of responsibility to God is at the helm'.[3] As late as in March 1918, when Ludendorff seemed to have achieved a breakthrough on the western front, the Kaiser exclaimed: 'The battle is won, the English are utterly beaten [and] if an English officer comes with a flag of truce he will first have to kneel before the Kaiser's standard, for this marks the victory of Monarchy over Democracy.'[4]

But how did he picture the '*German God-given* peace' to himself, for which Germany was fighting a 'crusade', as he said, on behalf of all mankind?[5] For him, as for the Reich's other leaders and large segments of nationalist opinion, a return to the status quo before the war was unthinkable. Theobald von Bethmann Hollweg, in his notorious war aims memorandum of 9 September 1914, which he had begun to draft as early as the middle of August,[6] defined the 'general aim of the war' as 'security for the German Reich in west and east for all imaginable time'. To this end, the document spelled out, 'France must be so weakened as to make her revival as a great power impossible for all time. Russia must be thrust back as far as possible from Germany's eastern frontier and her domination over the non-Russian vassal peoples broken.' France was to lose her army, her coal and iron fields, her colonies and a 'coastal strip from Dunkirk to Boulogne', Belgium to become a German vassal state with her ports in the hands of the German navy, and Poland and other satellite states under German control were to be established at Russia's expense in east-central Europe. The whole continent, from the Atlantic to the Urals and from Finland to Malta, would come under German economic domination, and in Africa a German colonial empire would stretch continuously from the west coast to the east to include the Belgian Congo.[7]

There is no doubt that Kaiser Wilhelm II shared Bethmann Hollweg's aims wholeheartedly, and in some cases pressed for even greater expansion, as did the generals and many industrialists, intellectuals and nationalist agitators. In the preamble to his 1914 September Programme, Bethmann recorded that for some time he had been under pressure to implement a pet idea of the Kaiser's, namely to pursue a policy of what we would nowadays call ethnic cleansing in Belgium and northern France. The Chancellor wrote:

His Majesty the Kaiser keeps harping on the idea that those parts of Belgium and France which might be annexed from Belgium and France should be evacuated and settled by military colonies in the form of land grants to deserving non-commissioned officers and men.[8]

In addition, the Supreme War Lord designated the coast of Flanders with the ports of Antwerp, Zeebrugge, Ostend, Dunkirk, Calais and Boulogne as 'the objective of my Navy', to serve as a base for the future invasion of England.[9]

The role that the Kaiser played in the creation of a Polish satellite state on the Reich's eastern border was just as decisive. Immediately after mobilisation in July 1914 he declared it to be his goal to found an 'independent' Polish state. As he saw it, the new Poland would of course be cut off from the Baltic, and its foreign policy, military and economic affairs would be directed by Germany; he personally would hold the supreme command of the Polish military forces, and the Polish railways would be integrated with the Prussian. The Polish kingdom that was proclaimed on 5 November 1916 was not least Kaiser Wilhelm's brainchild.[10]

To the Austrian foreign minister, Count Stephan Burián, Wilhelm II proclaimed in 1915 that he would put an end to the British balance of power policy and establish an unassailable central European bastion. Again in 1918 he declared, when Count Andrássy, Austria-Hungary's last foreign minister, offered himself as a peace broker on the basis of the European balance of power, 'Thanks very much! don't need one! We'll get there under our own steam! with the sword! Heaven save us from this!' He went on to comment that Andrássy should take a break at a sanatorium since he was evidently not quite right in the head.[11]

After the fall of the tsar in March 1917 Kaiser Wilhelm listed his breathtaking ideas of the new world order, and in so doing revealed what he was actually seeking in the First World War. In a memorandum of 19 April 1917 he demanded the capture of Malta, the Azores, Madeira and the Cape Verde Islands as naval bases for his fleet, the acquisition of the Belgian Congo and of the French ore field of Longwy-Briey and the annexation of Poland, Lithuania and Courland (southern Latvia) to the Reich. Furthermore, Ukraine, Livonia (northern Latvia) and Estonia were to become German satellite states. Reparations in terms of billions of marks were also to be demanded from Great Britain, the United States, France and Italy.[12] Such demands were not the Kaiser's alone; a few days later, at the war aims conference in Bad Kreuznach, they were formally adopted as Germany's guidelines. In a further memorandum of 13 May, Wilhelm II set out his 'minimum demands' for peace negotiations with Russia. Once again he demanded the annexation of Longwy-Briey and the capture of Malta, the Azores, Madeira and the Cape Verde Islands, as well as the return of the German colonies in Africa together with the entire Congo. He wanted to divide Belgium into Wallonia and Flanders and place it under German rule. In the east Poland, Courland and Lithuania should be directly or indirectly annexed and Ukraine become 'autonomous'. To the massive war reparations that he wished to impose on Britain, the United States, France and Italy were now added billions to be demanded from China, Japan, Brazil, Bolivia, Cuba and Portugal. Cyprus, Egypt and Mesopotamia (Iraq) were to be given back to Turkey, and Gibraltar to Spain.[13]

The Kaiser had already spoken of the necessity of revolutionising the Russian Empire before the war. When he heard that Lenin was being brought through Germany from Zürich to Petrograd, he joked that the Bolsheviks should be given a copy of his speeches to take with them. In January 1918, when the negotiations with Leon Trotsky began in Brest-Litovsk, he summed up his dizzying ambitions in both east and west in marginal comments: 'Germany's victory over Russia was the precondition for the [February] revolution, this in turn the precondition for Lenin, and that for Brest!'[14] Exactly the same must now happen in the west, he said. In the coming 'victor's peace' there could be no place for 'popularist ideas of world citizenship. . . [O]nly one's *own* naked self-interest and the guarantee of one's *own security* and greatness must count.'[15]

Naturally, such a reordering of the international states system was also fundamentally directed against Great Britain and the *Pax Britannica* that had hitherto held sway. The forcible abolition of the European balance of power, the seizure of Channel ports from Antwerp to Boulogne, the settlement of German veterans as farmers along the coast of Flanders, the reduction of France to the rank of a dependent state without an army and without coal, the entire continent from the Atlantic coast to the Black Sea and from Finland to Malta united economically in a 'German Central Europe', a ring of German satellite states from Estonia to the Caucasus, a railway line that was to stretch via Baghdad to Egypt and the Persian Gulf, German warships in Brest and Bordeaux, Madeira, the Azores and the Cape Verde Islands, the entire Congo, together with Togo, Cameroon, east and south-west Africa in German hands – in such a world proud Great Britain would have sunk into an insignificant island in the Atlantic, under constant threat from the Imperial High Seas Fleet and the U-boats with free access to the world's oceans. Far from being 'the wrong war' for her to be fighting, the First World War was, no less than the Second, for Britain too a struggle for existence in which everything was at stake.

When the expected breakthrough in the west did not happen, Kaiser Wilhelm II convinced himself that the defeat of Britain and the divinely ordered Germanic peace that he so ardently desired would be achieved only through 'a Second Punic War'. In September 1917 he astonished Bethmann Hollweg's successor as Reich Chancellor, Georg Michaelis, by declaring:

I know England and the English better than my countrymen do, certainly better than my officials and the For[eign] Office! If Y[ou]r Exc[ellency]'s predecessors in office had only listened to my suggestions and followed my advice instead of pursuing their continental political theories and ignoring what I told them, our treatment of these brutes would have been a different one and much would have turned out differently too! What Y[ou]r Exc [ellency] *needs to understand* is this: England is our bitter sworn *rival* full of hatred and envy and as such it speculated that it would surely win this contest; if it loses, its hatred will only grow deeper still; and the struggle will *continue mercilessly after the peace*, economically. [. . .] England has *not won* the First Punic War and – God willing – has therefore *lost* it; but we have *not defeated* it either and don't seem to be able to do so for the moment. Therefore the Second Punic War – hopefully under better conditions as far as our allies and prospects are concerned – must now be absolutely and *immediately* prepared for. *Because it is definitely coming*. Until one of the two of us has come out on top *alone* there will be no peace in the world! *Great Britain* will never accept a *condominium*; therefore it must be thrown out. It's the same situation we faced in '66 with Austria; which was the precondition for '70! [. . .] That's the way it is with England in the world. In order to *crush it* properly it is imperative that the necessary milit[ary] and *naval* preconditions are put in place now in the peace settlement.'[16]

CHAPTER 26

The impotence of the Supreme War Lord at war

Despite the fact that, during the war, Kaiser Wilhelm spent most of his time at Supreme Headquarters, it is clear that he was not involved with military operations. He was condemned to inaction, and his suite – to spare him – kept him only inadequately informed about the course of the war. He was subject to extreme mood swings, needed distraction, stayed away from Berlin and made not the slightest attempt to show, even symbolically, that he shared the sufferings of his people. In this way signs of the downfall of the Hohenzollern monarchy were already beginning to emerge in the first months of the war.[1] Nevertheless, the role that Wilhelm II played in the First World War, at least initially, should not be underestimated. Until the appointment of the third Supreme Army Command under Paul von Hindenburg and Erich Ludendorff in August 1916 he had a decisive influence both on personnel policy and in the conduct of the war at sea. Indeed, formally the kingship mechanism of the personal monarchy continued to function until the collapse in November 1918, and obliged the Kaiser, however difficult it often was for him, to have the last word in all important decisions regarding the war. As a result, the influence of the three Cabinet chiefs, on whose advice Wilhelm depended, grew even stronger during the war.

The chief of the Military Cabinet, Moriz Freiherr von Lyncker, played a decisive role in the replacement of the luckless chief of the General Staff, Helmuth von Moltke, by Erich von Falkenhayn in September 1914. After the defeat at the battle of the Marne Moltke suffered another nervous breakdown and his immediate dismissal became inevitable. Under pressure from Lyncker Wilhelm nominated Falkenhayn, the Prussian war minister, to succeed Moltke. Despite criticism and intrigues he held on to Falkenhayn until his replacement by the powerful and immensely popular duo of Hindenburg and Ludendorff in the summer of 1916 could no longer be avoided.[2]

Much to the regret of Grand Admiral Alfred von Tirpitz, the Kaiser exercised his power of command as Supreme War Lord directly in the conduct of the war at sea, this time with the advice of his Naval Cabinet chief, Admiral Georg von Müller.[3] He refused Tirpitz permission to send out the High Seas Fleet for a great battle in the North Sea and declared peremptorily that 'he had ordered the Fleet to stay at home and that was that'.[4] The question of U-boat warfare became increasingly critical for the Kaiser, especially after the sinking of the British liner *Lusitania* in May 1915, when almost 1,200 people, including many Americans, lost their lives. With the agreement of the Reich Chancellor, Müller and Falkenhayn, who were all anxious to avoid anything that could provoke the United States to enter the war, the Kaiser ordered that passenger ships should no longer be attacked, whereupon Tirpitz handed in his resignation. 'No! Stay and obey!' was Wilhelm's furious response.[5] He could not allow anyone 'in wartime to ask to be relieved from his post on account of differences of opinion concerning the deployment of warships over which I as Supreme War Lord and in full awareness of My responsibilities have the final say'.[6] Furthermore, he wrote, 'I have created and built up the Fleet as my weapon, how, where and when I decide to deploy it is solely my concern as Supreme War Lord.'[7]

On this occasion Tirpitz remained in office, and continued his campaign for the unrestricted use of U-boats. The Kaiser veered from one viewpoint to the other and complained that he was facing the most difficult decision of his life.[8] When Tirpitz handed in his resignation again in March 1916, Wilhelm reluctantly let him go. After the appointment of the third Supreme Army Command, under Hindenburg and Ludendorff, the pressure for unlimited U-boat warfare became unstoppable. On 8 January 1917 the Kaiser suddenly and very decisively declared himself in favour of the ruthless use of U-boats, even if Bethmann resigned over it. U-boat warfare, he now maintained, was 'a purely military matter' that was of no concern to the Chancellor.[9] 'Those English brutes must sue for peace! [. . .] Until they do so we must continue to thrash them and shoot them and fight them with our U-Boots! They must be made to swallow our terms!'[10] And, sure enough, the United States declared war two months later.

CHAPTER 27

Downfall: the collapse of the Hohenzollern monarchy

It is not without irony that the more bizarre his fantasies of world domination became, the more Wilhelm shrank into a helpless shadowy monarch in his own realm. A fundamental reform of the Prussian/German constitution, with its antiquated three-class franchise, the Crown's freedom to choose the Chancellor and the ministers at will and the Supreme War Lord's unrestricted power to command in military matters, had become imperative through the relentless dictates of total war. Yet Wilhelm II doggedly opposed Bethmann Hollweg's proposals for reform. The introduction of the parliamentary system would restrict the monarch's right to select and dismiss his ministers as he pleased, and, furthermore, to accept socialists or Catholic Centre Party members as ministers was simply 'unthinkable', he declared in June 1917.[1] The introduction of universal suffrage in Prussia could not be conceded until after the war, he insisted. Despite the threat to his personal monarchy represented by the takeover of power by Hindenburg and Ludendorff in 1916, Wilhelm preferred to take refuge in the shadow of the two generals rather than in the opening offered by a move towards parliamentary responsibility. 'You know, I'm in seventh heaven with these two men,' he remarked to one of his Flügeladjutanten.[2]

Relentlessly, both Kaiser and Chancellor became trapped between the grindstones of the increasingly self-confident Reichstag on the one hand and the military dictatorship of the Supreme Army Command on the other. On 12 July 1917 Wilhelm was warned to expect the resignations of Hindenburg and Ludendorff, as they could no longer work with Bethmann Hollweg. The Kaiser was outraged at this insubordination but had to recognise that it would be impossible to allow the two popular army commanders to go. The next day he accepted Bethmann Hollweg's resignation.[3]

Once again, as when Bülow had been dismissed in 1909, the Kaiser wavered helplessly over the choice of a new Reich Chancellor. On his resignation Bethmann had suggested the Bavarian prime minister, Count Georg von Hertling, as his successor, but Hertling refused the post on account of his age. Wilhelm raised 'lively objections' to Count Lerchenfeld's suggestion that he appoint the former ambassador Johann-Heinrich Count von Bernstorff, but, tellingly, he declared himself willing to put these objections aside 'should Hindenburg find him acceptable'. When the chief of the Civil Cabinet refused to ask the field marshal for his consent, Valentini was referred to the chief of the Military Cabinet, General von Lyncker. Valentini and Lyncker consulted together and became so desperate that they even resorted to the Almanach de Gotha in the search for possible candidates. As they were deliberating, the Kaiser's adjutant general, Hans von Plessen, joined them and recorded in his diary:

I chanced upon Valentini in the Military Cabinet. Clueless. Lyncker ditto. In my presence they went through all the possible and impossible candidates a second time: Dallwitz, Bülow, Tirpitz, Gallwitz, Bernstorff, Rantzau. All of them in Valentini's opinion unsuitable for this reason or that. Silent pondering. Then I proposed Dallwitz once again. Rejected, since he is supposed to have declared on an earlier occasion that he would always refuse this post. Then I proposed Hatzfeld. But H.M. didn't want him or Bülow or Tirpitz either. Then I suddenly thought of Undersecretary of State [Georg] Michaelis, whom someone had described to me as clever, lively and reliable! Valentini delighted! That would be a suitable fellow. Valentini, Lyncker and I go along with this proposal first to Hindenburg. He and Ludendorff are in full agreement. Thereupon all three of us to H.M. – The All-Highest declares himself in agreement even though he had seen him only once, saying he was short, a dwarf.[4]

In this way, after the Supreme Army Command had practically been asked for its prior approval, the highest office in the German Reich was entrusted to a man whom the Kaiser scarcely knew and who had no political backing and no experience in foreign affairs to show for himself. Michaelis held office only until October 1917, handing over his thankless task to Hertling, who had overcome his previous reservations. Wilhelm II's subordination to the powerful military duo of Hindenburg and Ludendorff reached its lowest point in January 1918 with the enforced replacement of Rudolf von Valentini, his long-standing and closest adviser, by the arch-conservative Friedrich Wilhelm von Berg as chief of his Civil Cabinet.[5]

After the failure of the Ludendorff offensive in the summer of 1918 the war was as good as lost. To the starving population and the army itself the Kaiser seemed an impediment to the end of the war for which they longed; a revolutionary mood developed with astonishing speed both at home and at the front. The new government under Reich Chancellor Prince Max of Baden worked desperately for a timely abdication by Wilhelm II in favour of a young Hohenzollern prince, with himself, Prince Max, as regent, so as to save at least the institution of monarchy in the hope of providing a focus of stability in the turbulent times ahead.[6] But it was in vain. Wilhelm declared: 'I am not going anywhere; if I were to, the Reich would fall apart. [. . .] The Chancellor is not on top of the job, the Foreign Office has completely filled its pants.'[7] On 1 November 1918 the Prussian interior minister, Bill Drews, was sent on the Chancellor's instructions to Supreme Headquarters in Spa in southern Belgium to suggest to the Kaiser that he should abdicate, but the monarch again responded with fury:

I will not abdicate. It would be incompatible with my duties, as successor to Frederick the Great, towards God, the people and my conscience. [. . .] My abdication would be the beginning of the end for all German monarchies. [. . .] But above all my duty as Supreme War Lord forbids me to abandon the army now. The army is engaged in a heroic struggle with the enemy. Its determined cohesion depends on the person of the Supreme War Lord. If the latter departs, the army will disintegrate and the enemy invade our homeland without let or hindrance. [8]

He was determined to answer the revolutionaries 'with machine-guns in the streets', and wouldn't dream of quitting his throne 'on account of a few hundred Jews or 1000 workers', he averred on 3 November 1918.[9]

On that day revolution broke out in Kiel – in Wilhelm's navy, of all places – and it spread like wildfire throughout Germany. The reigning German princely houses all abandoned their thrones; in Berlin, chaos and civil war loomed. A poll of divisional commanders in Spa revealed that the soldiers were 'completely exhausted and battle-weary'; they were not prepared to fight their compatriots for their Kaiser, to whom they were 'in fact quite indifferent'.[10] Hans von Plessen's suggestion that Wilhelm might abdicate as German Kaiser but remain King of Prussia was rejected as constitutionally impossible. While solutions such as this were being pondered in Supreme Headquarters, in Berlin Prince Max of Baden was forced to announce Wilhelm II's abdication as Kaiser and king on 9 November in a desperate attempt to keep control of the situation. A few hours later Philipp Scheidemann proclaimed the German Republic. Wilhelm Groener, who had succeeded Ludendorff as quartermaster general, later recalled the moment when it dawned on the Kaiser that the Hohenzollern monarchy was over. 'He said nothing, just looked – looked from one to the other, with an expression first of amazement, then piteous appeal, and then – just a curious wondering vagueness. He said nothing, and we took him – just as if he were a little child – and sent him to Holland.'[11]

PART VII

1918–1941: The Vengeful Exile

CHAPTER 28

A new life in Amerongen and Doorn

Early in the morning of Sunday 10 November 1918 a spectral little motor convoy appeared at the Belgian–Dutch border crossing at Eijsden. At daybreak the Kaiser had left Supreme Headquarters at Spa in the imperial train. Fearing an attack from his own troops, however, after only a few kilometres he and a small retinue had switched to two automobiles in the hope of reaching the neutral Netherlands unrecognised. In Eijsden Wilhelm II had to wait on the platform, enduring the insults of the angry local populace until the imperial train arrived with the remainder of his entourage and servants. After lengthy negotiations by telephone, Queen Wilhelmina granted the Kaiser asylum in the Netherlands, and Count Godard van Aldenburg-Bentinck agreed to offer him hospitality for three days at Kastell Amerongen, his moated castle in the province of Utrecht. In fact, the uninvited guests – the Kaiserin soon followed – spent the next eighteen months at Amerongen, until in May 1920 Wilhelm was able to move into the nearby property of Huis Doorn with its fifty-nine-hectare park, which he had bought from Baroness van Heemstra for 1.35 million guilders. On 28 November 1918 the Kaiser formally renounced 'for all time his rights to the Crown of Prussia and thereby to the rights to the German Imperial Crown bound to it'.[1]

Thanks to the generosity of the 'swinish' Weimar Republic, as he called it, the Kaiser was able to keep up an enviable lifestyle in exile, in comparison to his hard-pressed former subjects. As early as late November 1918 the revolutionary government in Berlin approved the transfer of millions of marks to the exiled monarch 'to maintain a life in accordance with his status': in the first year of his exile payments to him amounted to no less than 66 million marks. In May 1921 the minister of the Royal House demanded a further 10 million marks from public funds, which was approved. In addition, from the beginning the Kaiser had the contents of his imperial train at his disposal, which included 300 plates and the accompanying silverware. On 1 September 1919 the Prussian finance minister released 'furniture and other objects designated for the living quarters of the former Kaiser and King'.[2] No fewer than fifty-nine railway wagons were needed to transport the imperial 'removal goods' to the Netherlands. In vain the Social Democrats warned against treating this 'failed monarch', whom 'millions upon millions regard as one of the men most guilty for the war and all the suffering it has caused', with such generosity.[3]

After a plebiscite in June 1926 there was a final division of property between the state and the Hohenzollern family. Under a contract dated 29 October 1926 a third of the sixty former royal palaces and residences was awarded to the Hohenzollerns, including Schloss Bellevue (now the official residence of the president of the Federal Republic), Schloss Babelsberg on the outskirts of Potsdam, Monbijou, Königswusterhausen, Schloss Cecilienhof (scene of the Potsdam Conference in 1945), Schloss Oels in Silesia, the Palais of Kaiser Wilhelm I and the Niederländisches Palais on Berlin's Unter den Linden, the Prinz-Albrecht-Palais (later the headquarters of the Gestapo) in the Wilhelmstrasse and one-half of the Burg Hohenzollern at Hechingen in Württemberg, together with the hunting lodge at Rominten in East Prussia (later acquired by Hermann Göring), the Cadinen estate in West Prussia and that little jewel of a palace, the Achilleion, on Corfu. Wilhelm was even able to retrieve the saddle on which he had been accustomed to sit at his desk in the Stadtschloss in Berlin and use it in his tower room at Huis Doorn. When he died in 1941 his net estate was worth almost 13 million marks.

No other fugitive monarch in modern European history was able to enjoy as generous a settlement as Kaiser Wilhelm II. And yet his life in exile was marked by bitterness and depression. The lost war, the revolution at home, 'betrayal' by the generals at Spa, the flight over the border and the threat of being handed over to the victorious powers – it was more than enough to induce a nervous breakdown in December 1918, and, as he had often done previously, Wilhelm took to his bed. For six weeks he did not leave his room. Until March

1919 he wore a bandage round his head; it was said that his old ear complaint had become acute again. There were rumours of an attempted suicide. To more than one of his loyal visitors their Kaiser's existence seemed demeaning and they privately wished that death might put an end to his undignified situation.

With the death in April 1921 of the Kaiserin Auguste Viktoria, who had suffered for years from heart failure, Wilhelm's isolation affected him so severely that his personal physician, Dr Alfred Haehner, feared he was rapidly becoming a misanthropic recluse. He urged his patient to see more people, especially women. And soon all too many women appeared at Huis Doorn in the hopes of beguiling the sixty-two-year-old former monarch: a clairvoyant Finnish lady doctor, two lively Hungarian sisters, Princess Luise zu Solms, Ittel von Tschirschky, Hereditary Princess Marie Christine zu Salm-Salm, Catalina von Pannwitz and the widowed Auguste von Tiele-Winckler. Gabriele von Rochow came to visit him several times, and even persuaded him for a time that he could perhaps marry a woman from a middle-class or minor noble family rather than having to abide by the blue-blooded principle of *Ebenbürtigkeit* (equal birth). The twenty-five-year-old Cornelia (Lily) van Heemstra, distantly related to Audrey Hepburn and a former sweetheart of the Crown Prince, made the strongest impression on him; he called her his 'little sunshine'. He and Lily Heemstra often spoke of the possibility of marriage, but the difference in their ages was too great, and she moved on to Kronberg in the hope of marrying one of the four Hessian princes, the sons of Wilhelm's youngest sister, the Landgravine Margarethe of Hesse.

In Wilhelm's tiny entourage these comings and goings were watched with eagle eyes, but everyone was astonished when the Kaiser invited the widowed Princess Hermine von Schönaich-Carolath, daughter of Prince Heinrich XXII of Reuss, whom he had never seen, to Doorn in June 1922. She arrived on 9 June, and two days later she was engaged to Wilhelm. The wedding, which took place on 5 November in Doorn, was seen as a spectacular mésalliance, particularly by the imperial family. Not only was 'Hermo' scarcely older than Wilhelm's own daughter; she brought five children, of whom the youngest was only three years old, into the marriage; she insisted from the outset on being allowed to go back to Germany for several weeks twice a year; and she demanded

30 The ex-Kaiser with his second wife, Hermine von Schönaich-Carolath.

to be addressed as 'Your Majesty' by all. She proved to be quarrel-some and ambitious: Friedrich Wilhelm von Berg, the minister of the Royal House, was among those who were convinced that she had married the Kaiser only in the expectation of being enthroned one day as Germany's new Kaiserin, and some predicted that she would become embittered as soon as she realised how impossible a restor-ation would be.[4] But, then, Wilhelm too had chosen Hermine as his bride partly under the illusion that his marriage with a blue-blooded princess would improve his chances of returning to Germany as Kaiser and king.

CHAPTER 29

The rabid anti-Semite in exile

A return to the throne would have meant anything but jubilant celebrations. Instead, his restoration would almost certainly have sparked a bloody civil war, and probably also war with Poland, Czechoslovakia, France and Britain. Throughout the world Wilhelm was hated as the man whose overweening militarism on land and at sea and whose expansionist urge for supremacy had brought about the disaster of the Great War. He was wanted as a war criminal and probably escaped conviction and banishment to Devil's Island or its like only because the Dutch government refused to hand him over to the victorious powers, which were intending to try him in the Palace of Westminster. In Germany itself he had forfeited what remained of any veneration for the Hohenzollern monarchy after his thirty-year rule by his ignominious flight to the Netherlands. The revelation by the Bolsheviks of his correspondence with Tsar Nicholas II[1] and the publication of his marginal comments during the July crisis of 1914[2] and of the memoirs of his contemporaries[3] that followed the collapse in 1918 completely outweighed Wilhelm's own memoirs, which proved powerless against the weight of all this condemnation.[4] Soon he descended into a nightmare of violent paranoia, obsessed with the idea that satanic machinations had been at work to destroy him and everything noble for which he had chivalrously fought throughout his life, and was still fighting for: the true Germanic God, the Bible cleansed of Jewish and Roman contamination, the autocratic Prussian military monarchy of his illustrious forefathers, the German Reich restored to its former strength and freed from the chains of the Anglo-French Entente and from the dictated peace of Versailles, once again ready, with the aid of its glorious army, to assume its rightful place among the foremost powers of the world.

The revenge that the ex-Kaiser contemplated taking on his own people would have been fearful. The Germans, he said, had been guilty of 'betrayal, downright felony, cowardice' towards him;[5] he would most certainly return, 'but only if begged to do so on bended knee, and then heads would roll'.[6] The November revolution had been a 'betrayal of the ruling house & the army by the German people who had been deceived and lied to by the Jewish rabble!' and would be 'severely punished!'.[7] Wilhelm's *idée fixe* of a world conspiracy of Jews, Freemasons and Catholics against the Protestant German monarchy was confirmed in his eyes by the appointment of Walther Rathenau as a minister in Joseph Wirth's Catholic Centre-Party-led coalition government in May 1921. As he commented to his doctor: 'This showed once again the connection between Ultramontanism and international Jewish Freemasonry bent solely on keeping down the Prot[estant] Kaiserdom. [...] Behind it all were the Jesuits working at the behest of Rome and using Erzberger as their tool.'[8] When Matthias Erzberger, a politician who had opposed the war from 1917, was murdered in August 1921 Wilhelm danced for joy and called for champagne; nothing, he said, had given him greater pleasure since his arrival in the Netherlands. Not least, the Manichaean division of the world into good and evil, God and Satan, Christ and Antichrist, Protestantism and Catholicism, monarchy and democracy, German and Jew on which his thinking was based during his exile also found expression in a horrifying anti-Semitism.

In 1927 Wilhelm declared in a letter in English to his American friend Poultney Bigelow:

The Hebrew race are my most inveterate enemies at home and abroad; they remain what they are and always were: the forgers of lies and the master-minds governing unrest, revolution, upheaval by spreading infamy with the help of their poisoned, caustic, satyrical [sic] spirit. If the world once wakes up it should mete out to them the punishment in store for them, which they deserve.[9]

From such a view it was not a big step to the anti-Semitism of extermination. On 2 December 1919 Wilhelm wrote in his own hand to the most loyal of all his generals, Field Marshal August von Mackensen:

The deepest, most disgusting shame ever perpetrated by a people in history, the Germans have done unto themselves. Egged on and misled by the tribe of Juda whom they hated, who were guests among them. That was their thanks! Let no German ever forget this, nor rest until these parasites have been destroyed and exterminated from German soil! This poisonous mushroom on the German oak-tree![10]

In 1920 he shocked his one-time Flügeladjutant, General Max von Mutius, on a visit to his former Supreme War Lord at Doorn, by claiming that 'the world, and Germany in particular, would not rest in peace until all Jews had been clubbed to death or at least been driven out of the country'. When Mutius remarked that 'unfortunately it would not be practicable to club all of them to death', Wilhelm retorted angrily: 'My dear child, I *can* do it and *will* do it. Just you wait and see.'[11] In March 1921 he informed his perplexed dinner guests:

When a new era dawned once more in Germany the Jews would meet their fate in no uncertain terms. They had syphoned off some 80 milliards out of the country. They would have to repay all of this, the government must start by demanding 15 milliards immediately. They would have to forfeit everything, their art collections, their houses, all their property. They would have to be removed once and for all from all their public offices, they must be thrown completely to the ground.[12]

He called for a 'regular international all-worlds pogrom' as 'the best cure'.[13] And on 15 August 1927 he wrote, again in his own hand, in English, to his American friend Bigelow that the 'Press, Jews & Mosquitoes. . .are a nuisance that humanity must get rid of in some way or another. I believe the best would be gas!'[14]

CHAPTER 30

The Kaiser and Hitler

In spite of initial reservations about the *völkisch* movement, the exiled Wilhelm had great hopes of Adolf Hitler after the latter's swing to the right in 1928 and his pact with the press magnate Alfred Hugenberg in the 1929 campaign for a plebiscite against the 'war guilt lie' and the Young Plan fixing Germany's reparation payments for decades to come. The astonishing electoral successes of the National Socialist German Workers' (Nazi) Party and the transition to a presidential regime in Berlin seemed to clear the way for the restoration of the monarchy. The ex-Kaiser's son, Prince August Wilhelm of Prussia, joined the Nazis and the Sturmabteilung and was invited by Hitler to the Nuremberg rally as a guest of honour.[1] 'Kaiserin' Hermine also proved to be an ardent admirer of the Führer. She pleaded with Hitler to bring her husband back to Germany. Hermann Göring and his wife, Karin, came to spend two days with the imperial couple at Huis Doorn on 17 and 18 January 1931, the sixtieth anniversary of the proclamation of the German Reich at Versailles in 1871. Göring returned for a second visit on 20 and 21 May 1932. The Hohenzollerns believed they had almost reached their goal. 'For months now the only thing one hears in Doorn is that the National Socialists will put the Kaiser back on the throne,' Sigurd von Ilsemann, Count Bentinck's son-in-law, noted in his diary at Christmas 1931.[2]

After the Nazi 'seizure of power' on 30 January 1933 direct negotiations were held between Hitler and representatives of the House of Hohenzollern about the restoration of the monarchy. On 9 May 1933 Hitler made a telling statement of his views on the matter, which were as follows:

31 Hermann Göring on one of his visits to the Kaiser at Doorn in 1932.

(1) He regarded the monarchy as the culmination of his task. (2) For him there was only one German monarchy; he rejected monarchies in the federal states (the Länder). (3) For the monarchy only the House of Hohenzollern could be considered. (4) The time had not yet come for the reinstitution of the monarchy... (5) Hitler was....first and foremost a soldier. As such he believed it possible for the monarchy to come back through a plebiscite or something of that kind. Only the army could return the Kaiser to the throne after a victorious war.[3]

In discussions at the Reich Chancellery on 24 October 1933 with the representative of the House of Hohenzollern, General Wilhelm von Dommes, Hitler revealed his drastic long-term goals, which would, he said, make a restoration of the monarchy impossible for the present.

With regard to the form the state will take, he wanted to hold back for the time being. Naturally he was aware that a system could not rest upon one pair of eyes alone but needed to be founded on a House. He did not have a family, his name was engraved in Germany's history, in a few years it would be anchored there for all time. He had no ambition beyond achieving the tasks he had set himself: above all saving Germany from Bolshevism a[nd] liberating it from the domination of the Jews.

Hitler thought it doubtful that a monarchy could be robust enough to take on the bloody conflicts that would be inevitable, Dommes continued.

Very few people understood his position in the Jewish question... And here Hitler became very passionate: he went into great detail on how and why the Jews had become Germany's misfortune, had made the revolution etc. etc. The Jews would therefore have to be eliminated. This had been his aim from the beginning. He would not be blown off course. [...] The casting down [*Niederwerfung*] of Communism a[nd] Jewry were the tasks he had set himself a[nd] had to solve. He did not know how much time he would have to achieve his aims.

When Dommes asked with astonishment whether he was really of the opinion that 'the monarchy would be unsuited to solving the problems he had outlined', Hitler did not reply 'but instead returned to the Jewish question. Then he brought the conversation to an abrupt end.'[4]

Although this decision was deeply disappointing for Wilhelm, and although he sometimes expressed horror at the excesses of the Nazi regime, he greeted Hitler's foreign policy successes with glee, seeing them as a welcome continuation of his own hegemonic ambitions. Thus after the signature of the Munich Agreement in September 1938 he wrote:

It was an inspiration of God that influenced [Neville} Chamberlain to save the Peace! A clear proof of the influence of Heaven on Earthly affairs. The agreement of Munich which *enforced* Peace on War promoters has shattered Uncle Berties [i.e. King Edward VII's] Policy against us, & brought about by common consent of the People the *European Conclave* I vainly wished for for 30 Years!'[5]

And continuing in the same vein: 'If Grey in 1914 had behaved as Chamberlain did in 1938 there would have been no World War. But 1914 the British People *wanted* War, 1938 they *feared* it!'[6] A year later, however, when war broke out after all, Wilhelm exulted: 'The Polish Campaign was marvellous. Old Prussian spirit, the Leaders "My school"!'[7] As Hermine reported at the end of 1939: 'We do not doubt that he [the Führer] will succeed in bringing perfidious England to its knees and to conquer for Germany the place in the sun which it needs and deserves. [...] The Kaiser is proud of the young Wehrmacht and

32 Wilhelm as 'the gardener of Doorn'.

delighted at all the blows raining down on England.'[8] When the
German forces invaded the Netherlands in May 1940 Wilhelm refused
his cousin George VI's offer of asylum with the contemptuous remark
that he would rather allow himself to be shot than flee to England,
saying that 'he had no wish to be photographed alongside Churchill'.[9]

The retreat of the British army at Dunkirk and the capitulation of France led to wild rejoicing in Doorn. On 31 May 1940 Wilhelm crowed: 'The ordeal of Juda-England has begun. Destruction in Flanders.'[10] On the entry of German troops into Paris he sent the Führer a congratulatory telegram aligning this victory with the Prusso-German conquests attained by his own forefathers.

Under the deeply moving impression of France's capitulation I congratulate you and all the German armed forces on the God-given prodigious victory with the words of Kaiser Wilhelm the Great of the year 1870: 'What a turn of events through God's dispensation!' All German hearts are filled with the chorale of Leuthen, which the victors of [the battle of] Leuthen, the soldiers of the Great King sang [in 1757]: Now thank we all our God!'[11]

As with the Munich Agreement and the campaign against Poland, Wilhelm II saw the capitulation of France as the fulfilment of his own supremacist policy. Hitler's war, the ex-Kaiser exulted in September 1940, was

a succession of miracles! The old Prussian spirit of Fr[e]d[ericus] Rex, of Clausewitz, Blücher, York, Gneisenau etc. has again manifested itself, as in 1870–71. [. . .] The brilliant leading Generals in this war came from *My* school, they fought under my command in the [First] World War as lieutenants, captains and young majors. Educated by Schlieffen they put the plans he had worked out under me into practice along the same lines as we did in 1914.[12]

At last the balance of power policy that Britain had pursued against Germany since the time of Edward VII had been shattered and the Continent united under German domination. 'Over here the new U.S. of Europe are in formation, shaping the Continent into one block of Nations,' he wrote in November 1940.[13]

The hand of God is creating a new World & working miracles. To think that France has finally dropped the poisonous Entente Cordiale [of] Uncle Bertie's with Britain & sided with Germany & Italy in cooperation, ignoring the Kings [sic] appeal, is a *miracle*! We are becoming the *U.S. of Europe* under German leadership, a united European Continent, nobody ever hoped to see![14]

Britain's determination to hold out against the superior strength of Germany on the Continent was, for Wilhelm, readily explained in familiar terms: the Jews and the Freemasons were at work again! He

33 The wreath sent by the Führer, Adolf Hitler, for Wilhelm's funeral at Doorn in June 1941.

ranted about the necessity of freeing England too, the land of Satan, 'thoroughly contaminated' as it was by Jews and Freemasons, '*from the Antichrist Juda*'. Germany had to 'drive Juda out of England just as he has been chased out of the Continent. The *Antichrist Juda must be expelled* [*hinausgestoßen*] from England as well as from the Continent.' Twice – in 1914 and 1939 – the Jews had sparked off war against Germany with England's help and 'on the *orders* of Satan', in order to establish the 'world empire [*Weltreich*] of Juda', but 'then God intervened and *smashed* their plan!'. Now Europe was in the process of 'consolidating and closing itself off from British influence after the elimination [*Entledigung*] of the British and the Jews'. The 'United States of Europe!' would be the happy result.[15] In a letter written in the last year of his life the ex-Kaiser rejoiced: 'The Jews are beeing [*sic*] thrust out of their nefarious positions in all countries, whom they have driven to hostility for centuries.'[16] 'The feats of our brave troops are wonderful, God gave them success. – May He continue to help them to peace with honour, & the victory over Juda & Antichrist in British garb,' he wrote on 20 April 1941.[17] Even in this darkest hour for Europe, Wilhelm was incapable of grasping the extent of the colossal, worldwide catastrophe that was under way. While Hitler and the Wehrmacht were making their final preparations for the war of extermination in the east the Kaiser, self-righteous champion of God's Germanic cause to the bitter end, was dreaming happily of Nazi Germany's ultimate victory, her '*Endsieg*'. He died at Doorn on 4 June 1941.

Notes

PREFACE TO THE ENGLISH EDITION

1 John C. G. Röhl, *Wilhelm II.: Die Jugend des Kaisers 1859–1888*, Munich 1993 (English translation: *Young Wilhelm: The Kaiser's Early Life, 1859–1888*, Cambridge 1998); John C. G. Röhl, *Wilhelm II.: Der Aufbau der Persönlichen Monarchie 1888–1900*, Munich 2001 (English translation: *Wilhelm II: The Kaiser's Personal Monarchy, 1888–1900*, Cambridge 2004); John C. G. Röhl, *Wilhelm II.: Der Weg in den Abgrund 1900–1941*, Munich 2008 (English translation: *Wilhelm II: Into the Abyss of War and Exile, 1900–1941*, Cambridge 2014).

2 For the most recent and authoritative documentation on the decisions in all the capitals of Europe that led to war, see Annika Mombauer, ed., *The Origins of the First World War: Diplomatic and Military Documents*, Manchester 2013.

3 See, in particular, Christopher Clark, *The Sleepwalkers: How Europe Went to War in 1914*, London 2012; Herfried Münkler, *Der Große Krieg: Die Welt von 1914 bis 1918*, Berlin 2014.

4 David Lloyd George, *War Memoirs*, London 1938.

5 Kaiser Wilhelm II to Poultney Bigelow, 14 September 1940; cited below, p. 192.

1 THE 'SOUL MURDER' OF AN HEIR TO THE THRONE

1 Crown Princess Victoria's letters to her mother Queen Victoria were published in somewhat imperspicuous circumstances in 1928: see Sir Frederick Ponsonby, ed., *Letters of the Empress Frederick*, London 1928. Five further volumes of their correspondence, edited by Roger Fulford, followed in the years 1964 to 1981. Her ambitions for her adopted country and their failure are the subject of several archive-based studies, most notably Egon Caesar Conte Corti, *The English Empress*, London 1954; Hannah Pakula, *An Uncommon Woman: The Empress Frederick. Daughter of Queen Victoria, Wife of the Crown Prince of Prussia, Mother of Kaiser Wilhelm*, New York 1995;

Patricia Kollander, *Frederick III: Germany's Liberal Emperor*, Westport, CT, 1995; Rainer von Hessen, ed., *Victoria Kaiserin Friedrich (1840–1901): Mission und Schicksal einer englischen Prinzessin in Deutschland*, Frankfurt am Main 2002; Frank Lorenz Müller, *Our Fritz: Emperor Frederick III and the Political Culture of Imperial Germany*, Cambridge, MA, 2011.

2 Eduard Martin, Bericht über die Entbindung, 9 February 1859, Geheimes Staatsarchiv (GStA) Berlin-Dahlem, Brandenburg-Preußisches Hausarchiv Berlin-Dahlem (BPHA) Rep. 53a no. 9; copy in Royal Archives (RA) Windsor. See the detailed account of the birth in Röhl, *Young Wilhelm*, 4–11.

3 Wegner, report of 8 September 1859, RA Z63/133; Röhl, *Young Wilhelm*, 26f.

4 Clark, Jenner and Paget to Crown Prince Friedrich Wilhelm, 2 December 1865, folder Erzieher unserer Kinder, Archiv der Hessischen Hausstiftung (AdHH) Schloss Fasanerie; Gustav von Dresky, Bericht über die Mittel der Behandlung und die Fortschritte des Wachsthums des linken Armes Seiner Königlichen Hoheit des Prinzen Wilhelm, 3 July 1871, ibid.

5 Crown Prince's diary, 28 April 1863, AdHH Schloss Fasanerie.

6 Crown Princess to Queen Victoria, 28 April 1863, RA Z15/15. The letter is printed in Roger Fulford, ed., *Dearest Mama: Private Correspondence of Queen Victoria and the German Crown Princess 1879–1885*, London 1981, 203f.

7 See the details in Röhl, *Young Wilhelm*, 32–7, and the photograph of Wilhelm aged ten, figure 1 above.

8 Dresky's table showing the discrepancy in the dimensions of the prince's arms at the age of ten is printed ibid., 49.

9 Green to Passow, 26 December 1925, cited in Röhl, *Young Wilhelm*, 321f.

10 Irmgard Salzmann, 'Kaiser Wilhelm II.: Hatte er einen Hirnschaden? Eine Studie seiner Geburt und deren Folgen', dissertation, Tübingen 1991. Cf. Christopher Clark, *Kaiser Wilhelm II: A Life in Power* (rev. edn), London 2009, 31–4.

11 John C. G. Röhl, Martin Warren and David Hunt, *Purple Secret: Genes, 'Madness' and the Royal Houses of Europe*, London 1998.

12 Viscount Esher, diary entry for 21 November 1908, Esher Papers, Churchill Archives Centre, Cambridge, quoted ibid., 223f. For the disturbing predictions of Sir John Erichsen of March 1888 and their effect on later British assessments of the Kaiser's mental state, see Röhl, *Young Wilhelm*, 318f.

2 AMBIVALENT MOTHERHOOD

1 Crown Princess to Prince Albert, 18 August 1860, RA Z3/35. See also Crown Princess to Queen Victoria, 28 April 1863, RA Z15/15. For the

following, see the much fuller account in Röhl, *Young Wilhelm*, chap. 3, 'Ambivalent motherhood'.

2 Sigmund Freud, *Vorlesungen, Neue Folge: Studienausgabe*, vol. I, Frankfurt am Main 1978, 504 (English translation: James Strachey, ed., *The Complete Psychoanalytical Works of Sigmund Freud*, vol. XXII, *1932–6: New Introductory Lectures in Psycho-Analysis*, Harmondsworth 1979, 97f.).

3 Crown Princess to Queen Victoria, 28 April 1863, RA Z15/15; printed in Fulford, *Dearest Mama*, 203f.

4 Crown Princess to Prince Albert, 16 July 1859, RA Z2/28: see Thomas A. Kohut, *Wilhelm II and the Germans*, Oxford 1991, 32.

5 Crown Princess to Prince Albert, 27 January 1860, RA Z3/5: cf. Kohut, *Wilhelm II and the Germans*, 34.

6 Crown Princess to Queen Victoria, 28 April 1863, RA Z15/15.

7 Crown Princess to Queen Victoria, 23 May 1863, RA Z15/25; printed in Fulford, *Dearest Mama*, 216.

8 Crown Princess to Queen Victoria, 13 August 1864, RA Z16/73.

9 Crown Princess to Crown Prince, 4 March 1864, AdHH Schloss Fasanerie.

10 Crown Princess to Crown Prince, 9 May 1864, loc. cit.

11 Crown Princess to Crown Prince, 13 March 1880 [emphasis in original], loc. cit.

12 Crown Prince to Crown Princess, 11 March 1880, loc. cit.

3 A DARING EDUCATIONAL EXPERIMENT

1 Crown Princess to Queen Victoria, 16 August 1864 [emphasis in original], RA Z16/74.

2 Dr Georg Hinzpeter to Sir Robert Morier, 15 January 1866, folder Erzieher unserer Kinder, AdHH Schloss Fasanerie. For Hinzpeter's appointment and the principles he intended to adopt in educating Wilhelm, see Röhl, *Young Wilhelm*, 133ff. See also Yvonne Wagner, *Prinzenerziehung in der 2. Hälfte des 19. Jahrhunderts: Zum Bildungsverhalten des preußisch-deutschen Hofes im gesellschaftlichen Wandel*, Frankfurt am Main 1995.

3 Kaiser Wilhelm II, *My Early Life*, London 1926, 23f. 'The lesson was a cruel one', the ex-Kaiser claimed, 'and my brother Henry often howled with pain when compelled to witness the martyrdom of my youth.'

4 See the segment 'Riding lessons' in Röhl, *Young Wilhelm*, 151–4.

5 Ibid., 149ff., 179–82.

6 Crown Princess to Prince Wilhelm, 7 March 1870 [emphasis in original], GStA Berlin-Dahlem, BPHA Rep. 52T no. 13; Röhl, *Young Wilhelm*, 163ff.

7 Crown Princess to Prince Wilhelm, 29 April 1870, ibid.

8 Hinzpeter to Crown Prince, 30 December 1870, folder Erzieher unserer Kinder, AdHH Schloss Fasanerie.

9 Hinzpeter to Crown Prince, 2 April 1873, ibid.

10 Crown Princess to Crown Prince, 22 December 1870 [emphasis in original], AdHH Schloss Fasanerie; Röhl, *Young Wilhelm*, 171ff.

11 Crown Princess to Crown Prince, 13 and 16 August 1873, AdHH Schloss Fasanerie.

12 Hinzpeter to Anna Countess Görtz, 6 July 1874 [emphasis in original], Hessisches Staatsarchiv (HStA) Darmstadt, F23A no. 352/1; quoted in Röhl, *Young Wilhelm*, 195.

13 Hinzpeter to Crown Prince, 16 August 1874, folder Erzieher unserer Kinder, AdHH Schloss Fasanerie; quoted in Röhl, *Young Wilhelm*, 200.

14 Philipp Graf zu Eulenburg, note of 26 July 1897; cited in Röhl, *The Kaiser's Personal Monarchy*, 1047.

15 Hinzpeter to Emil Count Görtz, 12 February 1875, HStA Darmstadt, F23A 383/5; Hinzpeter to Crown Prince, 4 October 1874, folder Erzieher unserer Kinder, Schloss Fasanerie. See Röhl, *Young Wilhelm*, chap. 9, 'Experiment in Kassel'.

16 Prince Wilhelm to Emil Hartwich, 2 April 1885; printed in Wilhelm Preyer, *Unser Kaiser und die Schulreform*, Dresden 1900, 41f.; A. O. Klaussmann, ed., *Kaiserreden: Reden und Erlasse, Briefe und Telegramme Kaiser Wilhelms des Zweiten: Ein Charakterbild des Deutschen Kaisers*, Leipzig 1902, 275–7.

17 Ulf Morgenstern, *Lehrjahre eines neoabsoluten Monarchen: Kaiser Wilhelm II. als Kasseler Abiturient im Spiegel eines unbekannten Aufsatzheftes*, Friedrichsruh 2011.

18 Hinzpeter to Crown Princess, 7 November 1874, folder Erzieher unserer Kinder, Schloss Fasanerie; Hinzpeter to Crown Prince, 8 February 1876, copy, Morier Papers, box 55, Balliol College Oxford.

19 Hinzpeter to Sir Robert Morier, 9 February 1876, Morier Papers, box 55, Balliol College Oxford.

20 Alexander von Hohenlohe, *Aus meinem Leben*, Frankfurt am Main 1925, 368 [emphasis in original].

4 THE CONFLICT BETWEEN THE PRINCE OF PRUSSIA AND HIS PARENTS

1 Prince Wilhelm to his mother, 6 February [= March] 1875 [emphasis in original], AdHH Schloss Fasanerie [date corrected by reference to the Crown Princess's reply of 7 March 1875]; in Röhl, *Young Wilhelm*, 235f. See also Pakula, *An Uncommon Woman*, 363f.

2 Prince Wilhelm to his mother, 11 February [= March] 1875 [emphasis in original], AdHH Schloss Fasanerie; cited in Röhl, *Young Wilhelm*, 236.

3 Prince Wilhelm to his mother, 13 May 1875 [emphasis in original], loc. cit.

4 Prince Wilhelm to his mother, 6 June 1875, loc. cit.

5 Prince Wilhelm to his mother, 27 June 1875, loc. cit.

6 A facsimile of Wilhelm's letter of September 1874 is printed in Röhl, *Young Wilhelm*, 233.

7 Crown Princess to Prince Wilhelm, 8 February 1875, GStA Berlin, BPHA Rep. 52T no. 13; Röhl, *Young Wilhelm*, 236.

8 Quoted from Philipp Graf zu Eulenburg, 'Drei Freunde', unpublished manuscript in the possession of the Eulenburg family, Schloss Hertefeld, vol. I, part 3, 165f. See also Wilhelm II, *My Early Life*, 151–82.

9 Crown Princess to Queen Victoria, 17 July 1880, 5 August 1880; in Fulford, *Beloved Mama*, 83, 85.

10 As cited in Brigitte Hamann, 'Das Leben des Kronprinzen Rudolf von Österreich-Ungarn nach neuen Quellen', dissertation, Vienna 1977, 333.

11 Max Egon II Fürst zu Fürstenberg, diary entry for 6 April 1908; quoted in Peter Winzen, *Freundesliebe am Hof Kaiser Wilhelms II.*, Norderstedt 2010, 81f.

12 On this relationship and its troubled end, see Röhl, *Young Wilhelm*, 455–64; and Röhl, *The Kaiser's Personal Monarchy*, 197–9.

13 Otto von Bismarck, eds. Herman van Petersdorff, Friedrich Thimme and Willy Andreas, *Die gesammelten Werke*, vol. XV, *Erinnerung und Gedanke*, Berlin 1932, 545.

14 Ella Sommssics to Prince Wilhelm, summer 1887, cited in Röhl, *Young Wilhelm*, 485f.

15 See Röhl, *Young Wilhelm*, 484–9.

16 See Röhl, *Young Wilhelm*, chap. 19, '"W.W.W.": Wilhelm–Wedel–Waldersee'; and John C. G. Röhl, *Wilhelm II: Into the Abyss of War and Exile, 1900–1941*, Cambridge 2014, 526–8.

17 See, for example, Eulenburg to Lucanus, 3 April 1900, in John C. G. Röhl, ed., *Philipp Eulenburgs politische Korrespondenz*, 3 vols., Boppard am Rhein 1976–83, III, no. 1417.

18 See below, pp. 106–7.

19 Kaiserin Auguste Viktoria to Kaiser Wilhelm II, 19/20 July 1892 [emphasis in original], cited in Röhl, *The Kaiser's Personal Monarchy*, 623. Wilhelm insisted that his wife always wore gloves whenever she went out into the sun.

20 Crown Princess to Louise Duchess of Connaught, 2 January 1885 [emphasis in original], RA Add A15/4374; cited in Röhl, *Young Wilhelm*, 557.

21 Crown Prince to Crown Princess, 26 August and 17 September 1885; cited ibid., 558.

22 Alfred Graf von Waldersee, diary entries for 28 May and 10 June 1884, GStA Berlin-Dahlem, Papers; cited in Röhl, *Young Wilhelm*, 564.

23 Friedrich von Holstein, diary entry for 6 June 1884; cited in Norman Rich and M. H. Fisher, eds., *The Holstein Papers*, 4 vols., Cambridge 1956–63, II, 153ff.

24 See the detailed account of Wilhelm's two visits to Russia in Röhl, *Young Wilhelm*, 424–30, 570–84; but cf. Clark, *Kaiser Wilhelm II*, 12f.

25 Walter Goetz, ed., *Briefe Wilhelms II. an den Zaren, 1894–1914*, Berlin 1920.

26 See Röhl, *Young Wilhelm*, chap. 26, 'Prince Wilhelm and Queen Victoria's Jubilee'.

27 On Prince Wilhelm's deployment in the Auswärtiges Amt, see Röhl, *Young Wilhelm*, 584–98.

28 The ludicrous 'Vienna Incident' of 1888 and its repercussions are discussed at length in Röhl, *The Kaiser's Personal Monarchy*, chap. 4, 'An ominous family quarrel'.

29 For Wilhelm's attitude to foreign affairs at this early stage, see Röhl, *Young Wilhelm*, chap. 17, 'First steps in foreign affairs: Prince Wilhelm between England and Russia'.

30 Waldersee, diary entry for 25 January 1887, GStA Berlin-Dahlem, Waldersee Papers.

31 Holstein, diary entry for 13 May 1888; in Rich and Fisher, *The Holstein Papers*, II, 374f.

32 Prince Wilhelm to Eulenburg, 8 January 1887; in Röhl, *Philipp Eulenburgs politische Korrespondenz*, I, no. 102.

5 1888: THE YEAR OF THE THREE KAISERS

1 See Roggenbach's conversation with Waldersee of 3 April 1887; cited in Röhl, *Young Wilhelm*, 634f.

2 See ibid., 705ff.

3 Ibid., 763–72.

4 Prince Wilhelm to Eulenburg, 19 February 1888 [emphasis in original]; cited in Röhl, *Philipp Eulenburgs politische Korrespondenz*, I, no. 153; the letter is cited more fully in Röhl, *Young Wilhelm*, 782f.

5 See ibid., 785–7.

6 Crown Prince Wilhelm to Eulenburg, 12 April 1888; cited in Röhl, *Philipp Eulenburgs politische Korrespondenz*, I, no. 169; also cited in Röhl, *Young Wilhelm*, 804f.

7 See Frank Lorenz Müller, *Our Fritz: Emperor Frederick III and the Political Culture of Imperial Germany*, Cambridge, MA, 2011, 191–232.

6 DIVINE RIGHT WITHOUT END

1 Count Herbert von Bismarck, memorandum of 5 October 1888; in Johannes Lepsius, Albrecht Mendelssohn Bartholdy and Friedrich Thimme, eds., *Die große Politik der europäischen Kabinette, 1871–1914: Sammlung der diplomatischen Akten des Auswärtiges Amtes*, 40 vols., Berlin 1922, VI, no. 1352; Prince Otto von Bismarck to Herbert Bismarck, 5 October 1888; ibid., 346, note.

2 Kaiser Wilhelm II, sermon 'Ohne mich könnt ihr nichts tun!', spring 1925; cited in Willibald Gutsche, *Ein Kaiser im Exil: Der letzte deutsche Kaiser Wilhelm II. in Holland: Eine kritische Biographie*, Marburg 1991, 66f.

3 Kaiser Wilhelm II to Bismarck, telegram, 17 January 1890; cited in Röhl, *Philipp Eulenburgs politische Korrespondenz*, I, 420.

4 See John W. Wheeler-Bennet, *Wooden Titan: Hindenburg in Twenty Years of German History, 1914–1934*, London 1967; Wolfram Pyta, *Hindenburg: Herrschaft zwischen Hohenzollern und Hitler*, Munich 2007; Anna von der Goltz, *Hindenburg: Power, Myth and the Rise of the Nazis*, Oxford 2011.

7 BISMARCK'S FALL FROM POWER (1889–1890)

1 See Röhl, *Young Wilhelm*, chap. 28, 'The Stoecker Meeting and the break with the Bismarcks'.

2 Prince Wilhelm of Prussia to Prince Otto von Bismarck, 29 November 1887; printed in Bismarck, *Erinnerung und Gedanke*, 464f.

3 Holstein, diary entry for 13 May 1888; in Rich and Fisher, *The Holstein Papers*, II, 374f.

4 Count Kuno von Rantzau to Count Herbert von Bismarck, 29 August 1888, Bundesarchiv (BA) Koblenz, Bismarck Papers FC 3028 N.

5 Holstein, diary for 27 March 1888; in Rich and Fisher, *The Holstein Papers*, II, 365f.; see Röhl, *Young Wilhelm*, 796–800.

6 Count Herbert von Bismarck, 'Notizen V' and diary for 12 May 1889, BA Koblenz, Bismarck Papers FC3018 N.

7 Robert Freiherr Lucius von Ballhausen, *Bismarck-Erinnerungen*, Stuttgart 1920, 497.

8 Waldersee, diary entries for 7 and 26 December 1889, GStA Berlin-Dahlem, Waldersee Papers.

9 Holstein to Eulenburg, 3 July 1889; in Röhl, *Philipp Eulenburgs politische Korrespondenz*, I, no. 225.

10 Kaiser Wilhelm II to Emperor Franz Joseph of Austria, 3–5 April 1890, quoted in full in Röhl, *The Kaiser's Personal Monarchy*, 309–17.

11 Paul Kayser to Eulenburg, 6 and 7 February 1890; in Röhl, *Philipp Eulenburgs politische Korrespondenz*, I, nos. 310, 314.

12 Kayser to Eulenburg, 2 and 4 March 1890; in Röhl, *Philipp Eulenburgs politische Korrespondenz*, I, nos. 330, 333.

13 Waldersee, diary entry for 15 March 1890, GStA Berlin-Dahlem, Waldersee Papers.

14 See Otto von Bismarck, ed. Horst Kohl, *Gedanken und Erinnerungen*, 3 vols., Stuttgart 1919, III, 81ff. Clark, *Kaiser Wilhelm II*, 64, pre-dates this famous confrontation by one day to 14 March; the date is corrected to 15 March in the German edition (Munich 2008, 72), but not in the revised English edition of 2009.

15 Sir Edward Malet to Queen Victoria, 22 March 1890, RA VIC/MAIN/I58/33-4.

16 Waldersee, diary entry for 15 March 1890, GStA Berlin-Dahlem, Waldersee Papers.

17 Waldersee, diary entry for 19 March 1890, ibid.

18 See Lothar Machtan, *Bismarcks Tod und Deutschlands Tränen: Reportage einer Tragödie*, Leipzig 1998; and Robert Gerwarth, *The Bismarck Myth: Weimar Germany and the Legacy of the Iron Chancellor*, Oxford 2007.

19 Kaiser Wilhelm II to his mother, 25 September 1898 [emphasis in original], AdHH Schloss Fasanerie; the English text is printed in Bernhard von Bülow, *Memoirs*, 4 vols., London 1931, I, 235–7.

8 THE ESTABLISHMENT OF THE KAISER'S PERSONAL MONARCHY (1890–1897)

1 Eulenburg to Kaiser Wilhelm II, 7 March 1890; in Röhl, *Philipp Eulenburgs politische Korrespondenz*, I, no. 336.

2 On Caprivi's appointment and character, see Röhl, *The Kaiser's Personal Monarchy*, 320–4.

3 Kurd von Schlözer, *Letzte römische Briefe, 1882–1894*, Stuttgart 1924, 158.

4 For the decision not to renew the Reinsurance Treaty with Russia, see Norman Rich, *Friedrich von Holstein: Politics and Diplomacy in the Era of Bismarck and Wilhelm II*, 2 vols., Cambridge 1965, I, 307–24; see also Röhl, *The Kaiser's Personal Monarchy*, 334–43.

5 Clark, *Kaiser Wilhelm II*, 64f.

6 See John C. G. Röhl, *The Kaiser and His Court: Wilhelm II and the Government of Germany*, Cambridge 1994, 70–106.

7 John C. G. Röhl, *Germany without Bismarck: The Crisis of Government in the Second Reich*, London 1967, 176.

8 See Laurenz Demps, *Berlin-Wilhelmstraße: Eine Topographie preußisch-deutscher Macht*, Berlin 1994, espec. 144–64.

9 Prince Wilhelm of Prussia to Bismarck, 14 January 1888; printed in Bismarck, *Erinnerung und Gedanke*, 470.

10 Michael A. Obst, ed., *Die politischen Reden Kaiser Wilhelms II.: Eine Auswahl*, Paderborn 2011, no. 42. See the analysis in Michael A. Obst, *'Einer nur ist Herr im Reiche': Kaiser Wilhelm II. als politischer Redner*, Paderborn 2010, 121–53.

11 Court officials tried to explain away the gaffe by arguing that the Kaiser's inscription had been intended to stress the federal structure of the Reich by championing the divine right of the King of Bavaria. Their effort backfired badly when it was pointed out that the reigning King Otto of Bavaria, 'mad' King Ludwig's brother, was utterly insane and spent his days locked in a padded cell screaming at the walls.

12 Empress Frederick to Queen Victoria, 16 November 1891 [emphasis in original], RA Z51/46; cited in Röhl, *The Kaiser's Personal Monarchy*, 508.

13 Kaiser Wilhelm II, speech of 24 February 1892; Obst, *Die politischen Reden Kaiser Wilhelms II.*, no. 49; Louis Elkind, ed., *The German Emperor's Speeches: Being a Selection from the Speeches, Edicts, Letters and Telegrams of the Emperor William II*, New York 1904, 292–4.

14 Bernhard von Bülow, *Denkwürdigkeiten*, 4 vols., Berlin 1930–1, I, 316.

15 Holstein to Eulenburg, 3 March 1897; in Röhl, *Philipp Eulenburgs politische Korrespondenz*, III, no. 1300.

16 Robert Graf von Zedlitz-Trützschler, *Zwölf Jahre am deutschen Kaiserhof*, Stuttgart 1924, 68.

17 Lord Stamfordham to Freiherr Hugo von Reischach, 21 July 1929; quoted in Lamar Cecil, 'Der diplomatische Dienst im Kaiserlichen Deutschland', in Klaus Schwabe, ed., *Das Diplomatische Korps 1871–1945*, Boppard am Rhein 1985, 39.

18 Walter Görlitz, ed., *Der Kaiser: Aufzeichnungen des Chefs des Marinekabinetts Admiral Georg Alexander von Müller über die Ära Wilhelms II.*, Göttingen 1965, 109.

19 Kaiser Wilhelm II, marginal notes of 4 October 1912 on Bethmann Hollweg's submission of 3 October 1912 [emphasis in original]; cited in John C. G. Röhl, ed., *1914: Delusion or Design? The Testimony of Two German Diplomats*, London 1973, 41f.

20 These key developments are fully documented in Röhl, *The Kaiser's Personal Monarchy*, 371–87.

21 Eugen Richter, speech of 18 May 1897; in Erich Eyck, *Das persönliche Regiment Wilhelms II.: Politische Geschichte des Deutschen Kaiserreiches von 1890 bis 1914*, Zurich 1948, 171–2.

22 Kaiser Wilhelm II, speech to recruits on 23 November 1891; in Obst, *Die politichen Reden Kaiser Wilhelms II.*, no. 47.

23 Eulenburg to Bülow, 20–22 July 1899; in Röhl, *Philipp Eulenburgs politische Korrespondenz*, III, no. 1399.

24 Quoted in Zedlitz-Trützschler, *Zwölf Jahre*, 75.

25 Kaiser Wilhelm II, speech at the inauguration of the Alexander Regiment's barracks, 28 March 1901; in Obst, *Die politischen Reden Kaiser Wilhelms II.*, no. 132.

26 Eulenburg to Bülow, 9 August 1903; in Röhl, *Philipp Eulenburgs politische Korrespondenz*, III, no. 1499, with note 4.

27 August Bebel, speech of 22 January 1903, Stenographische Berichte über die Verhandlungen des Reichstages, 244th session, 7467ff.

28 Kaiser Wilhelm II to Anna Landgravine of Hesse, 7 August 1901, cited in *Vossische Zeitung*, nos. 159 and 160, 28 March 1914. The original of the Kaiser's supposed letter to his aunt has never been found. His fury at her conversion to the Catholic faith in 1901 is well documented, however, as is his decision to expel her from the Hohenzollern family. For the details, see Röhl, *Into the Abyss of War and Exile*, 151–5.

9 THE CHANCELLOR AS COURTIER: THE CORRUPT BÜLOW SYSTEM (1897–1909)

1 See Kurt Riezler's characterisation of Tirpitz as a 'Renaissance personality' and a 'Jesuit' in Karl Diedrich Erdmann, ed., *Kurt Riezler: Tagebücher, Aufsätze, Dokumente*, Göttingen 1972, 200.

2 Holstein to Eulenburg, 27 November 1894; in Röhl, *Philipp Eulenburgs politische Korrespondenz*, II, no. 1052; and in Rich, *Friedrich von Holstein*, II, 486. See also Röhl, *Germany without Bismarck*, 127; and Röhl, *The Kaiser's Personal Monarchy*, 539.

3 Eulenburg to Holstein, 2 December 1894; in Johannes Haller, *Aus dem Leben des Fürsten Philipp zu Eulenburg-Hertefeld*, Berlin 1924, 170–2. See also Rich, *Friedrich von Holstein*, II, 487f.

4 Eulenburg to Kaiser Wilhelm II, 15 April 1893 [emphasis in original]; in Röhl, *Philipp Eulenburgs politische Korrespondenz*, II, no. 791.

5 On the 'Liebenberg round table', see Isabel V. Hull, *The Entourage of Kaiser Wilhelm II, 1888–1918*, Cambridge 1982; and Röhl, *The Kaiser and His Court*, chap. 2, 'Philipp Eulenburg, the Kaiser's best friend'.

6 Bernhard von Bülow to Eulenburg, 13 March 1893; in Röhl, *Philipp Eulenburgs politische Korrespondenz*, II, no. 785.

7 For the latest and most authoritative account of Eulenburg's collaboration with Bülow, see Peter Winzen, *Im Schatten Wilhelms II.: Bülows und Eulenburgs Poker um die Macht im Kaiserreich*, Cologne 2011.

8 Bülow to Eulenburg, 23 July 1896; in Röhl, *Philipp Eulenburgs politische Korrespondenz*, III, no. 1245. Eulenburg read Bülow's letter to the Kaiser on 1 August: ibid., 1713.

9 Bülow, *Memoirs*, I, 3.

10 Bülow to Karl von Lindenau, 20 November 1897; quoted from Katharine Anne Lerman, 'The decisive relationship: Kaiser Wilhelm II and

Chancellor Bernhard von Bülow 1900–1905', in John C. G. Röhl and Nicolaus Sombart, eds., *Kaiser Wilhelm II: New Interpretations*, Cambridge 1982, 223.

11 On the Kaiser's 'Hun speech', see Bernd Sösemann, 'Die sog. Hunnenrede Wilhelms II.: Textkritische und interpretatorische Bemerkungen zur Ansprache des Kaisers vom 27. Juli 1900 in Bremerhaven', *Historische Zeitschrift*, vol. 222 (1976), 349–50; Obst, *Die politischen Reden Kaiser Wilhelms II.*, no. 117; and Obst, *'Einer nur ist Herr im Reiche'*, 223–54. Remarkably, a wax cylinder with a recording of the Kaiser's most notorious speech was recently discovered and published on the internet. As the speech itself was given in the open air in front of hundreds of marines, it could not have been recorded at that time. The supposition must therefore be that Wilhelm recorded his speech at some later date in a studio, though why he should wish to immortalise his bloodthirsty words, given the horrified reaction to them throughout the civilised world, remains a mystery.

12 Bülow to Holstein, 24 November 1899; cited in Lerman, 'The decisive relationship', 227.

10 THE CHALLENGE TO EUROPE: *WELTMACHTPOLITIK* AND THE BATTLEFLEET

1 The classic statement of this strategy was formulated by Bismarck at Bad Kissingen on 15 June 1877; see Lepsius, Mendelssohn Bartholdy and Thimme, *Die große Politik*, II, 154.

2 Kaiser Wilhelm II, speech of 26 February 1897; in Johs Penzler, *Reden Kaiser Wilhelms II.,* vol. II, *In den Jahren 1896–1900*, Leipzig 1904, 38–41; Obst, *Die politischen Reden Kaiser Wilhelms II.*, no. 84; Obst, *'Einer nur ist Herr im Reiche'*, 181–6.

3 Kaiser Wilhelm II, speech in Bremen of 22 March 1905; in Johs Penzler, *Reden Kaiser Wilhelms II.*, vol. III, *In den Jahren 1901–Ende 1905*, 240f.; Obst, *'Einer nur ist Herr im Reiche'*, 277ff.

4 Eulenburg's notes on a conversation with Kaiser Wilhelm II on 11 July 1892; in Röhl, *Philipp Eulenburgs politische Korrespondenz*, II, no. 688.

5 Minutes of the Prussian Crown Council of 18 February 1894, Geheimes Staatsarchiv Berlin-Dahlem.

6 Kaiser Wilhelm II to Crown Prince Gustaf of Sweden and Norway, 25 July 1895; in Chlodwig zu Hohenlohe-Schillingsfürst, *Denkwürdigkeiten der Reichskanzlerzeit*, Stuttgart 1931, 102–5.

7 Marschall, diary entry for 3 January 1896, Marschall Papers, Schloss Neuershausen, Baden. See Friedrich Thimme, 'Die Krüger-Depesche', *Europäische Gespräche*, vol. 2 (1924), 201ff.; Rich, *Friedrich von Holstein*, II, 466ff.; and Matthew S. Seligmann, *Rivalry in Southern Africa, 1893–1899: The Transformation of German Colonial Policy*, London 1998, 92ff.

8 The contrary view is taken by Christopher Clark, who downplays the Kaiser's personal role in the incident and attributes the ensuing 'torrent of outrage' in Britain to what was after all a 'mildly worded' telegram to British oversensitivities: Clark, *Kaiser Wilhelm II*, 181–3; Clark, *The Sleepwalkers*, 146f.

9 Clark, *Kaiser Wilhelm II*, 182f.

10 See, for example, Maximilian Harden's reaction to the Kaiser's letter to Lord Tweedmouth in 1908 as being even worse than the Krüger telegram; cited below, p. 95.

11 See below, p. 113.

12 Kaiser Wilhelm II to Auswärtiges Amt, 6 November 1897; in Lepsius, Mendelssohn Bartholdy and Thimme, *Die große Politik*, XIV, no. 3686.

13 On Wilhelm's role in the seizure of Kiaochow, see Röhl, *The Kaiser's Personal Monarchy*, 954–65. For an informative account of the operation and its international ramifications, see Charles Stephenson, *Germany's Asia-Pacific Empire: Colonialism and Naval Policy 1885–1914*, Woodbridge 2009, 17–30.

14 See Röhl, *Into the Abyss of War and Exile*, chap. 4, 'The Boxer Rebellion and the Baghdad Railway'.

15 On the Kaiser's progress through the Middle East in the autumn of 1898, see Röhl, *The Kaiser's Personal Monarchy*, 944–54. For his speech of 8 November 1898 in Damascus, see Penzler, *Reden Kaiser Wilhelms II.*, II, 126f.; and Obst, *Die politischen Reden Kaiser Wilhelm II.*, no. 101.

16 Kaiser Wilhelm II to Tsar Nicholas II, 20 October 1898; in Goetz, *Briefe Wilhelms II.*, 313–15.

17 Bülow to Kaiser Wilhelm II, 8 November 1899; cited in Röhl, *Into the Abyss of War and Exile*, 21f. On the 'tectonic shift' produced by the Kaiserreich's involvement in Micronesia and Samoa, see Stephenson, *Germany's Asia-Pacific Empire*, 49–66.

18 For Wilhelm's meeting with Cecil Rhodes, see Röhl, *The Kaiser's Personal Monarchy*, 987f. For the Kaiser's role in initiating the Baghdad Railway project, see Röhl, *Into the Abyss of War and Exile*, chap. 4.

19 Kaiser Wilhelm II, marginal note on telegram from Speck von Sternburg, 12 December 1903; quoted in Ragnhild Fiebig-von Hase, 'Die Rolle Kaiser Wilhelms II. in den deutsch-amerikanischen Beziehungen', in John C. G. Röhl, ed., *Der Ort Kaiser Wilhelms II. in der deutschen Geschichte*, Munich 1991, 244.

20 See below, pp. 96–7.

21 See Röhl, *Into the Abyss of War and Exile*, 231–5.

22 Volker R. Berghahn, 'Zu den Zielen des deutschen Flottenbaus unter Wilhelm II.', *Historische Zeitschrift*, vol. 210 (1970), 34–100; Volker R. Berghahn, *Der Tirpitzplan: Genesis und Verfall einer innenpolitischen Krisenstrategie unter Wilhelm II.*, Düsseldorf 1971; Michael Epkenhans, *Die wilhelminische Flottenrüstung 1908–1914: Weltmachtstreben, industrieller*

Fortschritt, soziale Integration, Munich 1991; Rolf Hobson, *Maritimer Imperialismus: Seemachtideologie, seestrategisches Denken und der Tirpitzplan 1875 bis 1914*, Munich 2004; Jan Rüger, *The Great Naval Game: Britain and Germany in the Age of Empire*, Cambridge 2007; Patrick J. Kelly, *Tirpitz and the Imperial German Navy*, Bloomington, IN, 2011; Matthew S. Seligmann, *The Royal Navy and the German Threat 1901–1914: Admiralty Plans to Protect British Trade in a War against Germany*, Oxford 2012.

23 Kaiser Wilhelm II, marginal note on Metternich's report of 16 July 1908; in Lepsius, Mendelssohn Bartholdy and Thimme, *Die große Politik*, XXIV, no. 8217; Kaiser Wilhelm II, marginal comments of 3 August 1908 on Metternich's dispatch of 1 August 1908, Politisches Archiv des Auswärtigen Amtes (PA AA) Berlin R 5780; both cited in Röhl, *Into the Abyss of War and Exile*, 631.

24 See Jonathan Steinberg, 'The Copenhagen complex', *Journal of Contemporary History*, vol. 1 (1966), 23–46.

25 Kaiser Wilhelm II, marginal note on a report from Eckardstein of 4 October 1902; cited in Röhl, *Into the Abyss of War and Exile*, 20.

26 These plans to invade Denmark in order to hoodwink the Royal Navy into exposing itself to an attack in the Baltic are described in greater detail in Röhl, *Into the Abyss of War and Exile*, 302–5.

11 THE RUSSO-JAPANESE WAR AND THE MEETING OF THE EMPERORS ON BJÖRKÖ (1904–1905)

1 Walter Goetz, ed., *Briefe Wilhelms II. an den Zaren 1894–1914*, Berlin 1920.

2 The Kaiser's original sketch, 'Nations of Europe, protect your holiest possessions!', is printed alongside the widely distributed finished version by Hermann Knackfuss in Röhl, *The Kaiser's Personal Monarchy*, 754–5.

3 Bülow to Kaiser Wilhelm II, 31 October 1904; in Lepsius, Mendelssohn Bartholdy and Thimme, *Die große Politik*, XIX/1, no. 6123.

4 Kaiser Wilhelm II to Tsar Nicholas II, 27 July 1905; in Goetz, *Briefe Wilhelms II.*, no. XLVIII, 373–6.

5 Kaiser Wilhelm II to Bülow, 28 December 1904; in Lepsius, Mendelssohn Bartholdy and Thimme, *Die große Politik*, XIX/1, no. 6146.

6 Kaiser Wilhelm II to Bülow, 11 August 1905 [emphasis in original]; in Lepsius, Mendelssohn Bartholdy and Thimme, *Die große Politik*, XIX/2, no. 6237.

12 WAR IN THE WEST? THE LANDING IN TANGIER AND THE FIASCO OF ALGECIRAS (1905–1906)

1 Kaiser Wilhelm II; cited in Röhl, *Into the Abyss of War and Exile*, 188.

2 Bülow, *Denkwürdigkeiten*, II, 72–6.

3 Notes by Hans Adolf von Bülow, 30 December 1904; printed in Rich and Fisher, *The Holstein Papers*, IV, no. 904 enclosure.

4 See Röhl, *Into the Abyss of War and Exile*, 310f.

5 Kaiser Wilhelm II to Bülow, 30 July 1905; quoted by Bülow to Auswärtiges Amt, 30 July 1905; in Lepsius, Mendelssohn Bartholdy and Thimme, *Die große Politik*, XIX/2, no. 6229. See Röhl, *Into the Abyss of War and Exile*, 325.

6 For further details of this murky threat, see Röhl, *Into the Abyss of War and Exile*, 311–13.

7 King Edward VII to Prince Louis of Battenberg, 1 Aprl 1905 [emphasis in original]; quoted in Roderick R. McLean, *Royalty and Diplomacy in Europe, 1890–1914*, Cambridge 2001, 114f.

8 See Rich, *Friedrich von Holstein*, II, 696–713.

9 Admiral Georg von Müller, diary entry for 4 February 1905; in Röhl, *Into the Abyss of War and Exile*, 791.

10 Cited in Bülow to Auswärtiges Amt, 8, 10, 12 October 1905; in Lepsius, Mendelssohn Bartholdy and Thimme, *Die große Politik*, XX/2, nos. 6874, 6875; Kaiser Wilhelm II, marginal comments on Metternich's dispatches of 9, 18 October 1905; ibid., nos. 6873, 6879.

11 Wilhelm von Hahnke to Wilhelm Groener, 26 April 1926 [emphasis in original], Bundesarchiv-Militärarchiv (BA-MA) Freiburg, Groener Papers, N46/38; quoted in Röhl, *Into the Abyss of War and Exile*, 793.

12 Kaiser Wilhelm II to Bülow, 31 December 1905; originally published in the *Berliner Tageblatt*, no. 487, 14 October 1928; quoted here from Josef Reimann, *Fürst Bülows Denkwürdigkeiten und die deutsche Marokkopolitik (1897–1909)*, Würzburg 1935, 110f.; cf. Bülow, *Denkwürdigkeiten*, II, 197f.

13 On the confusion of purpose among German leaders in Berlin and at the Algeciras conference, see Röhl, *Into the Abyss of War and Exile*, 1004ff.

13 THE INTENSIFICATION OF THE ANGLO-GERMAN CONFLICT

1 King Friedrich Wilhelm I of Prussia (1688–1740), the father of Frederick the Great, had forcefully recruited exceptionally tall men, his 'Lange Kerls', to act as his lifeguards.

2 See above, p. 83.

3 Waldersee, diary for 5 January 1904, GStA Berlin-Dahlem, Waldersee Papers; quoted in Röhl, *Into the Abyss of War and Exile*, 746f.

4 Waldersee, notes dated 5 January and 6 February 1904, GStA Berlin-Dahlem, Waldersee Papers, VI.HA-B.I no. 7 (Engelbrecht).doc, Blatt 206. On Moltke's appointment as chief of the General Staff, see the definitive account in Annika Mombauer, *Helmuth von Moltke and the Origins of the First World War*, Cambridge 2001, 42ff.

5 Kaiser Wilhelm II to Bülow, 15 July 1908, PA AA R 2099; quoted in Röhl, *Into the Abyss of War and Exile*, 1456f.

6 Kaiser Wilhelm II, marginal comments on Metternich's report of 16 July 1908 [emphasis in original]; in Lepsius, Mendelssohn Bartholdy and Thimme, *Die große Politik*, XXIV, no. 8217. Röhl, *Into the Abyss of War and Exile*, 1475.

7 Princess Marie Radziwill to General di Robilant, 14 March 1908; printed in Cyril Spencer Fox, ed., *This Was Germany: An Observer at the Court of Berlin: Letters of Princess Marie Radziwill to General di Robilant 1908–1915*, London 1937, 23f.

8 Radziwill to Robilant, 10 March 1908; printed in *Letters of Princess Marie Radziwill*, 22f.

9 Kaiser Wilhelm II to Bülow, 12 and 13 August 1908 [emphasis in original]; in Lepsius, Mendelssohn Bartholdy and Thimme, *Die große Politik*, XXIV, nos. 8225, 8226; quoted in English translation in Röhl, *Into thte Abyss of War and Exile*, 632–4.

10 Bülow, *Denkwürdigkeiten*, II, 321–4.

11 The Kaiser's interview with Dr Hale is printed (alongside the alarmed international correspondence it generated) in Peter Winzen, *Das Kaiserreich am Abgrund: Die Daily-Telegraph-Affäre und das Hale Interview von 1908. Darstellung und Dokumentation*, Stuttgart 2002, 344–8.

12 See the recent magisterial survey by Brendan Simms, *Europe: The Struggle for Supremacy, 1453 to the Present*, London 2013.

13 Sir Francis Knollys to Sir Charles Hardinge 13 November 1909; cited in McLean, *Royalty and Diplomacy*, 87.

14 Kaiser Wilhelm II, diary for 19 March 1907; in Zedlitz-Trützschler, *Zwölf Jahre*, 153. Kaiser Wilhelm II to Bülow, 17 January 1907; in Lepsius, Mendelssohn Bartholdy and Thimme, *Die große Politik*, XXI/2, no. 7203. See Röhl, *Into the Abyss of War and Exile*, 1102.

14 THE EULENBURG AFFAIR (1906–1909)

1 Max Weber to Friedrich Naumann, 14 December 1906 [emphasis in original]; in M. Rainer Lepsius and Wolfgang J. Mommsen, eds., *Max-Weber-Gesamtausgabe*, vol. II/5, *Briefe 1906–1908*, Tübingen 1990, 202.

2 Holstein to Eulenburg, 21 December 1895; in Rich and Fisher, *The Holstein Papers*, III, no. 515.

3 See Peter Winzen, *Im Schatten Wilhelms II.: Bülows und Eulenburgs Poker um die Macht im Kaiserreich*, Cologne 2011.

4 Peter Winzen, *Das Ende der Kaiserherrlichkeit: Die Skandalprozesse um die homosexuellen Berater Wilhelms II. 1907–1909*, Cologne 2010; Norman Domeier, *Der Eulenburg-Skandal: Eine politische Kulturgeschichte des*

Kaiserreichs, Frankfurt 2010. See also Peter Winzen, *Freundesliebe am Hof Kaiser Wilhelms II.*, Norderstedt 2010.

5 Holstein to Theodor Schiemann, 28 April 1906; in Rich and Fisher, *The Holstein Papers*, IV, no. 972.

6 Holstein to Eulenburg, 1 May 1906; in Rich and Fisher, *The Holstein Papers*, IV, no. 973.

7 See Röhl, *Into the Abyss of War and Exile*, 1296ff.

8 Harden to Holstein, 28 February 1907; in Rich and Fisher, *The Holstein Papers*, IV, no. 1012.

9 Extraordinary film footage has survived of the sailors of the imperial yacht *Hohenzollern* diving stark naked and attired only in women's wigs and headscarves into the sea off Norway to perform synchronised swimming for the Kaiser's pleasure: see Peter Schamoni, *Majestät brauchen Sonne*, 1999. Innocent fun, no doubt – but presumably this was not an isolated incident of this nature, and the high-ranking courtiers who authorised such entertainment must have been quite certain that it would meet with Wilhelm's approval.

10 Eulenburg to Bülow, 24 September 1900; in Röhl, *Philipp Eulenburgs politische Korrespondenz*, III, no. 1428. See also Eulenburg's letters to Bülow of 14 July 1898 and 20 July and 23 and 25 September 1900, cited in Röhl, *The Kaiser's Personal Monarchy*, 626–8.

11 Axel Freiherr von Varnbüler to Kuno Graf von Moltke, 15 April 1898; in Röhl, *Philipp Eulenburgs politische Korrespondenz*, II, no. 1366; cited in Röhl, *The Kaiser and His Court*, 58.

12 Holstein to Ida von Stülpnagel, in Helmuth Rogge, *Friedrich von Holstein: Lebensbekenntnis in Briefen an eine Frau*, Berlin 1932, 296.

13 On 30 December 1895 Eulenburg wrote to his mother from Vienna that he was about to come home to Liebenberg, where he would be expecting a rendezvous with Bülow to discuss important matters. 'Please think about the sleeping arrangements. I am bringing Emanuel [Bartsch] with me, who could sleep in my room behind a screen. Now I'd very much like to have a room for Bülow as well in the house. It would save me a lot of to-ing and fro-ing. But please don't mention this rendezvous to anyone.' Eulenburg to his mother, 30 December 1895; in Röhl, *Philipp Eulenburgs politische Korrespondenz*, III, no. 1182.

14 For details, see Röhl, *Into the Abyss of War and Exile*, 572–4.

15 Axel Freiherr von Varnbüler, unpublished memoirs; cited in Röhl, *Philipp Eulenburgs politische Korrespondenz*, III, 2150 note 2.

16 Varnbüler to Laemmel, 22 April 1908; in Röhl, *Philipp Eulenburgs politische Korrespondenz*, III, no. 1539. The letter is printed in part in Röhl, *The Kaiser and His Court*, 59f.

17 Kaiser Wilhelm II, marginal note on Metternich's report of 1 November 1907; cited in Röhl, *Into the Abyss of War and Exile*, 587f.

15 BÜLOW'S BETRAYAL OF THE KAISER: THE *DAILY TELEGRAPH* CRISIS (1908–1909)

1 Hildegard Freifrau von Spitzemberg, diary for 30 October and 1 November 1908; in Rudolf Vierhaus, ed., *Das Tagebuch der Baronin Spitzemberg: Aufzeichnungen aus der Hofgesellschaft des Hohenzollernreiches*, Göttingen 1989, 488ff. See Röhl, *Into the Abyss of War and Exile*, 674ff.

2 Harden to Holstein, 15 November 1908 [emphasis in original]; in Rich and Fisher, *The Holstein Papers*, IV, no. 1151.

3 Karl von Einem, *Erinnerungen eines Soldaten 1853–1933*, Leipzig 1933, 120f.

4 Bernhard Schwertfeger, ed., *Kaiser und Kabinettschef: Nach eigenen Aufzeichnungen und dem Briefwechsel des Wirklichen Geheimen Rates Rudolf von Valentini*, Oldenburg 1931, 101–2.

5 See Röhl, *Into the Abyss of War and Exile*, 598–600.

6 Colonel Stuart Wortley's letters to his wife recording the Kaiser's expectorations at Highcliffe are printed (in English) in Winzen, *Das Kaiserreich am Abgrund*, 94–9.

7 Kaiser Wilhelm II, marginal note on a report from London of 8 September 1908, received by Bülow on 16 September 1908; in Lepsius, Mendelssohn Bartholdy and Thimme, *Die große Politik*, XXIV, no. 8245; Winzen, *Das Kaiserreich am Abgrund*, 99f.

8 Winzen, *Das Kaiserreich am Abgrund*, no. 75. See Kaiser Wilhelm II, *Ereignisse und Gestalten aus den Jahren 1878–1918*, Berlin 1922, 99.

9 Charlotte Hereditary Princess of Saxe-Meiningen to Professor Ernst Schweninger, 18 November 1908; cited in Röhl, *Into the Abyss of War and Exile*, 691.

10 According to Rudolf von Valentini, who witnessed Hülsen's tragic death, the general was dressed not in a tutu, as widely reported, but in a brightly coloured balldress belonging to Princess Irma zu Fürstenberg and wearing a large ostrich feather hat: Röhl, *Into the Abyss of War and Exile*, 689.

11 Kaiser Wilhelm II to Fürstenberg, 23 December 1908; cited in Röhl, *Into the Abyss of War and Exile*, 733.

12 Kaiser Wilhelm II to Fürstenberg, 11 January 1909; cited in Röhl, *The Kaiser and His Court*, 206.

16 FROM BÜLOW TO BETHMANN HOLLWEG: THE CHANCELLOR MERRY-GO-ROUND (1909)

1 Kaiser Wilhelm II to Felix von Müller, 22 February 1909; printed in Winzen, *Das Kaiserreich am Abgrund*, no. 106.

2 Valentini, memorandum entitled 'Bülows Sturz, Bethmanns Ernennung, Juni/Juli 1909', BA Koblenz, Valentini Papers, Kl. Erw. no. 341-1, fol. 149;

printed with some modifications in Schwertfeger, *Kaiser und Kabinettschef*, 121.

3 Kaiserin Auguste Viktoria, view expressed to Dr Alfred Haehner on 26 October 1920, Haehner Papers, Stadtarchiv Köln, Tagebuch no. 8, Nachträgliche Aufzeichnungen, p. 158.

4 Carl Alexander Krethlow, *Generalfeldmarschall Colmar Freiherr von der Goltz Pascha: Eine Biographie*, Paderborn 2012, 264–6.

5 Schwertfeger, *Kaiser und Kabinettschef*, 122.

17 THE BOSNIAN ANNEXATION CRISIS (1908–1909)

1 Kaiser Wilhelm II, marginal comments on Bülow's submission of 13 November 1905; in Lepsius, Mendelssohn Bartholdy and Thimme, *Die große Politik*, XXII, no. 7566. See Holstein to Bülow, January 1906; in Rich and Fisher, *The Holstein Papers*, IV, no. 919. See also Röhl, *Into the Abyss of War and Exile*, 697f.

2 Kaiser Wilhelm II, marginal comment on Bülow to Rücker-Jenisch, 7 October 1908; in Lepsius, Mendelssohn Bartholdy and Thimme, *Die große Politik*, XXVI/1, no. 8992. See also his note on Marschall's telegram of 9 October 1908; ibid., no. 9002.

3 Kaiser Wilhelm II, marginal comments on Tschirschky's report from Vienna of 25 October 1908; ibid., XXVI/2, no. 9213.

4 Kaiser Wilhelm II, marginal comment on Bülow's submission of 5 October 1908; published in facsimile in Bülow, *Denkwürdigkeiten*, II, 336f. Cf. Lepsius, Mendelssohn Bartholdy and Thimme, *Die große Politik*, XXVI/1, no. 8939; and the Kaiser's marginal note 'Annexion!?' on Schoen to Bülow, 5 September 1908; ibid., no. 8927.

5 Kaiser Wilhelm II, marginal comment on Radolin to Auswärtiges Amt, 17 October 1908; in Lepsius, Mendelssohn Bartholdy and Thimme, *Die große Politik*, XXVI/1, no. 9050.

6 Count Ladislaus von Szögyény-Marich, telegram, 14 November 1895; cited in Helmut Krausnick, 'Holstein, Österreich-Ungarn und die Meerengenfrage im Herbst 1895: Persönliches Regiment oder Regierungspolitik?', in Richard Dietrich and Gerhard Oestreich, eds., *Forschungen zu Staat und Verfassung: Festgabe für Fritz Hartung*, Berlin 1958, 519f. See Lepsius, Mendelssohn Bartholdy and Thimme, *Die große Politik*, X, 203–7; and Röhl, *The Kaiser's Personal Monarchy*, 761–5.

7 Szögyény, report of 21 October 1908; in *Österreich-Ungarns Außenpolitik von der Bosnischen Krise 1908 bis zum Kriegsausbruch 1914: Diplomatische Aktenstücke des österreichisch-ungarischen Ministeriums des Äußern*, 9 vols., Vienna 1930, I, no. 362.

8 See below, p. 154.

9 Kaiser Wilhelm II to Fürstenberg, 1 December 1908, FFA Donaueschingen. See Röhl, *Into the Abyss of War and Exile*, 707–9.

10 Kaiser Wilhelm II, marginal comments on Pourtalès's report of 11 December 1908; in Lepsius, Mendelssohn Bartholdy and Thimme, *Die große Politik*, XXVI/1, no. 9152.

11 Kaiser Wilhelm II to Archduke Franz Ferdinand, 16 December 1908; cited in Röhl, *Into the Abyss of War and Exile*, 713f.

12 Moltke to Conrad, 21 January 1909; printed in Franz Conrad von Hötzendorf, *Aus meiner Dienstzeit*, 5 vols., Vienna 1922–5, I, 379. See Röhl, *Into the Abyss of War and Exile*, 716.

13 Kaiser Wilhelm II, comment on Tschirschky's report of 24 February 1909 [emphasis in original]; in Lepsius, Mendelssohn Bartholdy and Thimme, *Die große Politik*, XXVI/2, no. 9391. Cited in Röhl, *Into the Abyss of War and Exile*, 720.

14 Kaiser Wilhelm II, marginal note on Pourtalès's report of 17 March 1909; in Lepsius, Mendelssohn Bartholdy and Thimme, *Die große Politik*, XXVI/2, no. 9451.

15 Kaiser Wilhelm II, marginal note on Tschirschky's report of 26 March 1909; ibid., no. 9478.

16 Kaiser Wilhelm II to Archduke Franz Ferdinand, 9 April 1909; cited in Röhl, *Into the Abyss of War and Exile*, 725.

17 See Kaiser Wilhelm II's conversation with Prince Louis of Battenberg of 20 May 1911; cited ibid., 792–3.

18 THE 'LEAP OF THE *PANTHER*' TO AGADIR (1911)

1 David J. Hill, memorandum of 4 February 1910, Rochester University Library, Hill Papers; cited more extensively in Röhl, *Into the Abyss of War and Exile*, 777f.

2 Kaiser Wilhelm II, marginal comments of 24 December 1909 on Bethmann Hollweg's submission of 23 December 1909; in Lepsius, Mendelssohn Bartholdy and Thimme, *Die große Politik*, XXXII, no. 11668.

3 The photographs with the Kaiser's captions are reproduced in Stefan Loran, *The Life and Times of Theodore Roosevelt*, Garden City, NY, 1959.

4 Battenberg, 'Notes of a statement made by the German Emperor...on May 20th 1911, 23 May 1911', RA PS/GV/O/2580/1; cited in Röhl, *Into the Abyss of War and Exile*, 792–3.

5 H. H. Asquith to Lord Knollys, 24 May 1911; cited ibid., 793.

6 Sir William Tyrrell, 2 July 1911; cited in Zara S. Steiner, *Britain and the Origins of the First World War*, London 1977, 75.

7 On Kiderlen's character and career, see Ralf Forsbach, *Alfred von Kiderlen-Wächter (1852–1912): Ein Diplomatenleben im Kaiserreich*, 2 vols., Göttingen 1997, on his policy in the Agadir crisis, espec. II, 423ff.

8 *Die Post*, 4 August 1911; Maximilian Harden, 'Wilhelm der Friedliche', *Die Zukunft*, 5 August 1911. See Spitzemberg, diary for 7 August 1911; in Vierhaus, *Das Tagebuch*, 531f.; Jenisch to Auswärtiges Amt, 9 August 1911; in Lepsius, Mendelssohn Bartholdy and Thimme, *Die große Politik*, XXIX, no. 10699, note.

9 Müller, diary for 6 July 1911, BA-MA Freiburg, Müller Papers.

10 Kiderlen's letter of resignation, 17 July 1911; cited in Ernst Jäckh, ed., *Kiderlen-Wächter der Staatsmann und Mensch: Briefwechsel und Nachlaß*, 2 vols., Berlin 1924, II, 128ff.

11 Müller, diary for 29–30 July 1911, BA-MA Freiburg, Müller Papers; cited in Röhl, *Into the Abyss of War and Exile*, p. 807. See Jäckh, *Kiderlen-Wächter*, II, 497f.

12 Spitzemberg, diary for 8 August 1911; in Vierhaus, *Das Tagebuch*, 532.

13 Kaiser Wilhelm II to Kiderlen, 9 August 1911; in Lepsius, Mendelssohn Bartholdy and Thimme, *Die große Politik*, XXIX, no. 10696

14 Kaiser Wilhelm II, marginal note on Kiderlen to Jenisch, 17 August 1911; in Lepsius, Mendelssohn Bartholdy and Thimme, *Die große Politik*, XXIX, no. 10712.

15 Kaiser Wilhelm II, marginal note on Metternich's report of 3 August 1911; ibid., no. 10637.

16 Moltke, *Erinnerungen, Briefe, Dokumente, 1877–1916*, Stuttgart 1922, 362. See Mombauer, *Helmuth von Moltke*, 124.

17 Karl Freiherr von Bienerth to Franz Conrad von Hötzendorf, 10 October 1911; Bienerth to Blasius Schemua, 8 January 1912, Kriegsarchiv Wien, Gen. Stab, Mil. Att. Berlin nos. 11 and 12; cited in Röhl, *Into the Abyss of War and Exile*, 810.

19 THE BATTLEFLEET AND THE GROWING RISK OF WAR
WITH BRITAIN (1911–1912)

1 Tirpitz to Eduard von Capelle, 12 August 1911; cited in Alfred von Tirpitz, *Der Aufbau der deutschen Weltmacht*, Stuttgart 1924, 203–6.

2 Müller, draft of an autograph letter from Kaiser Wilhelm II to Bethmann Hollweg, 26 September 1911 [emphasis in original], BA-MA Freiburg, RM3/v 9; cited in Röhl, *Into the Abyss of War and Exile*, 820. See Jenisch to Bethmann Hollweg, 28 September 1911; in Lepsius, Mendelssohn Bartholdy and Thimme, *Die große Politik*, XXXI, no. 11308.

3 Admiral Harald Dähnhardt, memorandum of 16 October 1911; cited in Michael Epkenhans, *Das ereignisreiche Leben eines 'Wilhelminers': Tagebücher, Briefe, Aufzeichnungen 1901 bis 1920*, Munich 2004, 163, note 43. See also Epkenhans, *Wilhelminische Flottenrüstung*, 98–101; and Ivo N. Lambi, *The Navy and German Power Politics 1862–1914*, London 1984, 370f.

4 Müller, diary for 14 October 1911, BA-MA Freiburg, Müller Papers; cited in Röhl, *Into the Abyss of War and Exile*, 829.

5 Müller, diary for 10 and 15 January 1912; ibid., 836.

6 Allan Mallinson, *1914: Fight the Good Fight: Britain, the Army and the Coming of the First World War*, London 2013, 149ff. See Mombauer, *The Origins of the First World War*, no. 7.

7 Arthur J. Marder, ed., *Fear God and Dread Nought: The Correspondence of Admiral of the Fleet Lord Fisher of Kilverstone*, 3 vols., London 1952–9, II, 419.

20 DOOMED TO FAILURE: THE HALDANE MISSION (1912)

1 Müller, diary for 10 and 11 January 1912, BA-MA Freiburg, Müller Papers; cited in Röhl, *Into the Abyss of War and Exile*, 845.

2 Müller, diary for 7 February 1912; ibid.; cf. Görlitz, *Der Kaiser*, 112.

3 Walther Rathenau, diary for 13 February 1912; as quoted in Hartmut Pogge von Strandmann, ed., *Walther Rathenau: Industrialist, Banker, Intellectual, and Politician: Notes and Diaries 1907–1922*, Oxford 1985, 146–8. Cf. Haldane to his mother, 11 February 1912; as quoted in Dudley Sommer, *Haldane of Cloane: His Life and Times, 1856–1928*, London 1960, 263.

4 Kaiser Wilhelm II, notes for Tirpitz of 6 February 1912 [emphasis in original]; in Tirpitz, *Der Aufbau der deutschen Weltmacht*, 283f.

5 For Haldane's negotiations in Berlin, see Mombauer, *The Origins of the First World War*, nos. 19–28.

6 Kaiser Wilhelm II to Metternich, 5 March 1912; printed in Tirpitz, *Der Aufbau der deutschen Weltmacht*, 317.

7 Kaiser Wilhelm II, marginal comment of 31 March 1912 on Bethmann Hollweg's submission of 28 March 1912; in Lepsius, Mendelssohn Bartholdy and Thimme, *Die große Politik*, XXXI, no. 11422, annexe.

8 Müller, diary for 5 March 1912, BA-MA Freiburg, Müller Papers; cf. Görlitz, *Der Kaiser*, 116.

21 TURMOIL IN THE BALKANS AND A FIRST DECISION FOR WAR (NOVEMBER 1912)

1 Kaiser Wilhelm II, marginal note on Bethmann Hollweg's telegram of 1 October 1912; in Lepsius, Mendelssohn Bartholdy and Thimme, *Die große Politik*, XXXIII, no. 12192.

2 Kaiser Wilhelm II to Kiderlen-Wächter, 4 October 1912; printed in Jäckh, *Kiderlen-Wächter*, II, 189f.; and also in Lepsius, Mendelssohn Bartholdy and Thimme, *Die große Politik*, XXXIII, no. 12225.

3 Kaiser Wilhelm II, marginal comments of 3 November 1912 on Kiderlen-Wächter's submission of the same day; in Lepsius, Mendelssohn Bartholdy and Thimme, *Die große Politik*, XXXIII, no. 12320. Röhl, *Into the Abyss of War and Exile*, 887.

4 Kaiser Wilhelm II to Auswärtiges Amt, 1 December 1912; in Lepsius, Mendelssohn Bartholdy and Thimme, *Die große Politik*, XXXIII, no. 12468.

5 Kaiser Wilhelm II to Kiderlen-Wächter, 9 November 1912 [emphasis in original]; in Lepsius, Mendelssohn Bartholdy and Thimme, *Die große Politik*, XXXIII, no. 12348.

6 Tschirschky to Kiderlen-Wächter, 17 November 1912; Kiderlen-Wächter to Tschirschky, 19 November 1912; in Lepsius, Mendelssohn Bartholdy and Thimme, *Die große Politik*, XXXIII, no. 12397. See Hull, *The Entourage of Kaiser Wilhelm II*, 156.

7 Bienerth to Blasius Schemua, 4 December 1912; cited in Günther Kronenbitter, *'Krieg im Frieden': Die Führung der k. u. k. Armee und die Großmachtpolitik Österreich-Ungarns 1906–1914*, Munich 2003, 397.

8 Kaiser Wilhelm II, marginal notes on Tschirschky's telegram of 21 November 1912; Kaiser Wilhelm II to Kiderlen Wächter, 21 November 1912; in Lepsius, Mendelssohn Bartholdy and Thimme, *Die große Politik*, XXXIII, nos. 12404, 12405.

9 Schemua, 'Bericht über meinen Aufenthalt in Berlin am 22. d. M.', printed in E. C. Helmreich, 'An unpublished report on Austro-German military conversations of November, 1912', *Journal of Modern History*, vol. V (1933), 205–7; also published in Stephan Verosta, *Theorie und Realität von Bündnissen: Heinrich Lammasch, Karl Renner und der Zweibund (1897–1914)*, Vienna 1971, 627–31. See the English translation in Mombauer, *The Origins of the First World War*, no. 39. The Kaiser's and Moltke's meeting with the chief of the Austrian General Staff on 21 November 1912 is not mentioned in Christopher Clark's influential book *The Sleepwalkers*, which argues powerfully against any German or Austrian premeditation to begin a war.

10 See Röhl, *Into the Abyss of War and Exile*, 901. An extract from Bethmann Hollweg's speech is printed in Mombauer, *The Origins of the First World War*, no. 42.

22 WAR POSTPONED: THE 'WAR COUNCIL' OF 8 DECEMBER 1912

1 Kaiser Wilhelm II to Kiderlen-Wächter, 21 November 1912 [emphasis in original]; in Lepsius, Mendelssohn Bartholdy and Thimme, *Die große Politik*, XXXIII, no. 12405.

2 Prince Louis of Battenberg to King George V, 5 December 1912, RA GV/M 520 A/1 [emphasis in original]; cited in Röhl, *Into the Abyss of War*

and Exile, 902. Prince Heinrich's wife, Irène, was the sister of Princess Victoria of Battenberg and also of the Tsarina Alexandra of Russia.

3 King George V to Grey, 8 December 1912; printed in Harold Nicolson, *King George the Fifth: His Life and Reign*, London 1952, 206.

4 Prince Heinrich of Prussia to Kaiser Wilhelm II, 11 December 1912; cited in Röhl, *Into the Abyss of War and Exile*, 903f.

5 Karl Max Prince Lichnowsky, report of 3 December 1912; in Lepsius, Mendelssohn Bartholdy and Thimme, *Die große Politik*, XXXIX, no. 15612; Tirpitz, *Der Aufbau der deutschen Weltmacht*, 361f. On the orders of the Kaiser, Lichnowsky's dispatch was circulated to the General Staff, the Admiralty Staff and the Reich Navy Office; an English translation of Lichnowsky's report is printed in Mombauer, *The Origins of the First World War*, no. 43.

6 Kaiser Wilhelm II, marginal comments of 8 December 1912 on Lichnowsky's report of 3 December 1912; in Lepsius, Mendelssohn Bartholdy and Thimme, *Die große Politik*, XXXIX, no. 15612; Tirpitz, *Der Aufbau der deutschen Weltmacht*, 361f.

7 Hugo Count von Lerchenfeld to Georg Freiherr von Hertling, 14 December 1912; printed in Ernst Deuerlein, ed., *Briefwechsel Hertling-Lerchenfeld 1912–1917*, Boppard am Rhein 1973, 189ff; published in part in Karl Alexander von Müller, 'Neue Urkunden', *Süddeutsche Monatshefte*, July 1921, 293ff.

8 Kaiser Wilhelm II to Albert Ballin, 15 December 1912 [emphasis in original]; as cited in Bernhard Huldermann, *Albert Ballin*, Paderborn 2011, 273f.

9 See John C. G. Röhl, 'An der Schwelle zum Weltkrieg: eine Dokumentation über den "Kriegsrat" vom 8. Dezember 1912', *Militärgeschichtliche Mitteilungen*, vol. 21 (1977), 77–134. An English translation of Admiral von Müller's diary entry for 8 December 1912 is to be found in Mombauer, *The Origins of the First World War*, no. 44. For further evidence of the Kaiser's panicked reaction to Lord Haldane's warning of British intervention, see ibid., nos. 46–8.

10 From the first some historians, otherwise committed to giving due weight to newly discovered primary evidence, have outdone themselves in discounting the significance of Admiral Georg von Müller's eyewitness account of the 'war council' held by the Kaiser and 'his paladins from the army and navy' (as Bethmann Hollweg sarcastically called the meeting). Not only was Müller present throughout but his handwritten account – the lengthiest entry in his diary – was penned that same Sunday evening while the deliberations were still fresh in his mind. Repeatedly critics have seized on the admiral's supposed final words of that day, as published tendentiously by Walter Görlitz in 1965: 'This was the end of the conference. The result amounted to almost nothing' (Görlitz, *Der Kaiser*, 124f.). But it has long been established that these

were *not* Müller's last words at all. His final paragraph, omitted by Görlitz, makes clear how disappointed the chief of the Kaiser's Naval Cabinet was that the meeting had failed yet again to decide in favour of an immediate war against France and/or Russia. It reads: 'This was the end of the conference. The result amounted to almost 0. The Chief of the General Staff says: War the sooner the better, but he does not draw the logical conclusion from this, which is: To present Russia or France or both with an ultimatum which would unleash the war with right on our side.' See John C. G. Röhl, 'Admiral von Müller and the approach of war, 1911–1914', *The Historical Journal*, vol. 12 (1969), 661f.; Mombauer, *The Origins of the First World War*, no. 44. The truncated version of Müller's diary entry has been repeated time and again to support the argument that neither the Kaiser nor his military leaders entertained any premeditation of starting a war. See, for example, Clark, *Kaiser Wilhelm II*, 269–71; and Clark, *The Sleepwalkers*, 329f., 333, with notes 53–5 on 626f. Like some others, Clark mistakenly locates the war council at Potsdam rather than at the Schloss in Berlin; ibid., 354.

11 See Röhl, *Into the Abyss of War and Exile*, 917ff.

23 THE POSTPONED WAR DRAWS NEARER (1913–1914)

1 Bienerth to Conrad, 26 February 1913; cited in Röhl, *Into the Abyss of War and Exile*, 924.

2 Kaiser Wilhelm II, marginal notes on Karl Graf Kageneck's report of 5 April 1913; in Lepsius, Mendelssohn Bartholdy and Thimme, *Die große Politik*, XXXIV/2, no. 13095.

3 Kaiser Wilhelm II, marginal comments on Jagow's submission of 1 April 1913; ibid., no. 13060.

4 Jagow to Tschirschky, 28 April 1913; as cited in Fritz Fischer, *Der Krieg der Illusionen: Die deutsche Politik von 1911 bis 1914*, Düsseldorf 1969, 298.

5 Bienerth to Conrad, 20 May 1913; in Conrad, *Aus meiner Dienstzeit*, III, 328.

6 Kaiser Wilhelm II, marginal comment on Friedrich Graf von Pourtalès's report of 6 May 1913; in Lepsius, Mendelssohn Bartholdy and Thimme, *Die große Politik*, XXXIV/2, no. 13282. See also the Kaiser's marginal comments on Pourtalès's report of 17 May 1913; ibid., XXXIX, no. 15645.

7 Lord Stamfordham, 'Notes on a conversation with the German emperor', 25 May 1913, RA GV/M 450/18; cited in Röhl, *Into the Abyss of War and Exile*, 933–5.

8 'Notes of a conversation between Herr von Jagow & Lord Stamfordham', 28 May 1913, RA GV/M 450/18.

9 Franz Conrad von Hötzendorf, record of a conversation with Kaiser Wilhelm II on 8 September 1913; in Conrad, *Aus meiner Dienstzeit*, III, 431f. Conrad to Emperor Franz Joseph, 20 September 1913; ibid., annexe 4, 720–3.

10 Moltke to Conrad, 29 June 1913; in Conrad, *Aus meiner Dienstzeit*, III, 424–6.

11 Conrad, record of conversations with Moltke on 7 and 8 September 1913; in Conrad, *Aus meiner Dienstzeit*, III, 432f.

12 Botho Graf von Wedel to Auswärtiges Amt, 17 October 1913; in Lepsius, Mendelssohn Bartholdy and Thimme, *Die große Politik*, XXXVI/1, no. 14172.

13 Leopold Graf Berchtold, memorandum of 28 October 1913 on his conversation with Kaiser Wilhelm II on 26 October 1913; in *Österreich-Ungarns Außenpolitik*, VII, no. 8934.

14 Tschirschkly to Bethmann Hollweg, 28 October 1913 [emphasis in original]; as cited in Fischer, *Der Krieg der Illusionen*, 317.

15 Baron Beyens, *Deux années à Berlin, 1912–1914*, 2 vols., Paris 1931, II, 39f. See the careful textual analysis of this document in Jean Stengers, 'Guillaume II et le roi Albert à Potsdam en novembre 1913', *Bulletin de la Classe des Lettres et des Sciences Morales et Politiques*, vol. 6 (1993), 234f.

16 Kaiser Wilhelm II, marginal note on Wilhelm von Schoen's report of 26 November 1913 [emphasis in original]; in Lepsius, Mendelssohn Bartholdy and Thimme, *Die große Politik*, XXXIX, no. 15658. Stengers, Guillaume II et le roi Albert, 236–41.

17 Kaiser Wilhelm II, marginal comment on Pourtalès's report of 13 December 1913; in Lepsius, Mendelssohn Bartholdy and Thimme, *Die große Politik*, XXXVIII, no. 15483.

18 Kaiser Wilhelm II, marginal comments on Richard von Kühlmann's report of 10 October 1913 [emphasis in original]; in Lepsius, Mendelssohn Bartholdy and Thimme, *Die große Politik*, XXXIX, no. 15577.

19 Korvettenkapitän Max Schulz, memorandum on the speech made by Tirpitz on 9 October 1913; printed in Epkenhans, *Das ereignisreiche Leben eines 'Wilhelminers'*, 343, note 261.

24 THE KAISER IN THE JULY CRISIS OF 1914

1 Kaiser Wilhelm II, marginal comment on Wangenheim's report from Therapia of 8 June 1914; in Lepsius, Mendelssohn Bartholdy and Thimme, *Die große Politik*, XXXVI/2, no. 14603.

2 Ibid.

3 Bethmann Hollweg to Lichnowsky, 16 June 1914; in Karl Kautsky, ed., *Die deutschen Dokumente zum Kriegsausbruch*, 4 vols., Charlottenburg 1919, no. 3. See Willibald Gutsche, *Wilhelm II.: Der letzte Kaiser des deutschen Reiches: Eine Biographie*, Berlin 1991, 153 (an English translation is included in Mombauer, *The Origins of the First World War*, no. 97).

4 Georg Graf von Waldersee, memorandum of 18 May 1914; printed in Mombauer, *The Origins of the First World War*, no. 85.

5 Karl Ritter von Wenninger to the Bavarian minister of war, Kress von Kressenstein, 16 June 1914; cited in Röhl, *Into the Abyss of War and Exile*, 1015; also in Mombauer, *The Origins of the First World War*, no. 96.

6 Egmont Zechlin, 'Motive und Taktik der Reichsleitung 1914', *Der Monat*, vol. 209 (February 1966), 92; see Röhl, *Into the Abyss of War and Exile*, 1012. This vital piece of evidence receives no mention in Christopher Clark's book *The Sleepwalkers*, which is concerned to deny any German premeditation to begin a war.

7 See the conversations between the German and Austrian chiefs of General Staff, Moltke and Conrad von Hötzendorff, in mid-May 1914: Mombauer, *The Origins of the First World War*, nos. 84, 89.

8 Sigismund Graf von Berckheim to Alexander Freiherr von Dusch, 11 March 1914, Generallandesarchiv Karlsruhe, 233/34815. It is significant that Christopher Clark, who refers to this revealing document in his earlier book *Kaiser Wilhelm II*, 279, does not mention it at all in his controversial *The Sleepwalkers*. See John C. G. Röhl, 'Jetzt gilt es loszuschlagen!', *Die Zeit*, 22/2014.

9 Traugott Freiherr Leuckart von Weißdorf to the Saxon minister of war, 3 July 1914; printed in August Bach, ed., *Deutsche Gesandtschaftsberichte zum Kriegsausbruch*, Berlin 1937, no. 3 (an English translation is in Mombauer, *The Origins of the First World War*, no. 114).

10 Fritz Fischer, *Griff nach der Weltmacht: Die Kriegzielpolitik des kaiserlichen Deutschland 1914–1918*, Düsseldorf 1961, 51; Fischer, *Der Krieg der Illusionen*, 692; Willi A. Boelcke, ed., *Krupp und die Hohenzollern in Dokumenten*, Frankfurt am Main 1970, 222; Gutsche, *Wilhelm II.*, 160; Thomas Lindemann, *Die Macht der Perzeptionen und Perzeptionen von Mächten*, Berlin 2000, 177f.; Mombauer, *The Origins of the First World War*, no. 127.

11 See Bethmann Hollweg's comments to Lerchenfeld, 4 June 1914; in Mombauer, *The Origins of the First World War*, no. 94.

12 Christopher Clark asserts that the monarch returned to Berlin in the imperial yacht *Hohenzollern*, which is plainly impossible; see Clark, *Kaiser Wilhelm II*, 280.

13 Clark, *Kaiser Wilhelm II*, 280; Clark, *The Sleepwalkers*, 404; Christopher Clark, *Die Schlafwandler: Wie Europa in den Ersten Weltkrieg zog*, Munich 2013, 519; Lamar Cecil, *Wilhelm II: Emperor and Exile, 1900–1941*, Chapel Hill, NC, 198, with note 31; David Fromkin, *Europe's Last Summer: Why the World Went to War in 1914*, London 2005, 138.

14 See Leuckart to Saxon war minister, 3 July 1914; in Mombauer, *The Origins of the First World War*, no. 114.

15 Kaiser Wilhelm II, marginal comment on Tschirschky's report from Vienna of 30 June 1914 [emphasis in original]; printed in Kautsky, *Die deutschen Dokumente*, no. 7; Mombauer, *The Origins of the First World War*, no. 108.

16 On the Hoyos Mission to Berlin, see Fritz Fellner, 'Austria-Hungary', in Keith M. Wilson, ed., *Decisions for War 1914*, London 1995, 9–25; John D. Leslie, 'The antecedents of Austria-Hungary's war aims: policies and policy-making in Vienna and Budapest before and during 1914', *Wiener Beiträge zur Geschichte der Neuzeit*, vol. 20 (1993), 307–94; and Mombauer, *The Origins of the First World War*, 183–237.

17 Szögyény to Berchtold, 5 July 1914; in Imanuel Geiss, ed., *Julikrise und Kriegsausbruch 1914*, 2 vols., Hanover 1963–4, I, no. 21 (English translation in Mombauer, *The Origins of the First World War*, no. 120). See also Bethmann Hollweg to Tschirschky, 6 July 1914; in Kautsky, *Die deutschen Dokumente*, no. 15; and Berchtold to Tisza, 6 July 1914; in Geiss, *Julikrise und Kriegsausbruch*, I, no. 28.

18 See Röhl, *Into the Abyss of War and Exile*, 1024f.; and Mombauer, *The Origins of the First World War*, nos. 122, 123.

19 Hopman, diary for 6 July 1914; in Epkenhans, *Das ereignisreiche Leben eines 'Wilhelminers'*, 382–4.

20 Hopman to Tirpitz, 6 July 1914; printed in Volker R. Berghahn and Wilhelm Deist, 'Kaiserliche Marine und Kriegsausbruch 1914: neue Dokumente zur Julikrise', *Militärgeschichtliche Mitteilungen*, vol. 4 (1970), 37–58; Mombauer, *The Origins of the First World War*, no. 125.

21 Most of Germany's and Austria's leaders went on holiday in July 1914 'to obscure our intentions', as one of them said: see Josef Redlich's diary for 15 July 1914; in Mombauer, *The Origins of the First World War*, no. 157.

22 Moriz Freiherr von Lyncker to his wife, 21/22 July 1914; printed in Holger Afflerbach, ed., *Kaiser Wilhelm II. als oberster Kriegsherr im Weltkrieg: Quellen aus der militärischen Umgebung des Kaisers 1914–1918*, Munich 2005, 126, no. L 2 (printed in English translation in Mombauer, *The Origins of the First World War*, no. 183).

23 Bethmann Hollweg to Kaiser Wilhelm II, 20 July 1914; Kaiser Wilhelm II to Crown Prince Wilhelm, 21 July 1914; in Kautsky, *Die deutschen Dokumente*, nos. 84, 105. On this incident, see Röhl, *Into the Abyss of War and Exile*, 103f.

24 Müller, diary for 19 July 1914; cited ibid., 1036.

25 Müller, account of 27 November 1918; printed in Walter Görlitz, ed., *Regierte der Kaiser? Kriegstagebücher, Aufzeichnungen und Briefe des Chefs des Marine-Kabinetts Admiral Georg Alexander von Müller 1914–1918*, Göttingen 1959, 33.

26 Kaiser Wilhelm II, marginal notes of 25 July 1914 (afternoon) on Julius Freiherr von Griesinger's report from Belgrade of 24 July 1914; in Kautsky, *Die deutschen Dokumente*, no. 159. That the ultimatum was intended by the Austrians to be unacceptable was reported by the

German military attaché in Vienna as early as 7 July: see Kageneck to Moltke, 7 July 1914; in Mombauer, *The Origins of the First World War*, no. 132. See also Redlich's diary for 23–4 July 1914; ibid., no. 205.

27 Müller, diary for 25 July 1914; cited in Röhl, *Into the Abyss of War and Exile*, 1038.

28 Professor Rheindorf's record of a conversation with Kurt Riezler on 20 May 1931; printed in Bernd F. Schulte, *Die Verfälschung der Riezler Tagebücher*, Frankfurt am Main 1985, 175.

29 Kaiser Wilhelm II, marginal note of 26 July 1914 on Bethmann Hollweg's dispatch of 26 July 1914 [emphasis in original]; in Kautsky, *Die deutschen Dokumente*, no. 182; cited in Röhl, *Into the Abyss of War and Exile*, 1042.

30 Lyncker to his wife, 25 July 1914; in Mombauer, *The Origins of the First World War*, no. 231.

31 Kaiser Wilhelm II, marginal notes on Tschirschky's report from Vienna of 24 July 1914; in Kautsky, *Die deutschen Dokumente*, no. 155. The dispatch was received on the *Hohenzollern* at noon on 26 July.

32 Kaiser Wilhelm II, marginal notes on Pourtalès's report of 25 July 1914; in Geiss, *Julikrise und Kriegsausbruch*, I, no. 283.

33 Lyncker to his wife, 25–7 July 1914; in Afflerbach, *Kaiser Wilhelm II.*, no. L 6.

34 See Mombauer, *The Origins of the First World War*, nos. 266, 267, with notes.

35 Bethmann Hollweg to Kaiser Wilhelm II, 26 July 1914; cited in Gutsche, *Wilhelm II.*, 164.

36 Müller, diary for 27 July 1914, BA-MA Freiburg, Müller Papers.

37 Ibid. On the Chancellor's assessment of the situation on this day, see his telegram to Kaiser Wilhelm II of 27 July 1914; in Geiss, *Julikrise und Kriegsausbruch*, II, no. 489.

38 Falkenhayn, diary for 27 July 1914; in Holger Afflerbach, *Falkenhayn: Politisches Denken und Handeln im Kaiserreich*, Munich 1994, 154.

39 Lichnowsky to Jagow, 27 July 1914; in Mombauer, *The Origins of the First World War*, no. 251.

40 Kautsky, *Die deutschen Dokumente*, no. 293; Mombauer, *The Origins of the First World War*, nos. 276, 277.

41 See Geiss, *Julikrise und Kriegsausbruch*, II, 164ff.; Mombauer, *The Origins of the First World War*, 409, note 28.

42 Falkenhayn, diary for 29 July 1914; in Afflerbach, *Falkenhayn*, 156.

43 Prince Heinrich of Prussia, diary for 26 July 1914 with a later addendum, Marine- und Schifffahrtsmuseum Hamburg, Prince Heinrich Papers. Prince Heinrich to Kaiser Wilhelm II, 28 July 1914; in Mombauer, *The Origins of the First World War*, no. 281. For details of the meeting between Heinrich and King George V, see Röhl, *Into the Abyss*

of War and Exile, 1058–62; and Harold Nicolson, *King George V*, London 1967, 327.

44 Alfred von Tirpitz, *Deutsche Ohnmachtspolitik im Weltkriege*, Hamburg 1926, 2–4. See Hopman, diary for 29 July 1914; in Epkenhans, *Das ereignisreiche Leben eines 'Wilhelminers'*, 403f.

45 Bethmann Hollweg to Kaiser Wilhelm II, 28 July 1914; in Kautsky, *Die deutschen Dokumente*, no. 308.

46 Müller, diary for 30 July 1914, BA-MA Freiburg, Müller Papers. Cf. Müller, memorandum of 27 November 1918; printed in Görlitz, *Regierte der Kaiser?*, 37. See also Wenninger to Kress von Kressenstein, 30 July 1914; in Bernd F. Schulte, 'Neue Dokumente zu Kriegsausbruch und Kriegsverlauf 1914', *Militärgeschichtliche Zeitschrift*, vol. 25 (1979), 139.

47 For the Kaiser's panicked ravings of these days, see Röhl, *Into the Abyss of War and Exile*, 1073ff.; see also Mombauer, *The Origins of the First World War*, nos. 286, 296, 310, 322, 375.

48 King George V to Prince Heinrich of Prussia, 30 July 1914; in Mombauer, *The Origins of the First World War*, no. 310.

49 On Wilhelm's dramatic last-minute attempt to mediate, see Röhl, *Into the Abyss of War and Exile*, 1079–83.

50 Kaiser Wilhelm II, marginal comment of 31 July 1914 on Bethmann Hollweg's submission of 30 July 1914; in Kautsky, *Die deutschen Dokumente*, no. 466; Röhl, *Into the Abyss of War and Exile*, 1077–9.

51 Wenninger, diary for 30 July 1914; printed in Schulte, 'Neue Dokumente', 138f.

52 Szögyény to Berchtold, 2 August 1914; in Geiss, *Julikrise und Kriegsausbruch*, II, no. 1063.

53 Kaiser Wilhelm II, marginal note of 3 August 1914 to the telegram from King Constantine of Greece of 2 August 1914; in Kautsky, *Die deutschen Dokumente*, no. 702.

54 Valentini, diary for 30 July 1914, Bundesarchiv Koblenz, Friedrich Thimme Papers, no. 26.

55 Falkenhayn, diary for 30 July 1914; in Mombauer, *The Origins of the First World War*, no. 323.

56 Wenninger, diary for 31 July 1914; printed in Schulte, 'Neue Dokumente', 139f. See also Afflerbach, *Falkenhayn*, 161.

57 Falkenhayn, diary for 31 July 1914; in Afflerbach, *Falkenhayn*, 160f.; also in Mombauer, *The Origins of the First World War*, no. 351. See further Lyncker, diary for 31 July 1914; ibid., no. 341.

58 Müller, diary for 1 August 1914; in Röhl, 'Admiral von Müller and the approach of war', 670; Mombauer, *The Origins of the First World War*, no. 367. Cf. Görlitz, *Regierte der Kaiser?*, 38f., where this key passage has been changed to read: 'In both speeches the correct and entirely justified claim is made that we are the attacked.'

59 Kurt Riezler, diary for 14–18 August 1914; in Karl Dietrich Erdmann, ed., *Kurt Riezler: Tagebücher, Aufsätze, Dokumente*, Göttingen 1972, 193ff.

60 Kaiser Wilhelm II to Emperor Franz Joseph, 31 July 1914; in Kautsky, *Die deutschen Dokumente*, no. 503 (English translation in Mombauer, *The Origins of the First World War*, no. 353). See also Kaiser Wilhelm's marginal note of 5 August 1914 on Hans von Wangenheim's telegram of 4 August 1914; in Kautsky, *Die deutschen Dokumente*, no. 856; and Wenninger, diary for 31 July 1914; in Schulte, 'Neue Dokumente', 139f.

61 Wenninger, diary for 2 August 1914; in Schulte, 'Neue Dokumente', 142.

62 Moltke, *Erinnerungen, Briefe, Dokumente*, 19ff. See also Mombauer, *Helmuth von Moltke*, 216ff.

63 Moltke, *Erinnerungen, Briefe, Dokumente*, 19ff. Similarly, see Hans von Haeften, 'Meine Erlebnisse aus den Mobilmachungstagen 1914', BA-MA Freiburg, Haeften Papers, N 35/1, 32ff. The three Cabinet chiefs also recorded this conflict: see Müller, diary for 1 August 1914, BA-MA Freiburg, Müller Papers; Valentini, *Kaiser und Kabinettschef*, 127f.; and Lyncker, diary for 1 August 1914; in Afflerbach, *Kaiser Wilhelm II.*, no. L 8. See also Mombauer, *The Origins of the First World War*, nos. 372, 373.

64 Haeften, 'Meine Erlebnisse aus den Mobilmachungstagen 1914', BA-MA Freiburg, Haeften Papers, N 35/1, 32ff.; in Röhl, *Into the Abyss of War and Exile*, 1095.

65 Müller, diary for 1 August 1914, BA-MA Freiburg, Müller Papers. Cf. Görlitz, *Regierte der Kaiser?*, 38f. See Mombauer, *The Origins of the First World War*, no. 373.

66 For details of these extraordinary events, see Röhl, *Into the Abyss of War and Exile*, 1096f.

67 Haeften, 'Meine Erlebnisse aus den Mobilmachungstagen 1914', BA-MA Freiburg, Haeften Papers, N 35/1, 36ff.

68 Walter Page to President Wilson, 9 August 1914, Papers of Woodrow Wilson, XXX, 366–71.

69 Szögyény to Berchtold, 12 August 1913; in *Österreich-Ungarns Außenpolitik*, VII, 116–18.

25 THE KAISER'S WAR AIMS

1 Lyncker, diary for 25 April 1917; in Afflerbach, *Kaiser Wilhelm II.*, III, no. L 586.

2 Edward House, notes of 27 January 1916; in Charles Seymour, ed., *The Intimate Papers of Colonel House*, 2 vols., London 1926, II, 139.

3 Müller, diary for 14 August 1916; in Görlitz, *Regierte der Kaiser?*, 211.

4 Müller, diary for 23 and 26 March 1918; ibid., 365f.

5 Kaiser Wilhelm II to Houston Stewart Chamberlain, 15 January 1917 [emphasis in original], Chamberlain Papers, Bayreuth; printed in part in Houston Stewart Chamberlain, *Briefe 1882–1924 und Briefwechsel mit Kaiser Wilhelm II.*, 2 vols., Munich 1928, II, 250f.

6 Kurt Riezler, diary for 19 August 1914; in Erdmann, *Kurt Riezler*, 198ff.

7 Bethmann Hollweg to Clemens von Delbrück, 9 September 1914; printed in Fischer, *Griff nach der Weltmacht*, 110–13 (English translation: *Germany's Aims in the First World War*, New York 2007, 103–6).

8 Ibid.

9 Röhl, *Into the Abyss of War and Exile*, 1142f.

10 Ibid., 1144f.

11 Kaiser Wilhelm II, marginal note on an article by Gyula Graf Andrássy, 12 January 1918; in Werner Hahlweg, ed., *Der Friede von Brest-Litowsk: Ein unveröffentlichter Band aus dem Werk des Untersuchungsausschusses der Deutschen Verfassungsgebenden Nationalversammlung und des Deutschen Reichstages*, Düsseldorf 1971, no. 184.

12 Kaiser Wilhelm II, war aims programme of 19 April 1917; in Fischer, *Griff nach der Weltmacht*, 448f.

13 Kaiser Wilhelm II, war aims programme of 13 May 1917; in Fischer, *Griff nach der Weltmacht*, 457f.; Gutsche, *Wilhelm II.*, 183.

14 Kaiser Wilhelm II, marginal note of 10 January 1918; cited in Fischer, *Griff nach der Weltmacht*, 822.

15 Kaiser Wilhelm II, marginal note of 10 March 1918 [emphasis in original]; cited in Lothar Machtan, *Die Abdankung: Wie Deutschlands gekrönte Häupter aus der Geschichte fielen*, Berlin 2008, 90f.

16 Kaiser Wilhelm II to Georg Michaelis, no date [September 1917] [emphasis in original]; in William Michaelis, 'Der Reichskanzler Michaelis und die päpstliche Friedensaktion 1917: neue Dokumente', *Geschichte in Wissenschaft und Unterricht*, vol. 12 (1961), 433–4 (English translation in Röhl, *Into the Abyss of War and Exile*, 1148).

26 THE IMPOTENCE OF THE SUPREME WAR LORD AT WAR

1 For Wilhelm's role during the war, see the papers of his adjutant general, Hans von Plessen, and the head of his Military Cabinet, Moriz von Lyncker; in Afflerbach, *Kaiser Wilhelm II*. See also Holger Afflerbach, 'Wilhelm II as supreme warlord in the First World War', in Annika Mombauer and Wilhelm Deist, eds., *The Kaiser: New Research on Wilhelm II's role in Imperial Germany*, Cambridge 2003, 195–216.

2 See Afflerbach, *Falkenhayn*, 437–50.

3 Müller's wartime diaries are published in Görlitz, *Regierte der Kaiser?*.

4 Hopman, diary for 27 March 1915; in Epkenhans, *Das ereignisreiche Leben eines 'Wilhelminers'*, 586.

5 Kaiser Wilhelm II, marginal comment on Tirpitz's letter of resignation; Tirpitz, *Deutsche Ohnmachtspolitik im Weltkriege*, 350.

6 Alfred von Tirpitz, *Erinnerungen*, Leipzig 1919, 359.

7 Kaiser Wilhelm II, marginal comment on Tirpitz's submission of 7 September 1915; ibid., 428.

8 See Matthew Stibbe, 'Germany's "last card": Wilhelm II and the decision in favour of unrestricted submarine warfare in January 1917', in Mombauer and Deist, *The Kaiser*, 217–34.

9 Müller, diary for 8 January 1917; in Görlitz, *Regierte der Kaiser?*, 247.

10 Kaiser Wilhelm II, marginal notes of 14 May 1917; cited in Fischer, *Griff nach der Weltmacht*, 456.

27 DOWNFALL: THE COLLAPSE OF THE HOHENZOLLERN MONARCHY

1 Kaiser Wilhelm II to Bethmann Hollweg, 12 May 1917; printed in Wilhelm Deist, ed., *Militär und Innenpolitik im Weltkrieg 1914–1918*, 2 vols., Düsseldorf 1970, II, no. 296.

2 Friedrich Mewes to his wife, 9 December 1916, Mewes Papers, in private hands, Munich. Valentini also remarked on the Kaiser's relief at handing over responsibility to Hindenburg and Ludendorff: Valentini to his wife, 30 August 1916, BA Koblenz, Kl. Erw. 341–6.

3 For these events, see Röhl, *Into the Abyss of War and Exile*, 1166–9.

4 Plessen, diary for 13 July 1917; in Afflerbach, *Kaiser Wilhelm II.*, no. P 653. See Röhl, *Into the Abyss of War and Exile*, 1170f.

5 Ibid., 1166.

6 See Lothar Machtan, *Prinz Max von Baden: Der letzte Kanzler des Kaisers: Eine Biographie*, Berlin 2013, 400–69.

7 Sigurd von Ilsemann, diary for 25 October 1918; in Harald von Koenigswald, ed., *Der Kaiser in Holland: Aufzeichnungen des letzten Flügeladjutanten Kaiser Wilhelms II.*, 2 vols., Munich 1967, I, 25–7. See also Machtan, *Die Abdankung*, 187.

8 Bill Drews, report of his reception by Kaiser Wilhelm II in Spa on 1 November 1918; in Erich Matthias and Rudolf Morsey, eds., *Die Regierung des Prinzen Max von Baden*, Düsseldorf 1962, no. 115. See also Ilsemann, diary for 1 November 1918; in Koenigswald, *Der Kaiser in Holland*, I, 30–2.

9 Kaiser Wilhelm II, letter to a person unnamed; cited in Eugen Schiffer, *Ein Leben für den Liberalismus*, Berlin 1951, 135ff.

10 Wilhelm Groener, *Lebenserinnerungen: Jugend, Generalstab, Weltkrieg*, Göttingen 1957, 438.

11 Stewart Roddie, memorandum of 29 June 1921, RA GV/M 1515/36; cited in Röhl, *Into the Abyss of War and Exile*, 1187.

28 A NEW LIFE IN AMERONGEN AND DOORN

1 Kaiser Wilhelm II., abdication, 28 November 1918, GStA Berlin-Dahlem, BPHA Rep. 53 no. 203.
2 Hans Wilderotter, 'Haus Doorn: die verkleinerte Kopie eines Hofstaats', in Hans Wilderotter and Klaus-D. Pohl, eds., *Der letzte Kaiser: Wilhelm II. im Exil*, Gütersloh 1991, 119, with note 32. Further details in Röhl, *Into the Abyss of War and Exile*, 1190ff.
3 Speeches by Philipp Scheidemann and others at the SPD conference in September 1919; cited in Otmar Jung, *Volksgesetzgebung: Die 'Weimarer Erfahrungen' aus dem Fall der Vermögensauseinandersetzungen zwischen Freistaaten und ehemaligen Fürsten*, Hamburg 1990, 465f. See also Maximilian Harden in the *Zukunft* of 27 November 1920, 252f.
4 Dr Alfred Haehner, diary for 25 October 1923, Stadtarchiv Cologne.

29 THE RABID ANTI-SEMITE IN EXILE

1 Goetz, *Briefe Wilhelms II.*
2 Kautsky, *Die deutschen Dokumente.*
3 Most damaging of all was the posthumous publication of the third volume of Bismarck's *Gedanken und Erinnerungen*; Wilhelm covered the book with angry marginal comments.
4 See, among several other works, his *Ereignisse und Gestalten aus den Jahren 1878–1918*, Leipzig 1922; and *Aus meinem Leben 1859–1888*, Leipzig 1927.
5 Wolfgang Krauel, diary for 24 October 1919, *Mitteilungen der List Gesellschaft*, fasc. 6, no. 13, October 1968, 311–21.
6 Friedrich Karl Landgrave of Hesse, notebook for early February 1920; cited in Rainer von Hessen, ed., *Wolfgang Prinz von Hessen: Aufzeichnungen*, Kronberg 1986, 125; Lothar Machtan, *Der Kaisersohn bei Hitler*, Hamburg 2006, 103. See also Ilsemann, diary for 7 February 1920; in Koenigswald, *Der Kaiser in Holland*, I, 144f.
7 Kaiser Wilhelm II to Field Marshal August von Mackensen, 12 August 1920; cited in Röhl, *Into the Abyss of War and Exile*, 1221.
8 Haehner, diary for 4 June 1921, Stadtarchiv Cologne. See also the entry for 1 March 1923, ibid.
9 Kaiser Wilhelm II to Poultney Bigelow, 14 April 1927, New York Public Library, Bigelow Papers, IV; cited in Röhl, *The Kaiser and His Court*, 210.
10 Kaiser Wilhelm II to Mackensen, 2 December 1919; cited ibid.

11 Haehner, diary for 2 December 1920 [emphasis in original], Stadtarchiv Cologne.

12 Haehner, diary for 8 March 1921, ibid.; cited in part in Machtan, *Der Kaisersohn*, 144. The Kaiser was already expressing such views in autumn 1919. Krauel, diary for 24 October 1919, *Mitteilungen der List Gesellschaft*, fasc. 6, no. 13, October 1968, 311–21.

13 Kaiser Wilhelm II to Poultney Bigelow, 18 October 1927, New York Public Library, Bigelow Papers, IV; cited in Röhl, *The Kaiser and His Court*, 210.

14 Kaiser Wilhelm II to Poultney Bigelow, 15 August 1927; cited ibid.

30 THE KAISER AND HITLER

1 On Prince August Wilhelm ('Auwi') of Prussia's relationship with the Hitler movement, see Machtan, *Der Kaisersohn*.

2 Ilsemann, diary for 25 December 1931; in Koenigswald, *Der Kaiser in Holland*, II, 175f.

3 Wilhelm von Dommes, memorandum of 15 May 1933; printed in Willibald Gutsche and Joachim Petzold, 'Das Verhältnis der Hohenzollern zum Faschismus', *Zeitschrift für Geschichtswissenschaft*, vol. 34 (1986), 917–39.

4 Dommes, memorandum on his reception by Hitler on 24 October 1933, GStA Berlin, BPHA Rep. 53 no. 167/3; printed in Gutsche and Petzold, 'Das Verhältnis der Hohenzollern zum Faschismus', no. 7.

5 Kaiser Wilhelm II to Margarethe Landgravine of Hesse, 9 October 1938 [emphasis in original], AdHH Schloss Fasanerie.

6 Kaiser Wilhelm II to Margarethe Landgravine of Hesse, 7 November 1938 [emphasis in original], ibid.

7 Kaiser Wilhelm II to Margarethe Landgravine of Hesse, 18 October 1939, ibid.

8 Kaiserin Hermine to Beckmann, 29 December 1939; extract cited in the J. A. Stargardt catalogue no. 685 (2006), 425.

9 Kaiserin Hermine to Viktoria Luise Duchess of Brunswick, 15 July 1940, Archiv des vormals regierenden preußischen Königshauses, Burg Hohenzollern; cited in Gutsche, *Ein Kaiser im Exil*, 200f.

10 Kaiser Wilhelm II to Alfred Niemann, 31 May 1940; ibid., 204.

11 Kaiser Wilhelm II to Adolf Hitler, 19 June 1940, BA-MA Freiburg, Cramon Papers, N 266/47; in Gutsche, *Ein Kaiser im Exil*, 204. Hitler's letter of thanks of 25 June 1940 is printed ibid. See also Mackensen to Kaiser Wilhelm II, 18 January 1941, BA-MA Freiburg, Mackensen Papers, N 39/39.

12 Kaiser Wilhelm II to Poultney Bigelow, 14 September 1940 [emphasis in original], New York Public Library, Bigelow Papers, I; cited in part in Röhl, *The Kaiser and His Court*, 211.

13 Kaiser Wilhelm II to Poultney Bigelow, 21 November 1940, New York Public Library, Bigelow Papers, I.

14 Kaiser Wilhelm II to Margarethe Landgravine of Hesse, 3 November 1940 [emphasis in original], AdHH Schloss Fasanerie.

15 Kaiser Wilhelm II to Alwina Gräfin von der Goltz, 28 July and 7 August 1940 [emphasis in original]; printed in Willibald Gutsche, 'Illusionen des Exkaisers: Dokumente aus dem letzten Lebensjahr Kaiser Wilhelms II. 1940/41', *Zeitschrift für Geschichtswissenschaft*, vol. 10 (1991), 1028–32.

16 Kaiser Wilhelm II to Margarethe Landgravine of Hesse, 3 November 1940; cited in Röhl, *The Kaiser and His Court*, 211.

17 Kaiser Wilhelm II to Margarethe Landgravine of Hesse, 20 April 1941, AdHH Schloss Fasanerie.

Index